ENOLA GAY

AND THE COURT OF HISTORY

FRONTIERS IN **POLITICAL COMMUNICATION**

Lynda Lee Kaid and Bruce Gronbeck
General Editors

Vol. 8

PETER LANG
New York • Washington, D.C./Baltimore • Bern
Frankfurt am Main • Berlin • Brussels • Vienna • Oxford

Robert P. Newman

ENOLA GAY
AND THE COURT OF HISTORY

PETER LANG
New York • Washington, D.C./Baltimore • Bern
Frankfurt am Main • Berlin • Brussels • Vienna • Oxford

Library of Congress Cataloging-in-Publication Data

Newman, Robert P.
Enola Gay and the court of history / Robert P. Newman.
p. cm. — (Frontiers in political communication; v. 8)
Includes bibliographical references and index.
1. Hiroshima-shi (Japan)—History—Bombardment, 1945. 2. Enola Gay (Bomber)—
Exhibitions—Political aspects. 3. National Air and Space Museum—Exhibitions—
Political aspects. 4. Atomic bomb—Moral and ethical aspects. I. Title.
II. Series: Frontiers in political communication; v. 8.
D767.25.H6N48   940.54'2521954—dc22   2004005490
ISBN 0-8204-7071-6 (paperback)
ISBN 0-8204-7457-6 (hardcover)
ISSN 1525-9730

Bibliographic information published by **Die Deutsche Bibliothek**.
Die Deutsche Bibliothek lists this publication in the "Deutsche
Nationalbibliografie"; detailed bibliographic data is available
on the Internet at http://dnb.ddb.de/.

Cover design by Lisa Barfield

The paper in this book meets the guidelines for permanence and durability
of the Committee on Production Guidelines for Book Longevity
of the Council of Library Resources.

© 2004 Peter Lang Publishing, Inc., New York
275 Seventh Avenue, 28th Floor, New York, NY 10001
www.peterlangusa.com

Printed in the United States of America

To Paul Tibbets

*A great flier who dropped no bomb in anger, deplores
our overkill arsenal, and drives a Toyota*

CONTENTS

Acknowledgments ix

Preface xi

CHAPTER 1
Official Narrative #1—Truman Version 1

CHAPTER 2
Official Narrative #2—Nitze Version 28

CHAPTER 3
Stimson's Defense 50

CHAPTER 4
Blackett's Attack 62

CHAPTER 5
Cold War, Korea, Vietnam 75

CHAPTER 6
Enola Gay at Air and Space: Anonymity, Hypocrisy, Ignorance 97

CHAPTER 7
  A Transnational Narrative: Recognizing the Claims
  of Japan's Victims 134

AFTERWORD *Bruce E. Gronbeck*
  The Rhetorics of Foreign Policy Making,
  Implementing, and Remembering 153

  Notes 163

  Bibliography 185

  Index 195

ACKNOWLEDGMENTS

Where does one start? Probably with those great repositories of information, the National Archives, the (British) Royal Society Archives, various military archives, presidential libraries, university libraries, and similar collections that get immense exposure in the acknowledgments of every historian. I salute them all, and offer a note of special appreciation to the Smithsonian Institution archivists, who produced, miracle of miracles, a significant and usable collection of documents while the controversy over *Enola Gay* was still boiling. Could this openness and candor have come about had the Smithsonian not been bitterly divided over the affair of the cancelled exhibition?

And here is one former yellow dog Democrat who owes a debt of gratitude to Republican Senator Charles Grassley of Iowa. I have made a few demands of the Feds for documents that by virtue of overclassification have remained inaccessible well beyond the time set by various presidential directives; most of the documents, I think, eventually found their way to my mailbox. When I moved to Iowa in 1995, I thought I would see if Senator Grassley's record in support of whistleblowers and the public's right to know could be enlisted in behalf of a group of 1950s documents that I wanted *soon*. It could be so enlisted indeed. They arrived in what for a Freedom of Information Act request must be record time. I was heartened by the fact that even a busy senator would intervene with bureaucrats whose beliefs (especially those at the CIA) are of the minimum disclosure variety.

Three persons have been of inestimable help in prodding me away from heresies and banalities without end: Barton Bernstein, D. M. Giangreco, and Edward

Linenthal. I hope they are not disappointed with my conclusions. Sir Bernard Lovell of the Jodrell Bank Observatory has been more than helpful. Others, colleagues and students who have read and commented on various chapters: Rachel Avon, Ann Bauer, John Bonnett, Sue Breull, John Butler, Robert J. C. Butow, A. E. Campbell, Terry Check, Sheldon Cohen, Hilary Conroy, John Correll, Diane Crosby, David Depew, Ed Drea, Kathleen Farrell, Robert Ferrell, James A. Field, Walter Fisher, Robert Frank, Marc Gallicchio, Don Goldstein, Norman Graebner, Cecelia Graves, Robert Hariman, Mimi Harvey, Marouf Hasian, Waldo Heinrichs, Harold Hitchens, Sir Michael Howard, Thomas Kane, Wenshu Lee, Les Margolin, Martin Medhurst, Trevor Melia, Stuart Creighton Miller, Don Oberdorfer, Margaret Schwartz, Beth Smarts, Merrie Snell, Stephanie Steine, Mark Stoler, Mary Trachsel, Brian Villa, Philip Wander, McClain Watson, and Jennifer Wood.

At the University of Iowa, I am indebted to Jay Semel of the Obermann Center for Advanced Studies, John Nelson of the Project on the Rhetoric of Inquiry, and at the Communication Studies Department, Randy Hirokawa, Bruce Gronbeck, Jayne Lillig, Carol Schrage, and Jan Widmer.

Parts of this book have been adapted from articles in *The New England Quarterly*, *The Pacific Historical Review*, *Rhetoric and Public Affairs*, and my 1995 book *Truman and the Hiroshima Cult* published by Michigan State University Press.

PREFACE

Books such as this usually come about when someone begins to wonder "Now why in the world did *that* happen?" The "that" which first got under my skin was the audacity of a report issued by a prestigious, official United States Government fact-finding commission, the United States Strategic Bombing Survey (USSBS), charged by President Roosevelt in 1944 to investigate the effectiveness of strategic bombing in World War II. Such a survey was a good idea. We all wanted to know if bombing significantly contributed to German and Japanese surrender.

Since USSBS would have much influence on postwar organization and military budgets, much care was taken to make it appear to be run by civilians, not beholden to any military service. The chairman was an insurance executive. The Board of Directors included three men who later became prominent. They had a staff of some 1,000 people, mostly drawn from the Army Air Forces but augmented with navy personnel when it went to Japan.

When USSBS completed the European phase of their work, President Truman sent the survey to the Pacific. Of the directors, only Paul Nitze was willing to take on the Pacific survey. He and his crew arrived in Japan in October 1945, spent nine weeks hastily interrogating Japanese officials, then returned to Washington to write their reports.

Most reports were published the summer of 1946. At that time, few people viewed the United States Strategic Bombing Survey with a critical eye. Americans had not yet learned that prestigious fact-finding commissions could sometimes go astray. For example, the controversial report of the Warren Commission to investigate the assassination of John F. Kennedy was yet in the future. So was the useless report of the McCone Commission on the causes of the Watts riots in Los Angeles.

In the 1990s when I first read the USSBS, I was steeped in the mendacities of the Kennedy-Johnson-Nixon administrations. Confronted by Nitze's "official" report, to the effect that the USSBS had gathered "all the facts" about the role of the atom bombs in bringing about Japan's surrender, I thought it absurd. Were these really "All the facts," on so complicated a subject, from a brief foray into a wholly alien land by investigators innocent of Japanese history, language, and culture? And could those "facts" support a USSBS conclusion that Japan's decision to surrender was not significantly influenced by the destruction of Hiroshima and Nagasaki?

I spent a week at the National Archives in 1994, reading the USSBS files to see what "facts" this prestigious commission had to go on. The answer was astounding: no facts at all supported their claim. A great many facts indicated that the Bomb had shocked Japan, still intent on fighting through the scheduled American invasion, into surrender. Nitze wrote that the prime evidence he used was the interrogations of Japanese officials. I read them all. The story they told was the opposite of his claim.

There was a new "Why in the world" question: Why had Nitze issued such a mendacious report? I knew Nitze's beliefs well from studying the rhetoric of American officials during the cold war. Nitze was the quintessential hawk: until the 1990's he never met a weapon system that he did not like. He wrote NSC-68, the 1950 trumpet call to arms against the aggressive Soviet Union. He saw it as his major goal to demystify atomic weapons; to convince Americans that we could fight and win a nuclear war. Among other fire-breathing calls for maximum armament, he wrote the report of the Gaither Commission on how we should fight a future war. In 1957, on hearing this report, Dwight Eisenhower said, "You can't have this kind of war. There aren't enough bulldozers to scrape the bodies off the streets." Nitze was called the godfather of all the belligerent defense intellectuals. Why had such a person minimized the role of the atom in Japan's capitulation?

Now another conundrum arose. Why did the American Left, today heavily committed to opposing Truman's bomb decision, accept uncritically this implausible "all the facts" statement from a superhawk, making it the foundation text for attacks on Harry Truman? Paul Nitze as prime legitimator of anti-Hiroshima activism is an irony for the record books. And why did these anti-Truman activists endorse USSBS as an "official report" when they explicitly rejected Harry Truman's account of why he dropped the bombs simply because *it* was "official"?

When the USSBS operation finally got a thorough study in Gian Gentile's 1998 doctoral dissertation in history at Stanford, he found the Survey profoundly wrong, even though its claims were embedded by then in the historical establishment's conventional wisdom. Gentile writes, "The Survey's published reports, unfortunately, have taken on the mystique of 'biblical truth' about strategic bombing in World War II." The question remains: Why has this perverse report become biblical truth?

The power of Nitze's "atom was unnecessary" conclusion was uniquely demonstrated in 1994 when the National Air and Space Museum (NASM) under the leadership of Martin Harwit produced the first draft of a text to accompany the planned exhibit of *Enola Gay* scheduled to open in 1995, fifty years after her historic flight. Harwit and the curators he chose to plan the exhibit were of the New Left, anti-Truman persuasion. Harwit wanted to recast the image of NASM, deemphasizing its glorification of military aviation, showing instead what he called its "dark side" as exemplified by the *Enola Gay*. But Harwit had to avoid opposition from veterans who insisted *Enola Gay* be displayed "proudly." Harwit also had to avoid agitating the Japanese, from whom he needed to borrow artifacts showing the horrors of atomic bombing. The Japanese saw themselves as victims of the Pacific war; they had bought the 1948 contention of British Nobel laureate P. M. S. Blackett that Truman dropped the bombs not to speed the end of the war, but as the first act in the anti-Soviet cold war.

This left Harwit in a terrible bind. He promised American veterans he would celebrate their accomplishments in defeating Japan; at the same time, he promised the Japanese he would not celebrate American accomplishments, but would emphasize the "UnAmerican" nature of the Bomb. One of Harwit's curators, Tom Crouch, had the good sense to tell Harwit that he couldn't do both. Events proved Crouch correct.

In the process of putting the *Enola Gay* exhibit together, NASM became the storm center of a ferocious battle. My generation (World War II participants) and the majority of historians of the Pacific war generally opposed Harwit; we believed that ending the terror of that war justified use of the bomb. Here came the biggest mystery of all: Why did Harwit and his curators justify their text by claiming it was based on the best modern scholarly research about Japan's surrender, and then ignore all that research?

Harwit could have had material and advice from the top authorities whose work related to Japan's surrender: Pacific war historians, scholars of the Japanese surrender deliberations, nuclear arms race scholars, warfighting moralists, and Truman administration scholars. The first four categories were cut out of NASM deliberations almost entirely, and the fifth only lightly involved.

The foremost student of the Pacific war in this country is arguably Ronald Spector, whose office is five minutes away from NASM at George Washington University. Harwit did not contact him. The preeminent authority on the decisions of the Japanese war cabinet, Sadao Asada, was in Japan, and if Harwit had money to buy eight to ten tickets for his staff to go to Japan, he could have afforded to bring Asada to Washington. The top authority on the Soviet nuclear arms program, and hence on the nuclear arms race, David Holloway, could have been brought to Washington from Stanford, but he was similarly ignored. Since Harwit's exhibit was intended to be one long moral argument against use of the bomb, he could have brought Paul Ramsey from Princeton, instead of ignoring all the professional students of the morality of warfighting. And while Harwit did use the advice of Truman scholar Barton Bernstein, he never contacted any of the scholars who had written comprehensive biographies of Truman. His deliberate avoidance of top scholars remains a conundrum.

The final irritant that led to this book was the blatant ethnocentrism of the curators. They were strong supporters of the Japanese claims to have been victimized. However, for the vast majority of Asians who suffered under the Japanese empire—Koreans, Chinese, Filipinos, Malays, Vietnamese, Indonesians, Thais, Pacific Islanders—at least 20,000,000 of whom died at Japanese hands, there was not a glimmer of concern in NASM's exhibit. The Chinese who had been savaged by Japanese atrocities made an effort to get Harwit to acknowledge that the bombs ended *their* suffering, and they deserved a better shake than NASM's single-minded attention to the victims of Hiroshima and Nagasaki.

In this respect, unfortunately, American veterans were just as ethnocentric as the curators and the Japanese. All the Americans worried about was how many casualties they would have sustained had there been no bomb, and had the invasion gone forward. The ongoing carnage throughout Asia and the Pacific was exacerbated by the death throes of the Japanese empire. It was halted by the bomb; this did not enter the curators' minds.

At the very least, NASM had an obligation to probe thoroughly the extensive evidence bearing on what would have happened to the rest of Asia had there been no atomic shock. The gospel according to Nitze was simply inadequate on this vital matter.

These puzzles and inconsistencies are addressed in this book. Even though I argue that in August 1945 the two bombs were justified, this does not end the matter. However firmly the case is made that the bomb ended a vicious war and saved hundreds of thousands of Asian lives, the ethical question will remain for some. Pacifists and absolutists will say that this weapon is inherently intolerable, like poison gas and biological weapons. I will not argue with them, so long as they are consistent in applying their principles to all bombing of cities. My quarrel is with Martin Harwit and his curators who claimed to base their case on the best scholarship.

As this book was in process, the events of 11 September 2001 brought a new concern to the forefront of American consciousness—terrorism. This was to be countered militarily, said President George W. Bush, by an all-out war against the terrorists. Others said it was a criminal matter, to be avenged through a police-type international investigation and apprehension of the perpetrators. Some of the latter supported their position by claiming that Americans too had carried out terrorist acts. As one speaker at a Middle East Studies Association meeting put it, "We ought to be reminded of our responsibilities for Hiroshima and Nagasaki and understand that we're not so good."

Of course the missions of *Enola Gay* and *Bock's Car* were designed to shock Japan into surrender. The saturation raid of 10 March 1945 had no effect on the Japanese generals and admirals. They were still determined to fight to the bitter end, but the spectacular atom, and the threat of many more, shortened a war that the best evidence shows would have gone on into 1946 without the new and frightening weapon. There *can* be justified terror, as there can be just wars. The theorists of warfighting have gone over all this insightfully. Up to now, their conclusions have not figured significantly in the battles over *Enola Gay*. This book is designed to change that.

1

OFFICIAL NARRATIVE #1 — TRUMAN VERSION

MR. GRAY: I would like to ask a question, General Groves. This relates to a question Mr. Garrison asked about the urgencies, whether the urgencies had been stepped up with respect to having these weapons [atomic bombs] ready toward the end of the war. My recollection is that you said that there was not any acceleration as far as you were concerned?
GENERAL GROVES: No. My mission as given to me by Secretary Stimson was to produce this at the earliest possible date so as to bring the war to a conclusion. That was further emphasized by his statement that any time that a single day could be saved I should save that day. The instructions to the project were that any individual in that project who felt that the ultimate completion, insofar as he understood it, was going to be delayed by as much as a day by something that was happening, it was his duty to report it directly to me by telephone, skipping all channels of every kind. So that urgency was on us right from the start.
In the Matter of J. Robert Oppenheimer[1]

Harry S. Truman stepped into the role of commander in chief of a nation at war on 12 April 1945. He had not been among those with whom his predecessor had shared plans for winning the war and the peace that was to follow. He had, however, as a senator and then as presiding officer of the Senate known very well how Secretary of War Henry Stimson had been fighting hard to get a conscription bill through Congress that would furnish enough recruits to replace the mounting casualties. He was also acutely aware of the terrible blow to American hopes of having the

European part of the war over early in 1945 when the Germans mounted the Battle of the Bulge. Truman may have been new to the White House but he was a veteran of World War I who had kept his commission in the reserves and knew exactly the problem that Stimson and the Army Chief George Marshall faced.

Any disinterested researcher reading the Stimson diaries, or the planning documents from the Joint Staff Planners, or even the major newspapers, knew that the dominant imperative as the war ground on into 1945 was war weariness and the fear of increasing casualties. George Marshall and many others had observed how quickly the United States became tired of World War I; Marshall believed from the start of World War II that it would be a race between public intolerance of wartime controls and surrender of the Axis powers.[2] In a mere twelve months, Marshall was proven correct. The archives are full of alarms and protests about wartime restrictions, beginning in 1943. In *The War and American Culture* Perry R. Duis, studying wartime conditions in Chicago, devotes his chapter "No Time for Privacy" to the growing impatience of the homefront, 1943–1945. "During 1943 Americans began to lose their tolerance for home front substitutions at about the same rate that their optimism for an early victory, especially in the Pacific, disappeared."[3] There was a rising tide of impatience. Commentators complained about everything; Duis says, "as women joined the workforce and gained independent incomes, they were more prone to waste time and money shopping for frivolous clothes. There were also signs during 1943 of a growing intolerance of the rationing system. A chorus of complaints greeted the decision by the local Office of Price Administration to force Chicago's 560 undertakers to collect the ration books of the deceased. Chicago-area informants for the Federal Office of War Information noted rising anxiety and anger over the complexity of the new point system and a growing belief that the upper class used influence to get away with hoarding. The first newspaper accounts detailing a widespread black market also began to appear during 1943."

Half a century of cold war, Vietnam, and other crises has dulled American memory of how short our patience was in the "good" war. After the temporary anger over Pearl Harbor, when the realities of wartime rationing, conscription, casualties, and dislocations took hold, there was serious concern as to whether the country could stay the course. As early as 1943, after the battle against Rommel in Tunisia, rumors spread that the Americans who had participated in that campaign had "done their share" and would be sent home. General Omar Bradley wrote, "when the men were told emphatically that this was not true, there was widespread rebellion . . . many cases of self-maiming were reported."[4]

One window on the continual increase of home front discontent at wartime restrictions is provided by the reports of Colonel John Callan O'Laughlin, a friend of George Marshall and other military chiefs, who reported regularly to former President Herbert Hoover. The O'Laughlin letters to Hoover constitute a rich source of insight on the workings of the government during this period. O'Laughlin wrote a particularly pessimistic report on 30 December 1944, describing to Hoover the terrific effects of the Battle of the Bulge: "Because of the losses we have sustained and because they must be replaced and additions made to them for our hoped-for counter-offensive, there is the prospect that we will be unable to provide the Pacific and Asiatic theatres of war with the supplies they need. . . . Certainly the home front will be deprived of much of its requirements—the cancellation of ration stamps which has aroused the fury of housewives and brought the charge that the provident have been swindled, was due to the needs abroad."[5]

The war is going so badly, said O'Laughlin, that the White House and the High Command fear that unless Eisenhower gets a better strategy, "There will be an explosion that will rock the world, and ruin Eisenhower and Marshall, and gravely damage Roosevelt. Already the British are suggesting that General Alexander or Field Marshall Montgomery is more competent to handle troops than Eisenhower. . . ."

Thus toward the end of 1944, the Joint Chiefs of Staff (JCS) were pessimistic about winding up the war in Europe early in 1945. The failed northern crossing of the Rhine seriously altered the strategic timetable. On New Year's Day 1945, Admiral William Leahy, chief of staff to the president, thought obtaining Japan's unconditional surrender within the year was unlikely. On 11 January 1945, the JCS "diverted the last two fully trained divisions in the United States to the European Theater, divisions originally scheduled to go to the Pacific Theater in May." On 19 January the JCS informed the British that they had directed the Joint Staff Planners to reexamine operations against Japan, "in the event that prolongation of the European War requires postponement of the invasion of Japan until well into 1946."[6]

In January 1945, O'Laughlin was even more distraught. Stimson had recommended a National Service System, utilizing the four million men previously classified as 4-F (physically unfit). Congress was impressed with the urgency of the situation; draft boards had been ordered to review the farm deferments. Legislation would be forthcoming to "fix and hold ceilings on employment, deny labor to non-essential industries . . . and withhold jobs from men and women who quit work."[7] Clothing styles were to be regulated, there would be more restrictions on meat, butter, and other foods, the government had banned conventions except those regarded as necessary to defense, and hotels were being threatened with dire penalties if they failed to cancel unnecessary bookings.

American fears of low morale and possible desertions should the war go on much longer were fortified by a page one story from Ottawa in the *New York Times* of 21 January 1945: "6,300 Canadian Soldiers AWOL of 15,600 Called to go Overseas."[8] These were draftees; they were given embarkation leave for Christmas and New Years, half of them were AWOL at some time. The ships sailed without them. While Canadian authorities assured the public that enough troops had been sent to maintain unit strength, the absenteeism created a government crisis that threatened the tenure of Prime Minister Mackenzie King. George Marshall and other American officials who feared similar reactions among American troops kept a discreet silence.

The Battle of Iwo Jima in February 1945 was exceptionally traumatic. According to Geoffrey Perrett, "the cost of the war was beginning to wear on people's nerves. February brought a quarter of a million casualties, including more than 50,000 dead. For the first time in history the United States was in a war that would cost it more than 1,000,000 casualties. Letters and telegrams poured into government offices. One distraught woman wrote: 'Please, for God's sake, stop sending our finest youth to be murdered in places like Iwo Jima. It is too much to stand, too much for mothers and homes to take. . . . It is most inhuman and awful—stop, stop!' "[9]

The *San Francisco Examiner,* among other papers, took a dim view of the cost of taking Iwo Jima. In an editorial on 27 February 1945, the paper said American forces were paying too heavily for the island, and that they were "in danger of being worn out before they ever reach the really critical Japanese areas."[10]

John Toland writes that after Iwo Jima, "The War Department itself was searching for ways to reduce casualties on all fronts. The most controversial had already been suggested to Admiral Chester W. Nimitz by General Marshall's office, which had previously had similar recommendations for the European Theater of Operations: the use of poison gas. There were large quantities on hand. Nimitz pondered its employment on Iwo Jima but concluded that 'the United States should not be the first to violate the Geneva Convention.' "[11]

Morale among soldiers in the Pacific was particularly low. GIs felt that they would be kept there until they were physical wrecks, or until their bodies were buried with four or five more "in some dark jungle or scattered over the ground by artillery shells or bombs."[12] One combat veteran told Samuel A. Stouffer, who conducted the Social Science Research Council investigation of soldier morale, "If my company makes one more invasion you had better tell the medical corps to be sure and have 42 straight jackets for there are only 42 of us left."[13]

In April 1945, the Joint Intelligence Committee (JIC) deliberated extensively on the possibility that the blockade-bombardment strategy would force unconditional Japanese surrender. This would eventually happen, they concluded, but it would not happen "within a reasonable length of time."[14] Some analysts estimated that it might take many years. The JIC noted that Japanese military authorities believed that they would be able, as at Okinawa, to so punish American attackers that "disunity and war-weariness among the United Nations" would produce a negotiated settlement, which meant that the Allied aim of totally discrediting the Japanese military would not be achieved.

Hanson Baldwin of the *New York Times* worried on 2 April 1945 about America's staying power: "If we do not follow this course, as surely as the sun sets, twenty, thirty, fifty years from now, a rearmed and perhaps far more powerful Japan—bent on bloody revenge for her present defeats—will war upon us again."[15]

Marshall's alarm at lowered morale and American impatience to return to normalcy escalated during the spring and summer of 1945. Publicly, he told the American Academy of Political and Social Science in April that he feared a "general let-down in this country," and its effect on army morale.[16] Fred M. Vinson, Director of the Office of War Mobilization and Reconversion was "afraid of the unrest in the country," and he told the JCS in May that he had "never [seen] the people in their present frame of mind before."[17]

By May, Malvina Lindsay, a *Washington Post* columnist, identified what she called an alarming "back to normalcy" epidemic. "These symptoms include: a wave of public antagonism to OPA [Office of Price Administration] stirred up by the meat shortages, stepped-up military demands, and the low-cost clothing program; increased talk of 'lifting war controls,' and a drive on Congress to discredit controls, a letdown in moral standards by housewives who, in their zeal to get food, yield to black-market restrictions; a general war weariness and reaction against restriction."[18] Lindsay went on to project even worse: consumer groups fighting to keep the economy on an even keel were losing; post war inflation and a boom/bust cycle loomed.

The 95th Infantry Division had not endured the Normandy landings, but had been in action against Germany from October 1944 to the time the Germans surrendered. Their casualties were comparatively moderate. Nevertheless when they were shipped back to the United States on 29 June 1945, and sent to train for the invasion of Japan at Camp Shelby, Mississippi, the division commander wrote "After the Division's arrival in the U.S., there was a continuing and growing opposition to being ordered to the Pacific. A very disturbing situation arose approaching open sedition and mutiny."[19]

Samuel A. Stouffer, the lead author of *The American Soldier; Combat and Its Aftermath,* expected morale to drop after Germany's surrender, and it did: "In June 1945, just after VE Day, two-thirds of the returnees in the United States and not eligible for discharge under the point system reported themselves as unwilling to go overseas again while another fifth asserted they would be willing to go when needed."[20] But the fifth who were willing did not believe they would actually be sent.

By the summer of 1945, even the elite airborne divisions lacked any kind of martial spirit. Maxwell Taylor, commanding general of the 101st Airborne Division, tried to stir up enthusiasm for new missions among his Screaming Eagles, veterans of Normandy and Bastogne: "We've licked the best that Hitler had in France and Holland and Germany. Now where do we want to go?" "Home," they screamed in unison.[21]

Joseph W. Ballantine, Japanese specialist in the State Department, adds a confirming account of the final decision day when the Japanese said they would accept the Potsdam terms provided the prerogatives of the emperor would not be compromised. Ballantine was alarmed. "I heard that over the radio, the Japanese statement, and I rushed right down to the state department about 7:30 in the morning, got hold of Grew and Dooman, and I said: 'We can't agree to that, because the prerogatives of the emperor include everything and if you agree to that you're going to have endless struggle with the Japanese.' So Grew went in to see Byrnes, and Byrnes said, 'Oh, no, we'll accept that. We've got to accept that just as it stands, because the Army and Navy are sick of fighting, the President wants to get the surrender over with as fast as possible.'"[22]

Sick of fighting? Sick of the war, period. The old saying that "The business of America is business" is only partially true. The business of America is consumption: of goods and services, especially automobiles and of any gadget technology can produce to relieve boredom. The urge for normalcy—normal production and consumption—was overwhelming. It may have been as important as the concern of mothers and lovers that their men would never return from some foreign jungle, or would return maimed.

Although anti-Truman writers cannot have missed the massive outpouring of war weariness recorded in the media and archives, you will find no trace of it in their commentaries.

Truman's decision to drop the bomb was immensely popular in summer 1945. When he later came under attack, he made a serious rhetorical error. Instead of reminding his detractors that war weariness demanded use of any weapon that might speed the end of the war, Truman fell back on the visceral, but vulnerable claim that the bomb saved the lives of hundreds of thousands of American soldiers. It may have saved those lives. The invasion was on track and there would have been a tremendous slaughter as described in convincing detail in D. M. Giangreco's analyses of military casualty estimates.[23] While it cannot be proved that nothing would have intervened to call off the invasion, the belief of millions of GIs that the bomb saved their lives is reasonable. Those who minimize the probable casualties of an invasion do not have the evidence on their side; by falling back on the huge casualty argument, however, Truman laid himself open to challenge.

Conversely, the war weariness argument can be proved beyond a shadow of a doubt. In a democracy, this was compelling; the war had to be ended as soon as possible. Casualties were probable; war weariness was certain.

⌇ ⌇ ⌇

Stimson (and possibly Truman) was most influenced by the saving lives argument. Any administration had to confront the problem of escalating battle casualties. John Mueller has written a book seeking to prove that the only significant factor affecting popular support for a president in charge of a war is the casualties sustained, both injuries and deaths. Mueller claims that in the early stages of a war, people rally round the commander in chief, but as casualties rise, support for the war, and the president, drops. He has a formula apparently derived from the Korean War: "everytime the American casualties increased by a factor of ten, support for the war dropped fifteen percentage points."[24]

A close inspection of this conclusion about Korea does not bear out the rule; certainly it did not apply to World War II, public support for which remained high despite the complaining. We knew the Axis had to be defeated. As the Pacific fighting got closer to the Japanese home islands, the Japanese resistance seemed to stiffen, and public apprehension about casualties increased. Iwo Jima was perhaps the turning point, and when Okinawa followed hard on its heels, the whole government apparatus became casualty-shy. These battles were bloody beyond belief. U.S. losses on Iwo Jima were 6,821 marines killed and about 20,000 wounded for that tiny island. Nineteen of twenty-four battalion commanders were killed. All but about 22 of the 21,000 Japanese defenders were killed. On Okinawa, where the Japanese perfected kamikaze tactics, 7,000 U.S. soldiers were killed along with the commanding general. Ten thousand sailors were killed or wounded, a far greater loss in one battle than the U.S. Navy had ever sustained. Seventy thousand Japanese and 80,000 Okinawans died; only a handful surrendered.[25]

Ronald Spector describes the reaction to Okinawa: "An entire Japanese army had been destroyed, together with hundreds of planes and the greatest battleship of the Imperial Navy. Yet few Americans who took part in the campaign felt any exaltation when it was over. The general feeling was one of anxiety and dread before the tasks that lay ahead. If the capture of a base in the Ryukyus had been this bad, what would the assault on Japan itself be like?. . . Imperial Navy strategists, reviewing the damage, real and imagined, which the kamikazes had inflicted on American shipping, estimated that 30 to 50 percent of the American invasion fleet could be put out of action prior to a landing."[26]

These battles set the tone for casualty projections for OLYMPIC, the invasion of Kyushu scheduled for 1 November. Newspapers in the U.S. offered a drumbeat of pessimism. A 22 June Hanson Baldwin *New York Times* story was headlined, "Japan's Industrial Power: While Bombing Will Greatly Cut Output, New Denser Defenses Will Need Less."[27] Two days later, "Japan, Like Okinawa, Will Cost High Price. Our Soldiers, Sure of Final Victory, Expect Harder and Greater Battles" topped W. H. Lawrence's *Times* article. Soldiers headed for Kyushu "ask at once about the terrain. 'Are there caves?' That's all he wants to know. The Japanese will have to be dug out of caves all over Japan."[28]

"Japan's Civil Army Gets Suicide Order: Members Must Die Honorably to Avoid Captivity in Event of Invasion, Decree Says," was the *Times* headline 26 June. This was the message of "the latest of a series of handbooks being issued to the People's Volunteer Corps according to a Domei dispatch."[29] On 27 June, the *Times* headline read "Tokyo Chiefs Hail Okinawa Victory: Strategic Position Improved, Cabinet Declares."[30]

On the 29th, "Mass Suicide Corps Trained by Japan: Host of Secret Weapons, With Man to Ride Each to Doom, Ready for Showdown," read Gladwin Hill's story in the *Times*.[31] July was more of the same.

Some stories during this period ventured casualty estimates for the Kyushu invasion. One of the most publicized came in May from Kyle Palmer, just returned from the Pacific. Palmer wrote in the *Los Angeles Times* that the U.S. dare not slacken its war effort. That would bring needless casualties. Palmer thought that as things were then, between 500,000 and a million more soldiers and sailors would die before surrender was achieved.[32]

Truman read the daily press, and knew that such pessimistic projections were common. Casualty estimates within the government ranged from low (30,000 for the first 30 days of Operation Olympic) to high (one million or more to bring the

Japanese to capitulation). To say that Truman was alarmed at the estimates is an understatement. On 14 June he instructed Admiral Leahy to tell the Joint Chiefs to prepare for a meeting in four days to "reopen the question of whether or not to proceed with plans and preparations for Olympic."[33] Leahy's memo to the chiefs tells us exactly where Truman stood on the number one topic on his agenda:

> The President today directed me to inform [you] that he wishes to meet with the Chiefs of Staff in the afternoon of the 18th, in his office, to discuss the details of our campaign against Japan.
>
> He expects at this meeting to be thoroughly informed of our intentions and prospects for his discussion with Churchill and Stalin.
>
> He will want information as to the number of men of the Army and ships of the Navy that will be necessary to defeat Japan.
>
> He wants an estimate of the time required and an estimate of the losses in killed and wounded that will result from an invasion of Japan proper.
>
> He wants an estimate of the time and the losses that will result from an effort to defeat Japan by isolation, blockade, and bombardment by sea and air forces.
>
> He desires to be informed as to exactly what we want the Russians to do. . .
>
> It is his intention to make his decisions on the campaign with the purpose of economizing to the maximum extent possible in the loss of American lives.
>
> Economy in the use of time and in money cost is comparatively unimportant.
>
> I suggest that a memorandum discussion of the above noted points be prepared in advance for delivery to the President at the time of the meeting. . . .

If Truman's instructions to Leahy were not sufficient evidence of what mattered to the president, an entry in his diary 16 June is unmistakable. It reads "I have to decide Japanese strategy—shall we invade Japan proper or shall we bombard and blockade? This is my hardest decision to date."[34] These were not mutually exclusive choices, as Truman found out; he could, and did, plan for them all.

As part of his preparation for the meeting, General Marshall requested from MacArthur a casualty estimate for the first—and smaller—of two invasion operations, OLYMPIC, through the first ninety days. The answer came back from Pacific Headquarters: 105,000 battle and 12,600 non-battle casualties.[35]

Marshall was upset. The casualty matter was so sensitive, and Truman was taking so much heat about it, that Marshall wired back to MacArthur emphasizing Truman's concern, implying that the estimate was too high to be acceptable. MacArthur got the hint, and wrote a new, noncommittal answer, with no numerical estimate: "I believe the operation presents less hazards of excessive loss than any other that has been suggested, and that its decisive effect will eventually save lives by eliminating wasteful operations of a nondecisive character. I regard the operation as the most economical one in effort and lives that is possible."[36]

Edward Drea, who has exhaustively studied the planning for OLYMPIC, thinks MacArthur's response reflected his ambition to achieve eternal fame as the commander of the largest amphibious invasion in history (fourteen divisions as compared with Eisenhower's nine at Normandy). Drea writes that this history-making prospect "held overwhelming appeal to MacArthur's vanity."[37] He feared that if invasion loomed as too costly, Truman would simply wait for starvation to do the job.

So MacArthur's estimate was not presented at the meeting. In fact, the whole matter of casualties was treated with kid gloves; "casualties" was a dirty word. There is room here only for highlights of the recorded minutes, with Marshall reporting:

> We are bringing to bear against the Japanese every weapon and all the force we can employ, and there is no reduction in our maximum possible application of bombardment and blockade, while at the same time we are pressing invasion preparations. It seems that if the Japanese are ever willing to capitulate short of complete military defeat in the field, they will do it when faced by the completely hopeless prospect occasioned by (1) destruction already wrought by air bombardment and sea blockade, coupled with (2) a landing on Japan indicating the firmness of our resolution, and also perhaps coupled with (3) the entry or threat of entry of Russia into the war.
>
> *Casualties.* Our experience in the Pacific war is so diverse as to casualties that it is considered wrong to give any estimate in numbers.[38]

Nonetheless, Marshall presented a table of casualties for four battles in the Pacific war, showing Luzon cost 31,000 casualties during six months of combat and a ratio of one American casualty for every five Japanese. Following this,

> There is reason to believe that the first 30 days in Kyushu should not exceed the price we have paid for Luzon. It is a grim fact that there is not an easy, bloodless way to victory in war and it is the thankless task of the leaders to maintain their firm outward front which holds the resolution of their subordinates. . . .
>
> GENERAL MARSHALL said that it was his personal view that the operation against Kyushu was the only course to pursue. He felt that air power alone was not sufficient to put the Japanese out of the way. It was unable alone to put the Germans out. General Eaker and General Eisenhower both agreed to this. Against the Japanese, scattered throughout the mountainous country, the problem would be much more difficult than it had been in Germany. He felt that this plan offered the only way the Japanese could be forced into a feeling of utter helplessness.

Twice during the meeting, Truman said that he feared facing "an Okinawa from one end of Japan to the other."

The low-end estimates that Marshall seemed to feel would assuage Truman's fears were made on very shaky bases.[39] None of them reflected the knowledge only beginning to come from ULTRA that the Japanese knew which beaches we would probably invade; that despite what the air generals claimed, interdiction of Japanese troop movements was minimal. The 350,000 Japanese troops Marshall told Truman could be expected on Kyushu would rise to 900,000 by August, "with no end in sight." No one could know what fighting on their own soil for the first time would do to Japanese ferocity; nor could they know how many of the kamikaze planes, *kaiten* "human torpedoes," *shinyo* suicide boats, and other unique devices would get through to sink U.S. ships loaded with infantry.[40] No one could know how effective the satchel charges prepared for lone Japanese of all ages and sizes to explode under American vehicles would be. No one could know whether as many things would go wrong with OLYMPIC as went wrong with OVERLORD (Normandy).

Sadao Seno, an expert on kamikazes, with co-authors Denis and Peggy Warner, projecting what might have happened on Kyushu, concludes "Those casualty figures that were tossed about before the White House meeting on 18 June might have been surpassed in a single day. Just a handful of suicide planes caused doubts as to the wisdom of the Lingayen Gulf landing in January. This time the suicide planes would have numbered hundreds, if not the thousands the Japanese planned."[41]

Only an ideologue could find that Truman's claim to want to avoid high casualties was insincere. Nor were the high estimates Truman sometimes used mere postwar inventions.

At least six casualty projections for the invasion were in the million or more range. One forecast, important because it was read by Truman, came from former President Herbert Hoover, who had several channels to the military. These were described by Robert Ferrell at the 1999 meeting of the Society for Military History.[42] There were other channels to the former chief executive.

Herbert Hoover was never invited to the White House by Franklin Roosevelt. Truman, however, bore no grudges, and asked the former president to come discuss high policy. Hoover appeared at the White House 28 May 1945, talked with Truman about feeding Europe and other problems, and later sent a five-page "Memorandum on Ending the Japanese War." Most of this memo concerned ways in which the surrender formula could be modified to appeal to the peace forces in Japan; twice the brief, 900-word document warned of American casualties on a massive scale. Hoover maintains that making some changes would bring surrender, saying "We would have saved the lives of 500,000 to 1,000,000 American boys, the loss of which may be necessary by going on to the end." And "There can be no American objective worth the expenditure of 500,000 to 1,000,000 American lives."[43]

Truman wrote on the front page of this memo "From Herbert Hoover," and sent copies of it, asking for comment, to Secretary Stimson, Acting Secretary of State Grew, former Secretary of State Cordell Hull, and the war mobilization director, Vinson. Hull finessed comment on everything except what he regarded as Hoover's "soft" position on surrender terms. Grew wrote at length analyzing the suggested surrender terms. No one refuted the casualty statement and Grew confirmed that the Japanese "are prepared for prolonged resistance."

Stimson referred his copy to the staff, and it was dealt with by Lieutenant General Thomas T. Handy, chief of the Army Operations Division. Handy's comments echoed the army line: Hoover's numbers for American dead implied total U.S. casualties of up to 4,000,000—fully double the highest military estimate to date—and was "entirely too high *under the present plan of campaign*."[44]

A second estimate in seven figures was generated in the office of Secretary Stimson, and may have been what he relied on in his *Harper's* article of 1947. Working for Stimson's office was future Nobel Laureate William Shockley, a scientist credited with much of the success of the Allied anti-submarine campaign. When Shockley's anti-submarine work was completed, he was given the task of "gathering and organizing information bearing on the problem of casualties in the Pacific war." On 21 July 1945, while Stimson was in Potsdam, Shockley handed his superior, Edward L. Bowles, the head of Stimson's team of scientists, a lengthy report. In it Shockley complained about the eccentric casualty figures issued by G-1, G-2, Army Ground Forces, and the Army Surgeon General's Office; they were worthless.[45]

Shockley wrote that his investigations had been based on the assumption that if their nation were invaded, the Japanese would recapitulate the "fight to the death" behavior their soldiers had demonstrated in recent battles. In that event, he wrote, "the Japanese dead and inffectives at the time of defeat will exceed the corresponding number for the Germans. In other words, we shall probably have to kill at least 5 to 10 million Japanese. This might cost us between 1.7 and 4 million casualties including 400,000 to 800,000 killed."

Shockley's pessimistic report resides in the Bowles papers at the Library of Congress. We cannot be certain that Bowles showed it to Stimson, but Stimson did not get his figure out of thin air. Shockley was working with Quincy Wright of the University of Chicago and several competent scientists and military intelligence specialists. Startling as they were, his suggestions would not have been disregarded.

A third estimate of huge casualties came from John J. McCloy who, in his 1945 post of Assistant Secretary of War, had favored modifying unconditional surrender. He justified using the bomb "because an invasion would have cost terrible casualties . . . As to my own position, it was to bring the war to an end sooner than it would otherwise be ended, and thus to save American lives. The estimated American casualties for landing on Japanese shores were anywhere between 250,000 and 1,000,000, while the Japanese casualties were conservatively estimated to run as high as 10 million. . . . It is true we didn't need the bomb to win, but we needed it to save American lives."[46]

Despite Marshall's influence, some official War Department documents forecast more than a million casualties. As early as August 1944, the Joint Chiefs of Staff accepted a report from their planners stating that an invasion of the home islands "might cost us half a million American lives and many more times that number in wounded."[47]

A fourth estimate of huge casualties came from Rear Admiral Ellis Zacharias, an innovative psychological warrior who spearheaded an effort to convince the Japanese through radio broadcasts that the United States would not destroy their government if they surrendered. Zacharias's claims to having eased the way to surrender are highly speculative, but his estimate of the price was clear. In his 1946 postmortem on the war, he wrote that due to the work of his psywar team, "at least a million of our young men who would have been casualties had we invaded Japan now are living normal lives."[48]

Finally, Major General Charles Willoughby, MacArthur's chief of intelligence, told Philip Gustavson in 1945 that "our invasion of the home Japanese islands would have cost us at least 1,000,000 casualties." This appeared in Gustavson's *Saturday Evening Post* article, "What If We Had Invaded Japan?" on 5 January 1946.[49] Willoughby had at first taken seriously air forces' claims about being able to prevent reinforcement of Kyushu, and when he read the decrypts about steady additions to Kyushu's defense force, he panicked. On 28 July 1945 he informed his superiors that Japanese strength on Kyushu was growing so fast that if it was not checked, MacArthur's troops would "attack on a ratio of one (1) to one (1), which is not the recipe for victory."[50]

As Marshall's reluctance to pass on MacArthur's estimate to Truman shows, the army wanted to avoid written or official estimates that would encourage pessimism. But *some* authorities committed high estimates to paper; the median (perhaps a consensus) figure for casualties expected in the invasion of Japan was 500,000. The 500,000 figure is mentioned by dozens of those who were actively putting the plans for Olympic into effect.[51] Late twentieth century efforts to impugn Truman's memory or integrity by challenging these high estimates are unwarranted.

By late spring 1945, the terrible damage that the U.S. Navy had done to the Japanese fleet, and the steady pounding of Japanese cities by American bombers, caused the admirals and generals whose organizations achieved these results to think the Japanese had to be about ready to quit fighting. Sinking ships was what the navy did; when Japan could no longer get normal imports from abroad, of course she would surrender. Destroying buildings was what the strategic bombers did; when there was not a structure left standing in Japan, of course she would surrender. Curtis LeMay believed this absolutely. These men were applying Western tolerances of punishment to a Bushido society with quite different standards.[52]

The optimistic admirals and air generals were not running the war, however. George Marshall was, with the full backing of Secretary Stimson and President Truman. No American commanded the respect and prestige of Marshall, and Marshall's view of what was needed to secure Japan's surrender was the one that prevailed. Edward Drea, a historian fluent in Japanese and intimately familiar with tactics and strategy of both sides, gives an account of the run up to Japan's surrender as experienced by George Marshall; I depend on it here.[53]

At the time of the 18 June meeting with Truman, Marshall assumed that the claims of air generals that they could prevent Japanese reinforcement of Kyushu were valid. By July, ULTRA decrypts made a mockery of this assumption. New Japanese divisions were appearing and broadcasting orders to their subordinate units. Their locations in southern Kyushu indicated that the Japanese had accurately calculated what invasion beaches the United States had selected. From broadcasts of Japanese map maneuvers, Marshall learned that "Tokyo concluded a third of the assault troops would be destroyed at sea and another 15 to 20 percent of the first assault wave killed by artillery or beach defenses." By August, the buildup showed Japanese troops "stacked" on the scheduled landing beaches, in trenches, caves, bunkers, as they had been in dozens of minor islands where Americans had to flush them out with flame-throwers—when the Americans could get close enough.

This buildup, writes Drea, presented "Marshall's preview of hell. A professional soldier could easily visualize the bloody carnage along the beachheads. The assault troops needed every weapon America possessed to get them across the beaches and inland with the fewest possible losses." One potent new weapon that would be available: the atomic bomb.

On 30 July Marshall got a report from Groves on the possible tactical use of the atom: the blast would clear the enemy entirely from an area 2,000 feet in diameter, and paralyze enemy troops in an area five miles in diameter; seven of the bombs would probably be ready for OLYMPIC, in addition to those to be used against strategic targets—which use might bring surrender. But no one knew, of course.

The first atomic bomb on Hiroshima did not shock the Japanese into surrender. In Drea's account:

> Codebreakers read dispassionate eyewitness Japanese Military assessments from Hiroshima downplaying the enormous destruction. One vivid ULTRA description of 100,000 casualties actually seems to have affected Truman more than Japan's warlords. While they looked for countermeasures for atomic bombs, he secretly ordered no more bombs to be used without his express approval. Marshall saw Hiroshima against a larger backdrop of strategic bombing. According to a deciphered message, an earlier air raid had killed 100,000 Japanese people in the capital of Tokyo in a single night, but seemingly had no effect whatsoever on Japanese determination to fight on. . . . An invasion was still likely. Indeed ULTRA had located three more Japanese divisions on Kyushu the day the Hiroshima bomb was dropped. The Sixteenth Area Army now had 600,000 troops on Kyushu and expected even more.[54]

As the United States discovered later in Korea and Vietnam, strategic bombing could not prevent a determined enemy from infiltrating thousands of troops into wooded areas almost at will. So fearsome was the Japanese strength on Kyushu that on 6 August the JCS requested its planners to provide a scenario for bypassing Kyushu and attacking northern Honshu. The Joint War Plans Committee took this request seriously; a 96-page plan for this was ready by 9 August.[55]

Marshall again wanted the judgment of MacArthur, and sent an "eyes only" message on 7 August. As Drea describes Marshall's inquiry, he wanted to know "Did it make sense to attack into the teeth of the Japanese defenses? Maybe it was better to shift Olympic to less well fortified places like Tokyo [Honshu], Sendai, and Ominato? What did MacArthur think? Imagine Marshall sending such a cable to Eisenhower asking him to consider switching the Normandy invasion to Norway just three months before D-Day! MacArthur's reply, received two days later, dismissed reports of reinforcements as 'greatly exaggerated.'. . .his air campaign would isolate and weaken Japanese defenses on Kyushu before the invasion."[56]

An alternative site was not popular with MacArthur. Marshall explored the atomic option further. Marshall's plan was to clear the beaches with bombs while the troops were still six miles offshore; a few days later the invaders would land and go straight through the bombed area, preferably by truck but by foot if necessary. Marshall was almost totally unaware of the possibility of radiation damage. Drea summarizes: "An atomic attack on such a scale along Kyushu's shores would have rendered Hiroshima and Nagasaki mere footnotes to history. The atomic hell on the beaches would have seared both ways . . . Olympic would not have invaded the land of the gods but the world of the dead."[57]

The hundreds of thousands of troops scheduled for Olympic might never have gone ashore, but they were justified in believing that if they had, the carnage would have been terrible. All postwar inspectors of the still-uncompleted defenses in Kyushu, and all soundings of the determination of the Japanese to kill at least a third of the invaders while still seaborne, support the conclusion of Edward J. Winslett, an intelligence officer with Sixth Army. Winslett reported "after a personal survey of the areas in which our invasion landings were scheduled to take place, I am convinced that the greatest battle the American Armies have ever won was the one which was never fought: the INVASION OF KYUSHU."[58]

⊱ ⊱ ⊱

A second imperative for Truman when he took office was carrying out Franklin Roosevelt's vow to secure unconditional surrender of the Axis powers. Unconditional surrender was not a mere slogan thought up by Roosevelt at Casablanca as some Roosevelt critics maintain.

Roosevelt was an active participant in the settlement of World War I. He was assistant secretary of the navy from 1913 to 1920, when he absorbed the "big stick" philosophy of his cousin Theodore Roosevelt, disagreeing with Woodrow Wilson's 1917 "peace without victory" speech. As Earl Pomeroy shows in his article, "Sentiment for a Strong Peace, 1917–1919," the Wilsonian program, with its Fourteen Points, did not have widespread support. Theodore Roosevelt, Henry Cabot Lodge, William Howard Taft, and other prominent politicians wanted a hard peace, and American military leaders were of a like mind.[59]

General John Pershing was perhaps the most adamant of those demanding the complete destruction of German armies. His pressure on President Wilson was partially effective, and Wilson told the Germans on 23 October 1918 that the United States would deal with the "military masters and the monarchial autocrats of Germany" only on the basis of surrender. But the Allies nonetheless granted an armistice. Pershing, in his memoirs, complained that "Instead of requiring the German forces to retire at once, leaving materiel, arms and equipment behind, the Armistice terms permitted them to march back to their homeland with colors flying and bands playing, posing as the victims of political conditions. . . . The surrender of the German armies would have been an advantage to the Allies in the enforcement of peace terms and would have been a greater deterrent against possible future German aggression."[60]

Laurence Stallings, in his study of World War I, repeated some of Pershing's more colorful language: "Foch . . . wanted the Germans on the ropes when he, as referee, would stop the bout, but Pershing wanted the German champion stretched cold on the canvas for the count of ten. . . . At Paris, there was a meeting of the Allied Supreme War Council, three members keeping it secret from the fourth [Wilson]. Clemenceau and Lloyd George and Orlando quietly steamed the stamp from a fresh deck and began to mark the cards."[61] Wilson was out of it. And as Pershing told a friend in 1923, "They never knew they were beaten in Berlin. It will all have to be done all over again."[62]

Franklin Roosevelt was in sympathy with Pershing. As acting Secretary of the Navy in 1918, he dealt with the disposition of the German fleet. Against heavy opposition he recommended that the fleet be surrendered rather than simply interned. He convinced Wilson to back him, and the armistice so provided. But it was a minor success.[63] There should have been no armistice until the Germans were forced back to their own soil, visibly defeated, completely foreclosed from future claim that they did not lose the war on the battlefield.

General Pershing's eighty-third birthday was 13 September 1943; American forces were then struggling in their ill-fated invasion of Italy. Roosevelt sent Pershing a birthday greeting: "Today brings forcibly to mind that you wanted to go through to Berlin in 1918."[64]

Roosevelt did not impose the doctrine on unwilling subordinates. It also bubbled up from below. The best account of how it developed during World War II comes from Iokibe Makoto, professor of history at Kobe University, in an article in the *Japanese Journal of American Studies*. As Iokibe tells us, the influential Council on Foreign Relations (CFR) began studying postwar policy as soon as the war broke out. On 8 April 1942, Grayson Kirk, then professor of government at Columbia University, presented a paper, "The Armistice Negotiations, 1918," to a meeting of the CFR in New York. Kirk's conclusion could have come from the lips of Franklin Roosevelt:

> It is clear that if, instead of an armistice, there had been an unconditional surrender including, as implied, a speedy conclusion of a military settlement of the war, recovery might have been expedited, the peace conference would not have had hanging over it the fear of a renewal of hostilities by Germany, and German resentment over military aspects of the settlement might not have been so intense or prolonged.[65]

Kirk's paper was sent to the newly formed State Department Advisory Committee on Postwar Foreign Policy, a subcommittee of which was headed by Norman H. Davis, president of CFR and an intimate of President Roosevelt. This subcommittee rapidly endorsed the CFR's conclusions. On 20 May 1942, Davis told his group that he had discussed surrender with the president, who agreed with the committee's position.[66]

America's allies were fully aware of Roosevelt's intentions. The United Nations Declaration, signed 1 January 1942, did not use the unconditional surrender phrase, but said the same thing in other words: "The governments signatory hereto . . . Being convinced that complete victory over their enemies is essential . . . Declare . . . [etc.]."[67]

Shortly before the Casablanca Conference, Roosevelt discussed unconditional surrender with his Joint Chiefs of Staff (JCS). The minutes of the meeting of 7 January 1943 record: "The President said he was going to speak to Mr. Churchill about the advisability of informing Mr. Stalin that the United Nations were to continue on until they reach Berlin, and that their only terms would be unconditional surrender."[68]

At Casablanca, Roosevelt did speak with Churchill, who approved the idea and suggested that they issue a statement about it after the British cabinet was consulted. This was done, the Cabinet approved and suggested that Italy be included in the public statement.[69] Roosevelt was to make the statement at the end of the conference, and a script was prepared for him to read:

> The President and the Prime Minister, after a complete survey of the world war situation, are more than ever determined that peace can come to the world only by a total elimination of German and Japanese war power. This involves the simple formula of placing the objective of this war in terms of an unconditional surrender by Germany, Italy and Japan. Unconditional surrender by them means a reasonable assurance of world peace, for generations. Unconditional surrender means not the destruction of the German populace, nor of the Italian or Japanese populace, but does mean the destruction of a philosophy in Germany, Italy, and Japan which is based on the conquest and subjugation of other peoples.[70]

For some unknown reason, Roosevelt scuttled this script at the news conference and ad-libbed. What came out was a reference to "Unconditional Surrender Grant" plus a reasonably coherent statement about what the policy could mean, and *not* mean, for the Axis powers. He concluded, "This meeting is called the Unconditional Surrender meeting."[71]

Roosevelt did not say that the policy had been discussed in twenty-one meetings of a CFR study group, that it had been approved by a committee of the U.S. State Department, that it had been discussed with his Joint Chiefs of Staff, nor that Churchill had approved it and gained the approval of the British cabinet. No listening reporter knew that he and Churchill had written out a statement about it in advance. William M. Franklin's statement that "In 1943, unconditional surrender was a newly publicized slogan for an already well-known policy," is accurate.[72]

Roosevelt's casual handling of the announcement left the door open for all kinds of silliness. Churchill was the worst offender; his memory played tricks on him and he wrote to Robert Sherwood "I heard the words 'unconditional surrender' for the first time from the President's lips at the [news] conference."[73]

Roosevelt's memory was hardly better. He told Sherwood, "We had so much trouble getting those two French generals together that I thought to myself that this was as difficult as arranging the meeting of Grant and Lee — and then suddenly the press conference was on, and Winston and I had had no time to prepare for it, and the thought popped into my mind that they had called Grant 'Old Unconditional Surrender' and the next thing I knew, I had said it."[74]

Elliott Roosevelt added to the confusion, Samuel Roseman and E. L. Woodward gave misleading versions of the background. The accurate version was published in Sherwood's *Roosevelt and Hopkins* in 1948: "What Roosevelt was saying was that there would be no negotiated peace, no compromise with Nazism and

Fascism, no 'escape clauses' provided by another Fourteen Points which could lead to another Hitler. . . . He wanted to ensure that when the war was won it would stay won."[75]

There were other reasons for using the phrase; it was intended as a morale booster for the Allies, and specifically for the Soviet Union. Stalin was outraged at continual postponement of a second front on the European continent. He feared the United States and Britain were unwilling to bear their share of the fighting and casualties, when the Soviet Union had already paid in torrents of blood on the Eastern Front. Roosevelt wanted some gesture of reassurance for Stalin, and unconditional surrender, which committed the Western powers not to compromise with the Nazis, seemed to be such a gesture.[76]

Partly because of Roosevelt's sloppy introduction of the phrase, much uncertainty existed as to exactly what it meant. One effort to clarify its application to Japan came at the Cairo Conference on 1 December 1943. The declaration of this Anglo-Sino-American gathering read "The three Great Allies are fighting this war to restrain and punish the aggression of Japan. They covet no gain for themselves and have no thought of territorial expansion." The declaration goes on to indicate that Japanese conquests (Manchuria, Formosa, and "all other territories which she has taken by violence and greed") should be taken away from her and the independence of Korea granted.[77]

Both Roosevelt and Churchill provided definitions of a sort. They usually distinguished between the Axis leaders and the common people, as in this Roosevelt statement in 1943: "The people of the Axis-controlled areas may be assured that when they agree to unconditional surrender they will not be trading Axis despotism for ruin under the United Nations. The goal of the United Nations is to permit liberated peoples to create a free political life of their own choosing and to attain economic security."[78]

Similarly, Churchill told the House of Commons in February 1944:

> The term "unconditional surrender" does not mean that the German people will be enslaved or destroyed. It means however that the Allies will not be bound to them at the moment of surrender by any pact or obligation. There will be, for instance, no question of the Atlantic Charter applying to Germany as a matter of right and barring territorial transferences or adjustments in enemy countries. No such arguments will be admitted by us as were used by Germany after the last war, saying that they surrendered in consequence of President Wilson's Fourteen Points. Unconditional surrender means that the victors have a free hand . . . If we are bound, we are bound by our own consciences to civilization. . .[79]

In the United States, Japan was the object of more hostility than Germany. Every public opinion poll showed that large majorities wanted Japan thoroughly beaten and the emperor deposed or tried as a war criminal.[80] That the soft peace advocates ultimately won their main objective, the retention of the emperor, was due to Truman's sagacity in realizing that peace would not come without some flexibility on that topic. The slogan had to stay; the policy could give just a bit.

Opposition to unconditional surrender in the United States came from two groups: 1) the military, fearful of the huge casualties should Japan not capitulate before the scheduled invasion. 2) Japanophiles, mostly conservative, felt that however mistaken Japan's rampage through the Pacific had been, Japan (not China) was the most plausible bulwark against the spread of Communism in Asia. If unconditional surrender was held to strictly, and the Japanese state was reduced to anarchy and impotence, the Soviet Union would assume hegemony in that area.

Foremost among the Japanophiles were Joseph Grew, the last pre-war American ambassador to Japan, Joseph Ballantine and Eugene Dooman of the state department, Harry Kern of *Newsweek,* Hanson Baldwin of the *New York Times,* economist James Lee Kauffman, and a dozen others who later formed the American Council on Japan (ACJ).[81] These people wanted no mention of unconditional surrender, but rather a clear statement that the Japanese could choose their own form of government, which meant retention of the emperor system.

The most influential force for modifying unconditional surrender came from the military. During 1944, worried that the casualties likely to be caused by strict adherence to unconditional surrender would be unacceptable, General George Strong, an army planner, drafted two sample surrender documents, both of which implicitly allowed the emperor to continue to function under the control of American occupiers. These drafts were presented to Under Secretary of State Joseph Grew. In February 1945, the new State-War-Navy Coordinating Committee (SWNCC) considered and modified them, since they seemed to weaken unconditional surrender.[82]

SWNCC deliberations were overtaken by the Anglo-American discussions at Malta and Yalta, 30 January to 11 February 1945. Here the military leaders of the United States and Britain came to grips with problems of the Pacific war, including plans, logistics, and surrender policy. Churchill was then in favor of mitigating the harshness of unconditional surrender. He said this "would be worthwhile if it led to the saving of a year and a half of war in which so much blood and treasure would be poured out."[83] After the defeat of Germany, Churchill wanted the Allies to issue an ultimatum to Japan, retaining the unconditional surrender wording, but defining it to allow retention of the emperor. Brian Villa believes this proposal of Churchill's was the true origin of the Potsdam Declaration.[84]

From Yalta until the Potsdam Conference in July, the question of surrender terms was rarely off the agenda of SWNCC, the Joint Staff Planners, the Joint Intelligence Staff (JIS), the War Department Operations Division, the Department of State, or the desks of Grew, Stimson, Byrnes, and even President Truman. Military advice was strongly against a strict interpretation of unconditional surrender. On 7 April, for instance, the Joint Intelligence Staff distinguished between defeat and surrender, claiming that the literal meaning of unconditional surrender "is unknown to the Japanese." And even if a Japanese government surrendered unconditionally, the JIS thought, Japanese resistance would cease only if the people and army believed the emperor approved the surrender.[85]

Harry Truman, taking over the presidency 12 April, gave his first address to Congress 16 April. He had not been privy to Roosevelt's decision making, but he knew Roosevelt's rationale for unconditional surrender, and affirmed his own commitment in his speech to Congress. In his *Memoirs,* Truman notes that "There were many indications of approval of what I said. I was applauded frequently, and when I reaffirmed the policy of unconditional surrender the chamber rose to its feet."[86] Few events could have confirmed his support of the doctrine more indelibly.

Nonetheless, military efforts to clarify the doctrine were felt in the White House. On 8 May, in his V-E Day press conference, Truman went further than Roosevelt had in explaining what unconditional surrender meant for Japan, and subtly modified the doctrine. Instead of assuming Japan to be monolithic, he separated the people from their political and military leaders. He did not demand surrender of Japan, but only of the military and naval forces:

Just what does the unconditional surrender of the armed forces of Japan mean for the Japanese people?

It means the end of the war.

It means the termination of the influence of the military leaders who brought Japan to the present brink of disaster.

It means provision for the return of soldiers and sailors to their families, their farms and their jobs.

And it means not prolonging the present agony and suffering of the Japanese in the vain hope of victory.

Unconditional surrender does not mean the extermination or enslavement of the Japanese people.[87]

This change was noted in Japan. Advocates of peace saw a significant softening of the Casablanca attitude. The die-hard Japanese military ignored the change.

On 28 May, in a conference with the primary advocate of retaining the emperor system, Joseph Grew, Truman said he had been thinking of further modification of surrender terms, but he refused to include in his upcoming Memorial Day address the statement Grew suggested specifically allowing for continuance of the "present dynasty." Instead, Truman wanted the matter referred to the JCS and SWNCC.[88]

The military advised against any such statement. American forces were then being butchered by the fanatic defenders of Okinawa, and modifying the surrender terms at that time would be seen by the Japanese as a sign of weakness. Consequently, on 1 June, Truman issued a militant call for unconditional surrender. He was back on the same wavelength as his predecessor.[89]

But the controversy continued. Unconditional surrender dominated the meetings of the secretaries of war, state, and navy in June. On the 12th, Secretary Stimson mentioned the letter former President Herbert Hoover had written to Truman advocating flexibility on the surrender issue. Stimson said the unconditional part should be abandoned if the United States could secure its strategic objectives without it.[90] On 18 June, Truman met with the JCS and the service secretaries; Stimson tried to get Truman to publicly define "surrender" to allow retention of the emperor. He was supported by Truman's chief of staff, Admiral William Leahy. They failed. The minutes of the meeting report Truman saying, "he had left the door open for Congress to take appropriate action with reference to unconditional surrender. However, he did not feel that he could take any action at this time to change public opinion on this matter."[91]

On 19 June, the three secretaries (Artemus Gates sitting in for Navy Secretary James Forrestal) went over the same ground with the same results. Surrender simply had to be clarified before any invasion. Once American troops landed, it would be too late; they would face "cave-by-cave" battle to the bitter end.[92]

Truman agreed to appoint a high-level committee to word a public surrender demand. Drafting of the statement was in the hands of a group chaired by McCloy; at this stage, everybody in the War Department got into the argument. Brig. Gen. George Lincoln, Col. Charles Bonesteel, Col. Dean Rusk, and many others all had a say.[93] A Lt. Col. Fahey wrote a substantial memo saying, "It should be made perfectly clear that a Japanese 'Yes' or 'No' is the only type answer sought, and that no Allied-Jap negotiations will be tolerated."[94] Mark Howe, in Stimson's office, advised that "Although present plans being formulated . . . are based on the assumption that unconditional surrender will include the total capitulation of the Japanese Government and the emperor (JCS 1275), the United States is neither committed to that assumption, nor to any particular definition of unconditional surrender. It is clear, however, that any modification of tacitly assumed policy would be unacceptable if it substantially jeopardized the objectives of the United States. It would be short-sighted in the extreme to save the lives of this generation only to lose those of the next."[95]

So the famous Potsdam Declaration (officially it was a proclamation, but that label did not stick) went out on 26 July 1945.[96] The first paragraphs warned the Japanese that unless they seized the opportunity to end the war, they would be devastated as was Germany. Paragraph five was also tough: "Following are our terms. We will not deviate from them. There are no alternatives. We shall brook no delay." Japan's diplomats immediately saw that the terms the U.S. imposed were not punitive. Nor were the terms a surprise, following on the heels of various Truman speeches and the Cairo Declaration: eliminate the power of the militarists, submit to occupation until a peaceful and responsible government is established, give up all conquered territories, and "proclaim now the unconditional surrender of all the Japanese armed forces."

All this was demanded of Japan. But there were also promises: the disarmed military would be permitted to return home and lead productive lives; freedom of speech, religion, and thought would be established; civilian industries would be permitted; international trade would be permitted eventually; and the Allied occupation would be ended when the new government was established.

The word "unconditional" was still there, but the rhetoric had softened. How much it had softened was revealed in an anonymous memo produced in McCloy's office on 4 September. The memo was headed "Rights and Powers over Japan."[97] The first paragraph observed that although MacArthur had full power to "take

such steps as he deems proper to effectuate the surrender terms," he was nevertheless bound by the Potsdam Declaration. Then:

2. In the sense in which "Unconditional Surrender" has been used in relation to Germany, the Japanese surrender is not an unconditional surrender. On the contrary it
   is based on the terms of the Potsdam Declaration, the exchange of notes resulting
   in the acceptance of those terms, and the surrender instrument, which itself con-
   stitutes an acceptance of those terms.
3. A moment's consideration of the effect of those documents will make this clear:
   Under the Potsdam Declaration we have bound ourselves to continue Japanese
   sovereignty in the home islands (par 8); to permit Japanese military forces "to return to their homes with the opportunity to lead peaceful and productive lives"
   (par 9); not to enslave the Japanese race, and to establish freedom of speech, of religion, and of thought. . . .

The rest of the Potsdam conditions were reviewed, and the memo concluded:
"All of these are expressly 'terms' which were offered to Japan in order to induce
her to surrender, and which were accepted by Japan. No such situation arises in our
relations with Germany."

Potsdam can of course be interpreted different ways. Writers who wish to put
Truman in the wrong see the declaration as just another instance of American and
British vindictiveness. Martin Sherwin, for instance, says, "The Potsdam Declara-
tion of July 26 calling for the surrender of Japan was decidedly unhelpful to those
Japanese who were searching for a means of bringing the war to a conclusion."[98]
Leon Sigal, in *Fighting to a Finish,* is contemptuous of the Potsdam Declaration:
"Adding little to the threats and promises that might alter Japan's calculations to
continue the war, the declaration was also released in a way that denied time for ra-
tional choice . . . Neither conciliation nor ultimatum, the Potsdam Declaration was
no more than propaganda."[99]

Careful inspection of the attitudes of leaders of the Japanese peace party yields
different conclusions. They saw in the Potsdam terms an acceptable alternative to
the destruction Japan would otherwise sustain.

Foreign Minister Togo Shigenori was foremost among them: "It appeared also
that a measure of consideration had been given to Japan's economic position; at a
time when such Draconian retribution upon Germany as the Morgenthau Plan for
her reduction to a pastoral state was being proposed, I felt special relief upon see-
ing that the function of Japan as a processing nation, as contemplated by Secretary
Hull during the Japanese-American negotiations [of 1941] would be recognized,
and that to this end severe reparations would not be imposed."[100]

Baron Hiranuma Kiichiro, president of Privy Council, said, "Following the
Potsdam Declaration, I felt that we should accept it at once since it did state that
the position of the Imperial House would be maintained."[101]

Kase Toshikazu, officer for American affairs in the Japanese Foreign Office in
1945, discusses the declaration in *Journey to the Missouri:*

Instead of demanding unconditional surrender from our government the last item significantly called upon it to proclaim the unconditional surrender of all our armed forces. *This was a deft move,* as it spared the imposition of indignities upon His Majesty's government . . . The Army at first opposed the publication of the proclamation, but it was finally prevailed upon by the Foreign Office to agree to it . . . Also, the newspapers were encouraged to denounce the proclamation as a device to intimidate our people into submission.

The popular reaction, however, was that the terms were far more lenient than had been generally expected . . . I remember that quite a few people came to see the foreign minister in order to urge upon him the necessity of immediately accepting the offer.[102]

In his book *The Lost War,* reporter Kato Masuo offers similar interpretations of the declaration: "Foreign Office Officials quickly interpreted it as offering Japan considerable latitude, even though it called for 'unconditional surrender.' Actually, aside from purely military considerations, the Allied demand was far from 'unconditional.' It left Japan no sane alternative but acceptance."[103]

Shigemitsu Mamoru, an active member of the peace party and foreign minister before Togo, told Samuel Eliot Morison that despite the absence of an explicit statement about the emperor, the "reference in paragraph 7 to withdrawing occupation forces after 'a peacefully inclined and responsible government' had been set up indicated to the Japanese that they would be permitted to determine their own future government."[104]

The Japanese officials in Switzerland, led by Minister Kase Shunichi and director of the Bank for International Settlements, Kitamura Kojiro, after initial negative reaction to the Potsdam Declaration, decided that it was an "astute document which left a possible way out." According to an Office of Strategic Services (OSS) report sent to Truman through channels, the Kase-Kitamura group cabled Tokyo on 30 July stressing the favorable terms from Potsdam.[105]

The Japanese government finally decided on 10 August, after the atomic bombing of Hiroshima and Nagasaki and Russia's entry into the war, to accept the Potsdam terms with the understanding that "the prerogatives of His Majesty as a sovereign ruler" would remain.[106] This was unacceptable to the Americans, but peace was too tantalizing to let the opportunity slip by. Truman and Byrnes did not promise the emperor could keep his throne, they did imply that he would not be immediately overthrown: his authority, however, "shall be subject to the Supreme Commander of the Allied Powers." They did not say for how long the emperor would have this authority. Truman handled this deftly; he kept the slogan, appeared to keep the policy, and finessed the details. He conceded what was necessary to end the war, while maintaining the appearance of toughness.

Did the unconditional surrender doctrine delay Japanese capitulation? There is no evidence that it did. After reading the defiant statements of the Japanese generals and admirals after the war, it is clear that unless they got major concessions, they had intended to do exactly as they had done on Okinawa, on a massive scale; punish the attackers so severely that the *attackers* would sue for peace. The holdouts demanded no change in the government, no general occupation, no war crimes trials by outsiders, and self-disarmament. To secure these demands, they defied the peace party, and until the very end, even the emperor. Only when the emperor made it a matter of loyalty did they bow to the imperial order.

Suppose Truman had scuttled unconditional surrender in June, when anti-Truman writers claim he could have obtained surrender? Certainly relations with the Soviet Union would have been further embittered. Stalin would have been confirmed in his suspicion that the United States simply wanted to keep Russia out of postwar affairs in the Pacific by securing an early surrender. The domestic consequences in the United States could have been explosive. (Dean Acheson, Cordell Hull, and Archibald McLeish attest to this.) Secretary Byrnes put it bluntly: he told Truman the American people would crucify their president if unconditional surrender were publicly renounced.[107] British historian A. E. Campbell emphasizes Roosevelt's sensitivity to Woodrow Wilson's failures at the end of World War I: Wilson "failed to carry either the Allied leaders or his own countrymen with him in his grand design."[108] Truman was well advised to heed a strong public demand for unconditional surrender; it would have been unrealistic to reverse policy in the spring of 1945. Only the atom, and the startling reversal of the Japanese position to acceptance of the Potsdam terms made it possible for Truman and Byrnes, on 11 August, to offer the Japanese "slight reassurance" that the emperor could remain.[109]

The Allies had conflicting objectives in the summer of 1945. They desperately wanted to end the war without a bloodbath on Kyushu. This objective required the cooperation of Hirohito. But they also wanted to defeat Japanese forces so convincingly as to make a renewal of Japanese militarism unlikely.

Did they achieve both objectives? About the first there can be little doubt. Despite U.S. Army estimates at the conclusion of the Okinawa slaughter that Japan could not be brought down until late 1946, with the aid of the August shocks (the atom and Soviet entry) the war was over long before that.

About the second, the answer is a qualified "Yes." One of the best discussions of how the American occupation of Japan worked out is John Dower's landmark work, *Embracing Defeat*. MacArthur instituted a "revolution from above," intended to establish democratization and demilitarization. Writes Dower:

> This was an extraordinary, and extraordinarily fluid, moment—never seen before in history, and, as it turned out, never to be repeated . . . many Japanese would indeed welcome the revolution from above. It kindled their hopes and sparked their imaginations. The American regimen cracked open the authoritarian structures of the old society in a manner that permitted unprecedented individual freedoms and unanticipated forms of popular expression to flourish.[110]

None of this would have happened had the war ended on other terms. Dower again: "Had men of influence from the emperor on down been left to their own devices, they would never have dreamed of initiating anything even remotely approximating such drastic reforms; and had the government actually been conceded a 'conditional' surrender in the closing stages of the war, it might have been in a position to cut American reformers off at the knees."[111]

As the Cold War took hold, these early reforms were circumscribed, but no one can say Japan is not the better for what was achieved in the early years.

※ ※ ※

The third imperative confronting Truman in 1945 was getting the United Nations underway, avoiding the mistakes Woodrow Wilson made with the League of Nations after World War I, and setting the world on course toward an organization that would make war less likely. Roosevelt had laid the foundation for this too; Truman followed through with only minor problems. Dealing with atomic matters was a separate, though related process, and here Truman ran into difficulty. Eventually he was accused of having started the nuclear arms race, which we will consider in chapter six.

In 1945, however, the country was overwhelmingly supportive of Truman's achievements. The war was over sooner than expected. There was no costly amphibious landing in a hostile Japan. All Axis powers were convincingly defeated. War crimes trials were underway. The United Nations was beginning to function.

As to the ten percent in Gallup's poll of 16 August 1945 who said they disapproved of the atomic bombings, some opposition was to be expected. The bomb was a horrible weapon. Pacifists and some religious leaders were sure that atomic bombs should be outlawed, like poison gas. We had used them against noncombatants.

Anti-bomb dissenters often had powerful voices. Dwight MacDonald, first off the block with criticism in the August 1945 *Politics,* titled his piece "The Decline to Barbarism." We were on a moral level with the beasts of Maidenek, and the American people were as responsible for this horror as the Germans had been for the death camps.[112]

On 17 August 1945, *The United States News* carried editor David Lawrence's "What Hath Man Wrought?" Lawrence told us "God did not provide this new weapon of terror. Man made it himself with the God-given brains and skill of the scientist . . . Military necessity will be our constant cry in answer to criticism, but it will never erase from our minds the simple truth that we, of all civilized nations, did not hesitate to employ the most destructive weapon of all times indiscriminately against men, women, and children."[113]

The editors of *Commonweal,* in the issue of 24 August 1945, noted "There were names of places in Europe which from the early days of the war were associated with the German idea that by disregarding the rights of civilians you could shorten the war. These names of places—Rotterdam, Coventry—were associated . . . with a judgment of German guilt and German shame. . . . The name Hiroshima, the name Nagasaki, are names for American guilt and shame."[114]

Christian Century acknowledged that the bomb saved the lives of more than one million American and 250,000 British soldiers, but "What the use of poison gas did to the reputation of Germany in World War I, the use of the atomic bomb has done for the reputation of the United States. . . . Japanese leaders . . . reiterated that Japan has won a moral victory by not stooping as low as her enemies, that a lost war is regrettable but not necessarily irreparable, that the United States has been morally defeated because she has been driven to use unconscionable methods of fighting."[115]

Norman Thomas in *Human Events* said we had made guinea pigs of thousands upon thousands of Japanese, and "This destruction of Nagasaki was the greatest single atrocity of a very cruel war."[116] Stuart Chase and Milton Mayer in *Common Sense*, and Lewis Mumford in *The Saturday Review of Literature* made similar objections.[117] All these criticisms were based on absolutist morality.

One major absolutist criticism of the bomb decision was described in the *New York Times* of 6 March 1946. A Special Commission of the Federal Council of Churches reported the conclusions of a group of prestigious theologians, including Reinhold Niebuhr and Henry P. Van Dusen of Union Theological Seminary, H. Richard Niebuhr and Roland Bainton of Yale Divinity School, Harvey Branscomb of Duke University, and Bishop Angus Dun of the Washington D.C. Protestant Episcopal Diocese. This group emphasized the impossibility of avoiding large noncombatant casualties in using atomic bombs, and deplored their use without warning on a Japan whose strategic position was already hopeless. Also, "it was virtually certain that she had not developed atomic weapons of her own. Even though use of the new weapon last August may well have shortened the war, the moral cost was too high. As the power that first used the atomic bomb under these circumstances, we have sinned grievously against the laws of God and against the people of Japan."[118] This Federal Council of Churches report was a major stimulus in creating the Stimson narrative of the bomb decision (see chapter three).

Also influential was a major attack on the bomb decision by Norman Cousins, editor of *The Saturday Review of Literature* and, during the war, a strong supporter of strategic bombing. Well before the mission of *Enola Gay*, Cousins explained to his readers why, even though it was immoral to *unleash* "such terrors of warfare as mass bombing of cities, poison gas, bacteriological warfare, and whatever other scientific hells might be devised . . . once the enemy *starts* it, it becomes no longer a moral but a military question, no longer a matter of argument but a matter of action. The weapons have been dictated by the enemy."[119] Cousins is writing at this time about Allied bombing of Germany, which was warranted by Nazi attacks on Dutch, Polish, and British cities; he took the same line justifying American attacks on Japan until Hiroshima.

Then, on 15 June 1946, Cousins changed his mind. He and Thomas K. Finletter coauthored an article in *Saturday Review* entitled "A Beginning for Sanity." The main focus of the Cousins-Finletter article was an attack on the use of atomic bombs in Japan.[120] This was a new position for Cousins, heretofore, a hawk. It was a temporary belief for Finletter, previously a Washington attorney holding various assignments in defense-related posts, but destined in 1947 to head a committee on air force strength that recommended "an air-atomic strategy" and a vast expansion of nuclear-capable aircraft. And shortly after the article with Cousins, Finletter was appointed secretary of the United States Air Force.

Here, in "A Beginning for Sanity," the former hawk-turned-dove and the dove-soon to be hawk agreed on one thing: "the military advantages and the saving of American lives achieved by the sudden use of atomic bombs against Japan may be outweighed by the ensuing loss of confidence and by a wave of horror and revulsion sweeping over the rest of the world." We should first have made a demonstration of the bomb, since the "war was on the very verge of being won." Cousins and Finletter suggested that a major Truman motive was limiting Soviet expansion in Asia, but did not develop this idea. The article had little impact at the time or later.

In addition to these relatively isolated moralistic attacks on the bomb decision, a prominent ultraconservative poet-historian, Hermann Hagedorn, went on a crusade against Truman with a poem in book form entitled *The Bomb That Fell on America*, published 25 March 1946.[121] It was distributed by Hagedorn to a stellar group of opinion leaders and presented at many poetry-readings in private homes on the East and West coasts. Many of the readings were under the auspices of Moral Re-Armament, Frank Buchman's anti-Communist quasi-religious cult.

Hagedorn controlled his political beliefs, and the poem-book is largely an emotional reaction to the atomic danger. His basic thrust is clear from these lines on pages 18–19:

Who loosed this terror upon mankind?
We know, and the world knows.
It is America, the idealist among the nations. The people with the great humanitarian dream, the friend of the underdog, the protester against persecutions and atrocities, the supporter of the Hague and Geneva conventions, the lover of peace. . . .
The people who used the Boxer indemnity from China to educate Chinese youth in the United States.
The people who were indignant when German armies marched into neutral Belgium, a quarter century ago, who cried out at Germany's warfare against the innocent, who were outraged at Hitler's persecution of the Jews.

Hagedorn's conclusion is an entirely conventional appeal to piety; Americans should dedicate "one hundred and thirty-five million lives, bearing witness, To the power of God and the power of the soul that the rays of God have split open."[122]

The Hagedorn Papers at Syracuse University Library contain letters of appreciation to Hagedorn for complimentary copies he sent Henry Wallace, Dorothy Canfield Fisher, Lewis Mumford, Robert Oppenheimer, Reinhold Niebuhr, Senator Glen Taylor, Lowell Thomas, Nicholas Roosevelt, and Henry Stimson, among others. Most of these letters praise Hagedorn's book. Only the letter from Nicholas Roosevelt is negative; he asks what is the difference between "the dropping of an atomic bomb on a city and the dropping within a day or two of two thousand or more blockbusters?"[123] Don Hollenbeck gave an abbreviated reading of Hagedorn's book on the ABC Network. The book went into at least nine printings, yet neither all this publicity, nor the similar gripping prose of John Hersey's *Hiroshima*, published in 1946, changed American opinion about the rightness of Truman's decision.

One reason is American reluctance to embrace abstract, absolutist values; we prefer instrumental, consequentialist values. The bomb was awful, but it ended an awful war. Racism is often invoked to explain the popularity of Truman's decision, and it may have been a factor, but the charge that the atom would not have been used against Germany is without warrant. Dresden proves we were equally willing to incinerate Germans; American bombs contributed substantially to the destruction of that city. Colonel Tibbets' original orders were to develop the capability to drop bombs on both Germany and Japan.[124]

Truman sent *Enola Gay* and *Bock's Car* out to end the war, save American lives, and achieve a surrender that would enable the Allies to eradicate Japanese militarism. Americans believed these to be good reasons, and they believed the bombs did what was expected of them. Barton Bernstein says the decision to use them was overdetermined; several legitimate reasons supported the decision, with no significant objections.[125]

For at least a year after the end of the war the only challenge to use of the bombs was that of the moral absolutists: the bomb was an intrinsically evil weapon, used against noncombatants. This attack on Truman's decision did not affect American opinion. Only the claim that use of the bomb was not necessary to end the war quickly, which claim was made by an "official" source in July 1946, began to erode Truman's overwhelming support.

2

OFFICIAL NARRATIVE #2 —
NITZE VERSION

SECRETARY ACHESON said . . . If we must go ahead with hostilities against the Chinese [in Korea] we must resist a suggestion of a cease fire. In that case, we would have to try to get a condemnation of the Chinese and have them branded as an aggressor. . . .
MR. NITZE said we would be better off if we had no hostilities with the Chinese if we could do this with honor and then get ready for the Soviet Union.
                    Foreign Relations of the U.S., 1950, 7, 1332

In the twelve-month period from August 1945 to July 1946, an official investigative commission, appointed and tasked by the president of the United States, directed by "impartial" civilians, studied American strategic bombing in Japan. The important commission reports came out in July 1946. This commission, unlike that of the Federal Council of Churches, did not conclude that the use of the bombs had been immoral. It claimed something that in the long run was far more potent: *the bombs were unnecessary.* This conclusion of the United States Strategic Bombing Survey (USSBS) written by Paul H. Nitze, appeared in preemptive form:

> Based on a detailed investigation of all the facts, and supported by the testimony of the surviving Japanese leaders involved, it is the Survey's opinion that certainly prior to December 31, 1945, and in all probability prior to November 1, 1945, Japan would have surrendered even if the atomic bombs had not been dropped, even if Russia had not entered the war, and even if no invasion had been planned or contemplated.[1]

One would expect that this startling claim, appearing to invalidate the official reason for using the bombs given by President Truman, would have attracted widespread attention. In July 1946, however, Americans were absorbed in conflicts with the Soviet Union, strikes in major industries, coming elections, inflation, and continued shortages of consumer goods. The newspaper of record, *The New York Times* carried two accounts of USSBS findings by Anthony Leviero. On 30 June 1946, the headline read "Atom Bomb Survey Cites Peril to U.S.," and the story presented the findings of physical damage to Hiroshima and Nagasaki, comparing them to New York City as a possible target. The second *Times* story, on 14 July, dealt with the causes of Japan's defeat and her decision to surrender; the incendiary paragraph "Based on a detailed investigation of all the facts" was given in full. There appeared to be little or no response.

U.S. News had extensive coverage in the issues of 5 and 19 July, but did not cite the early surrender conclusion. *Newsweek* and *Time* ignored USSBS, to concentrate on events such as the Crossroads series of nuclear tests in the Pacific and the disclosure of a major Soviet spy ring in Canada.

But if the public was not attentive, every observer for whom the bomb decision was significant, pro- and anti-Truman, paid very close attention. The early surrender hypothesis entered the archival stream in capital letters. As an "official" government report, couched in the most arresting language possible, enjoying the privilege of top secret protection for the data on which it was based (it dealt with atomic damage), the USSBS paragraph found its way into every subsequent discussion of Truman's decision. Fifty years later, when the National Air and Space Museum put together the text for its *Enola Gay* exhibit, the USSBS paragraph got top billing. It was easily the most important single text ever to appear in discussions of the bomb decision. How this paragraph came to be written demands attention.

✍ ✍ ✍

The United States had no independent air force during World War II. The Army Air Forces operated uneasily under Chief of Staff George C. Marshall. General Henry H. (Hap) Arnold commanded the fliers, with considerable leeway. This did not keep the fliers from looking to the postwar situation; everybody could see from the great achievements of the fliers during the war that air power was the force of the future. Not only did air power advocates covet independent status on a level with Army and Navy, they coveted a much greater share of the defense dollar.

Consequently it was vital to General Arnold and his associates to be able to prove that air power won the war. As early as 1943, Army Air Forces personnel were talking about a survey effort much more elaborate than the usual military after-action reports. Soldiers and sailors could measure the success of their operations by ground gained or warships sunk. Measuring the success of strategic bombing was much more complicated, and would require time and resources as soon as evaluators could enter enemy territory.

Specific proposals for evaluating the bombing offensive came from AAF officers in March 1944. Settling the many problems that arose (Was there to be a joint U.S.-British survey? What level of control would air forces people have? What exactly would the survey measure?) took much time and discussion, and it was not until 9 September 1944, that President Roosevelt was induced to write Secretary of War Stimson ordering the creation of the United States Strategic Bombing Survey.[2]

Everyone realized that the survey had to appear to be objective, not controlled by the airmen, but by a civilian. Assistant Secretary of War Robert Lovett was instrumental in getting the survey underway; he wanted a university president as chairman, but all the candidates approached turned it down. Finally on 21 October, Franklin D'Olier, president of the Prudential Life Insurance Company, accepted the job.

D'Olier and his air forces advisors set up a civilian board of directors, each director being in charge of a specific investigation: effects of bombing on transportation, equipment, munitions, physical damage, morale, aircraft, oil, and overall economic effects. Each division was to have military staff working under the director.

USSBS became noteworthy not only because of its controversial conclusions, but because three of its directors later had prominent careers: George Ball, John Kenneth Galbraith, and Paul Nitze.

The survey's first task was to follow Eisenhower's armies into Germany. This was a congenial operation for many of the survey's Eurocentric directors. Galbraith's account of his exploits, particularly the interviews he, Ball, and Nitze conducted with Albert Speer, the German economic czar, is lyrical.[3] Inevitably the civilian investigators gave less credit for victory to the strategic bombers than the air forces claimed. Galbraith's Overall Economic Effects Division was particularly unimpressed with bombing damage to industry. Only when massive bombing of transportation and petroleum facilities began in mid-1944 was the operation held to be cost-effective. This evaluation was influenced by conclusions of the British Bombing Survey Unit, which were hotly contested.[4]

In June 1945, Nitze, Ball, and several air forces generals were brought from Europe to Washington to advise on the most effective bombing plan for Japan. No final reports had been written on their European findings, but as Nitze put it, "we had accumulated sufficient information to draw tentative conclusions." Nitze's later account of his conferences with the Joint Target Group (JTG) is crucial to an understanding of the explosive USSBS publications a year later:

> A concentrated air attack on the essential lines of transportation, including railroads . . . would isolate the Japanese home islands from one another and fragment the enemy's base of operations. I believed that interdiction of the lines of transportation would be sufficiently effective so that additional bombing of urban industrial areas would not be necessary. My plan of air attack on Japan was approved but not my estimate of when it would cause Japan's capitulation. . . . I concluded that even without the atomic bomb, Japan was likely to surrender in a matter of months. My own view

was that Japan would capitulate by November 1945. However, the Joint Chiefs saw matters differently. The upshot was that they unanimously recommended that plans go forward for an early invasion of the Japanese home islands.[5]

On 15 August 1945, President Truman asked D'Olier to continue USSBS operations in the Pacific. The authorization this time was broader, and since the U.S. Navy had played a major role in bombing Japan, the Pacific group was to include Navy as well as Army Air Forces personnel. Also, USSBS was to study more than just the effects of strategic bombing: Truman's letter to D'Olier instructed him to consider postwar military planning. Then there was what is now called "mission creep"; USSBS attempted to evaluate the unique impact of atomic bombs, investigate why the Japanese attacked Pearl Harbor, and why they ultimately surrendered.[6]

With the war over, D'Olier had trouble persuading Survey employees to transfer to the Pacific. Of the civilian directors, only Nitze was willing to take a major responsibility for the Pacific Survey; he was in effect CEO. D'Olier put in a perfunctory appearance. Galbraith came over to Japan for a month.

Paul Nitze welcomed the chance to give the world its first official and comprehensive evaluation of atom bombs, and he arrived in Japan with some opinions already formed. In addition to his belief that Japan would surrender by November without the bombs, he was ambivalent about the bomb itself. As Strobe Talbott puts it in his biography of Nitze: "By the time he arrived at Hiroshima and Nagasaki, Nitze was already an experienced observer of what bombs could do. He had seen places in Germany where more people were killed by conventional explosives than by the A-bombs . . . Nitze saw it as his task to demystify the bomb, to treat it as another weapon rather than the 'absolute weapon.' While others believed that nuclear weaponry was truly something new under the sun, Nitze believed that the measurements of the Survey at Hiroshima and Nagasaki showed the effects to be roughly the equivalent of an incendiary bombing raid by 220 B-29s."[7]

It was a belief he never changed. The United States might avoid nuclear war by maintaining a preponderance of power, but if it came, it would not be Armageddon.

Nitze was in Japan from 27 September until 4 December. For some of this time he had a thousand people working for him. In December, most Survey employees returned to Washington, D.C. where they processed their data and wrote reports. There were hundreds of reports from various divisions of the Survey, but only three had the imprimatur of the chairman's office (and hence Nitze): *Summary Report (Pacific War), Japan's Struggle to End the War,* and *The Effects of Atomic Bombs on Hiroshima and Nagasaki.*

These reports, and most of the documents supporting them, are now in USSBS files (National Archives microfilms of these papers, M1654 and M1655, run to 514 rolls). By 1991, they all appeared to be declassified. Most of the documents concern production, shipping, armed force strength, photos of bombed sites, and such like. These data are probably as accurate as could be expected when agents of a foreign enemy swarm over a defeated nation trying to find out in two months "what made that alien culture tick," and what happened to it under siege. Nitze and his crew asked and answered questions about Japan's motives and intentions. And it was in the official reports from the chairman's office that Nitze was able to get back at the JCS, Truman, and their wrongheaded preference for invasion or nuclear weapons.[8]

Flushed with victory, walking the streets of Japan as conquerors, the surveyors were manic in their claims: "On the basis of all the facts . . ." One needs only to think about it to realize its absurdity. One thousand persons, all but a tiny handful of them Caucasians, from a land whose customs, language, lifestyles, *everything* was profoundly different from the land to be investigated, are going in a mere two months to gather *all the facts,* and in *detail,* about why the Japanese began the war, how they prosecuted it, what internal conflicts kept Minister of War Anami from agreeing with the so-called peace party that the war had to end, how strong the national commitment to fight to the death really was—all these and the ultimate conjecture: when would Japan have surrendered with no bombs and Russians—these 1,000 investigators could accomplish all this?

Every student of the Pacific war knows that, extensive as the USSBS files are, they do not contain even a tiny fraction of the "facts" that have since been uncovered about the Japanese participation in that war, and about ultimate acceptance of defeat. The Japanese history of the war runs to more than one hundred volumes, mostly untranslated, but they were read by American Japanologists as they became available. Many linear feet of interviews with Japanese authorities conducted by specialists, after USSBS was through, when MacArthur's occupation set out to learn about the war, are also in Archives files. Hundreds of historians, both Japanese and American, have since 1946 added significant information to our knowledge about Japan's war. The (Japanese) Pacific War Research Society, the (U.S.) Far East Command's intelligence section, the staff of the International Military Tribunal for the Far East (Tokyo War Crimes Court) have produced tens of thousands of pages of information, including more extensive and revealing interrogations of Japanese wartime leaders than USSBS obtained. And most of what USSBS obtained was not "facts" in any accepted sense, but only opinion and data that needed to be interpreted.

But this "all the facts" rhetoric, coming from a presumably nonpartisan, objective fact-finding commission, effectively skewered Truman, General Marshall, and all the military leaders who had contemplated invasion and had unleashed the atom. Truman stood indicted as trigger-happy, indifferent to civilian casualties, dropping atomic bombs simply to frighten the Russians, or out of spite, malice, racism, or inertia.

As if the magnitude of the task were not overwhelming, Nitze had the typical type A, gung-ho attitude toward it. According to an in-house USSBS history by Major James Beveridge, at the 28 November 1945 staff meeting, "Mr. Nitze congratulated the whole group on the conduct of what he called the fastest moving, hardest hitting post-war organization on record."[9] Fast moving it no doubt was; whether this allowed the materials gathered to be digested is another matter.

Several items in the USSBS files indicate that moving fast influenced the composition of reports, if not content. In early 1947, the USSBS report titled *Japanese*

Air Weapons and Tactics was sent to the Air War College at Maxwell Field. On 3 March 1947 USSBS personnel were still involved in tying up loose ends. On that date, Major John J. Driscoll wrote USSBS chairman D'Olier a scathing letter: "A preliminary reading of a copy of the subject report just received has disclosed over one hundred and fifty (150) typographical errors, the majority of which are serious enough to nullify the potential value of this extensive study."[10]

Driscoll thought the data in the study would be of great value to students at the Air War College, but "in its present form the value of this report is nullified, and the seriousness of the typographic errors reflect upon the authority of the entire survey. The multiplicity and complexity of the errors, and the nature of this confidential report, preclude the practicability of adding an errata sheet." From reading the details in Driscoll's letter, one suspects that Major Driscoll was toning down his criticism. In addition to typos, there were some substantive errors. D'Olier's' office, in its response, pleaded guilty to 18 errors that needed to be rectified "for clarification of the report."[11] The rest were just harmless typos. Driscoll was not mollified. He wanted them all corrected. The correspondence does not reveal who prevailed.

By the time all were published, there were 108 reports in the USSBS Pacific war series. The crucial one, written by Nitze, is *Japan's Struggle to End the War,* dated 1 July 1946. It consists of thirteen pages of text and twenty-three pages of appendices. Gian Gentile, who has done the most thorough analysis of USSBS, believes that *Japan's Struggle* was written in April, and included the early surrender counterfactual in the first draft. The second paragraph of *Japan's Struggle* says:

> Fortunately, most of the pertinent questions relating to how Japan was brought to acceptance of the Potsdam Declaration find their answers in the simple chronology of events which can now be narrated in some detail for the period from the collapse of Tojo in July 1944, to the imperial rescript of 15 August 1945. The evidence is chiefly in the testimony obtained by Survey interrogation of the Army, Navy, Government and Imperial Household leaders who participated or were influential in the struggle within Japan over whether to continue the war or to accept surrender.[12]

Unfortunately, the relevant testimony, with its allegedly corroborating evidence, is not presented in this USSBS document in any fashion: no verbatim quotes, no paraphrases, no summaries. Appendix B is "Biographies of Japanese Leaders," and twenty-four persons are profiled. The purpose of this section is obscure; no light is thrown on the effects of American bombing, or on Japan's decision to surrender. About 65% of the space is devoted to routine listings of dates and places of birth, education, offices held.

Many of these leaders were interrogated by USSBS. This appendix would be an appropriate place to present in at least skeleton form their observations on the surrender decision process. Marquis Kido Koichi, for instance, the Lord Privy Seal, who was interviewed at length by the Survey and was a defendant in the Tokyo War Crimes Trial, has half a page in this appendix. We are told the place and date of birth, schooling, inherited title, his service with the Agriculture Ministry, the

Fishery Bureau, the Industrial Bureau, the Commerce and Industry Ministry, and a string of other irrelevant posts up to 1940, when he became Privy Seal. But what did he observe during this last, crucial capacity? He was closer to the emperor than any other person during the whole of the Pacific war. He was a member of the so-called "Peace Party" toward the end. His testimony to the war crimes trial occupies 775 pages; his diary, a major source for every student of wartime Japan, contains 5,920 entries.[13] Surely something he said could be given in this half page, instead of uninformative details. There is only this: "A member of the Tokyo aristocracy, he had long been associated with Prince Konoye, Fuminaro, and was backed by the latter and by the Army for the Post of Lord Keeper of the Privy Seal, to replace Yuasa, Kurakei, whom the Army considered to be too liberal an adviser to the emperor."[14] In the transcript of his interrogation, never printed in a USSBS report, we find Kido saying many highly significant things. Why are none of them given here?

USSBS interviewed fourteen of the leaders they list in the appendix. Six of these interviews dealt with Japan's decision to surrender. Prince Konoye, for instance, interviewed just before his suicide, had much to say. Frame 0503 of the transcript shows the interrogator drawing from Konoye the statement that the main obstacle to ending the war was opposition in the army. He claimed that, even in July 1945, had the emperor tried to end the war, there would have been an uprising. Only in August was there a "decrease in the risk of disorders in the event of an Imperial rescript."[15] And what factors contributed to the improved situation in August? Konoye did not hesitate: "The big thing was the deterioration of the war effort; then with the entry of Russia in the war, and the dropping of the atomic bomb, it did a lot to prepare the way for the next move."

Were this not plain enough, frame 0504 of the transcript has this exchange:

Q: How much longer do you think the war might have continued had the atom bomb not been dropped?
A: It is a little hard for me to figure that out.
Q: What would your best estimate be?
A: Probably it would have lasted all this year.
Q: It would not have been terminated prior to November 1 — is that correct?
A: Probably would have lasted beyond that.

The questioner — probably Nitze — was not happy with this answer, and worried the matter for two more pages. The final discussion, from frame 0506:

Q: Could Japan have continued to fight with these increasing attacks of the B-29's?
A: There was bound to be a limit as to what she could do.
Q: Yet you said if it weren't for the emperor's statement [surrender rescript] they would be fighting today, did you not?
A: Of course, that was a conditional statement. There was a limit to what they could do. They would do what they could.
Q: Hadn't they almost reached the limit?
A: Of course, they were nearing the limit, but the army would not admit it. They wouldn't admit they were near the end.

Q: Would they not have been forced to surrender, therefore, even if Russia had not come in or even though we had not dropped the atomic bomb?

A: The army had dug themselves caves in the mountains and their idea of fighting on was fighting from every little hole or rock in the mountains.

Konoye had more to say. He thought the emperor would attempt to prevent a last-ditch stand, but did not say when. He was candid about the class interest motivating the peace party: "These were all of the upper rank of men—of higher classes of men who carried on such activities. As far as I know, there was none of the lower ranks. . . . They were afraid of a revolution—a sort of communistic revolution" (frame 0501).

The answer to the question "Why were not the pertinent remarks of Prince Konoye included in the USSBS report?" becomes clear: they contradicted Nitze's views. Likewise with the rest of the testimony, with the single exception of the Privy Seal Marquis Kido.

Kido was interrogated 10 November 1945. At first, he would not accommodate the obvious wish of the interrogator. The main obstacle to surrender was the army's determination to continue the fight. And the bomb? "The atomic bomb had a strong effect upon bringing those—for want of a better term I would use 'fence sitters'—to the view that the war must be stopped. . . . To answer the question which of the two—the entry of Russia and the dropping of the atomic bombs—had the greatest effect on the army I can not say."[16]

There was more discussion of the role of the cabinet in the surrender and of the problem of securing army compliance. Then the interrogator went directly to his main point:

Q: In the event that atomic bombs had not been dropped and Russia had not entered the war, how long in your opinion might the war have continued?

A: As I have stated, our decision to seek a way out of this war was made in early June before any bomb had been dropped and Russia had not yet entered the war. It was already our decision.

Q: The dropping of the atomic bombs and the entry of Russia into the war apparently did speed the agreement of the services ministries to end the war. What we would like to get is the degree to which this was speeded up.

A: It was not the time factor. It was the fact that it made the task easier to bring the war to a close by silencing those who would advocate the continuation of the war. If there had been no dropping of the atomic bomb or entry of the Soviet Union into the war, I am inclined to be very doubtful whether the policy to bring the war to a close would have progressed as smoothly. A rather large-scale outbreak within the armed forces could easily be imagined.

Q: Is it proper then to interpret it as being your opinion that the war might have been over in any case prior to November 1st even without the entry of Russia and the dropping of the atomic bombs?

A: I personally think that the war would have ended prior to November 1, as every possible effort was being exhausted to terminate the war.

Here was the first, *and only,* affirmation by one of Japan's wartime leaders of the early surrender hypothesis. It took a bit of badgering and just a hint of suggestion, but Kido said it. He also said the effect of the atomic bombs was much greater than conventional bombing; Nitze did not want to hear that. But this was not the last word from Kido.

On the witness stand on 16 October 1947, at the Tokyo War Crimes Trial (International Military Tribunal for the Far East, or IMTFE), under questioning by an interrogator not possessed of USSBS biases, Kido made a statement contradicting what he had told the Survey. He identified the Nagasaki bomb as a "great shock to the nation, together with the Soviet Union's participation in the Pacific War. . . . I thought there would be no course left but to broadcast an Imperial rescript to the nation . . . terminating the war."[17] And free of USSBS badgering, he clearly indicated that he did not believe the war would have ended before invasion: "It is my inward satisfaction that I was instrumental in saving another twenty million of my innocent compatriots from war ravages and also the Americans tens of thousands of casualties, which would have been caused had Japan gone on fighting to the bitter end . . . " If he kept Japan from fighting to the bitter end, he could not have believed in Nitze's early surrender hypothesis.

Toyoda Soemu, chief of the naval general staff at the end of the war, thought the atom and Soviet entry "did enable us to bring the war to a termination without creating too great chaos in Japan."[18] Baron Hiranuma, president of Privy Council, had been wounded by an assassin in 1941, and was one of the most important of the elder statesmen who engineered the surrender. He was interrogated 20 and 23 November. Hiranuma claimed to be one of several Japanese leaders who advocated immediate acceptance of the Potsdam Proclamation. As to causes of surrender, "The biggest factor . . . there came the atomic bomb, so that the country was faced with terrible destructive powers and Japan's ability to wage war was really at an end."[19]

Neither interrogation is mentioned by USSBS. Both refute Nitze's early surrender conclusion.

The chief cabinet secretary at the time of surrender was Sakomizu Hisatsume, one of the peace activists. His interrogation on 11 December is one of the most interesting in the whole USSBS series. David B. Truman was in charge, and approached the surrender by asking Sakomizu what he thought when news of the Hiroshima bomb arrived:

A: When this news came on the morning of the 7th I called the Prime Minister on the phone and reported the announcement. Everyone in the government and even in the military knew that if the announcement were true, no country could carry on a war. Without the atomic bomb it would be impossible for any country to defend itself against a nation which had the weapon. The chance had come to end the war. It was not necessary to blame the military side, the manufacturing people, or anyone else—just the atomic bomb. It was a good excuse. Someone said that the atomic bomb was the kamikaze to save Japan.

Q: How long do you think the war would have continued if the atomic bomb had not been used?

A: We had already asked the Russians to intercede, and we could expect that they would eventually give us some answer. If it had been unfavorable there was just one way to bring peace and that was to broadcast direct to the United States. But it would have been difficult to find a good chance to do so. I think you can understand. Suzuki tried to find a chance to stop the war and the atom bomb gave him that chance.[20]

Admiral Baron Suzuki Kantaro, Premier at the time of surrender, was interviewed 26 December. Here, of all people, was the witness who might have been able to support the early surrender hypothesis. The civilian leadership of USSBS was back in Washington, D.C. Generals Anderson and Gardner, civilians Paul Baran and Burton Fisher asked the questions. Suzuki was responsive, even to questions about his instructions from the emperor. About his plight when he became premier (on 7 April 1945) Suzuki said:

It seemed to me unavoidable that in the long run Japan would be almost destroyed by air attack so that merely on the basis of the B-29s alone I was convinced that Japan should sue for peace. On top of the B-29 raids came the Atomic Bomb, immediately after the Potsdam Declaration, which was just one additional reason for giving in and was a very good one and gave us the opportune moment to make open negotiations for peace. I myself on the basis of the B-29 raids felt that the cause was hopeless. The Supreme War Council, up to the time the Atomic Bomb was dropped, did not believe that Japan could be beaten by air attack alone. They also believed that the United States would land and not attempt to bomb Japan out of the war. On the other hand there were many prominent people who did believe that the United States could win the war by just bombing alone. However the Supreme War Council, not believing that, had proceeded with the one plan of fighting a decisive battle at the landing point and was making every possible preparation to meet such a landing. They proceeded with that plan until the Atomic Bomb was dropped, after which they believed the United States would no longer attempt to land when it had such a superior weapon—so at that point they decided that it would be best to sue for peace.[21]

No clearer, nor more probative, statement exists giving the reason why Japan surrendered when she did.

The List of "Japanese Leaders" used in *Japan's Struggle* is incomplete. Several important generals and admirals not listed by USSBS as "leaders" gave opinions on what led to surrender. On 8 December, Field Marshal Hata Shunroku, commanding general of the 2nd General Army (Hiroshima) in 1945, was interrogated. Here was another bitter-ender. He stressed to his troops that Japan would win the final decisive battle of the homeland. The army would dig in deeply to survive preliminary bombing: "We intended to stand and fight on the beaches. . . . However, when the atom bomb was dropped on Hiroshima, I believed there is nothing more we can do, we might as well give up."[22]

Fleet Admiral Nagano Osami, who had been chief of naval general staff at the time of the Pearl Harbor attack, and was supreme naval advisor to the emperor at the end of the war, was interrogated on 30 November. Most of this interrogation concerned the beginning of the war, but the questioner did get around to the vital question: "Admiral, could the war have been brought to a close, in your opinion . . . without the entry of Russia into the war and without the employment of either atom bomb?"[23] Nagano acknowledged that even without these two events, Japan could not win, but "Speaking very frankly, I think we would have been able to extend the war for a considerable time at considerable sacrifice on your part."

On November 15, Rear Admiral Tomioka Sadatoshi, operations officer of the naval general staff after November 1944 was interrogated. Tomioka was conversant with Japanese intelligence and planning, and heavily involved in the defenses of Iwo Jima, Okinawa, and Kyushu. After the fall of Saipan, he did not think that Japan would win the war: "Our only hope was that we could discourage you by inflicting great damage on your forces. We estimated that we would destroy 30–40% of the initial assaulting forces when you hit the homeland." He expected the invasion of Kyushu in July or early August 1945, since "We felt that your home front pressure would require you to move fast and try to end the war as quickly as possible . . . You couldn't bomb us into submission, I thought, and therefore you would have to land on the home islands."[24] No hint of early surrender here.

All these officials said the war would have gone on absent the Hiroshima and Nagasaki bombings, and some said Soviet entry was also important. There is no contradictory testimony in USSBS files. Nitze made up the testimonial basis for the early surrender claim out of whole cloth.

～ ～ ～

While Nitze says most of the pertinent questions about Japan's surrender decision are answered by the testimony of Japanese officials, he does allow for some of the facts to be gathered elsewhere. Even in the great bulk of data gathered, however, there are no "facts" that directly support the early surrender thesis. Instead, buried in the 108 Pacific war reports are dozens of palpable errors, illegitimate inferences, and stark denials of the early surrender belief.

Perhaps the most remarkable of the denials is in a document issued by the Urban Areas Division, *The Effects of Air Attack on Japanese Urban Economy—Summary Report*. This was not issued until March 1947. No reason for its late appearance is given, but the substance may explain it. This report was the work of social scientists, who wanted to go beyond the subjective opinions sought in interrogations. As stated in the preface to this Urban Areas report, "The Urban Areas Division endeavored to measure the effects of those raids on the urban economy and determine the extent to which that bombing program contributed to Japan's surrender."[25] In other words, here's some hard evidence, statistics.

Statistics they got, but when it came to the bottom line trying to connect the statistics to Japan's will to fight on, somebody had to draw conclusions. Death and destruction had not brought German surrender; some powerful reasoning would be needed to show that the Japanese were different. The Urban Areas people went to the president of Tokyo Imperial University. The president appointed a committee under Professor Dr. C. Maiide to investigate the surrender, and USSBS published the resulting report as an appendix, "in its entirety (with some grammatical corrections) as it was submitted to the Survey on 23 December 1945."

> The following Report is a result of the Scientific Research of the members of the Committee on "The Effects of the Urban Area Bombing on Japanese Wartime Economy," which was conducted by our Faculty under the order of the President of the University.
>
> Our report is rather abstract and not statistical enough, but this does not mean that it is merely the product of dogmatic judgment. On the contrary, it is a product of statistical survey and scientific research by the following committee. In this connection, we feel it may be necessary to explain the method by which the research was made and the course of the studies which we undertook.
>
> At first, in order to study the important and extensive problems which were raised in your letter, we formed the above mentioned committee which consisted of the following persons: Chairman, Prof. C. Maiide (Dean of the Faculty), Prof. T. Arisawa (Prof. Of Statistics), Prof. Y. Wakimura (Commerce and Industry), Prof. M. Yamada (Agriculture), Prof. N. Yanagawa (Theory of Distribution), Prof. F. Kitayama (Credit and Finance), Prof. K. Okochi (Labour and Society Problems), Prof. S. Takamiya (Business Management), Assistant Professor G. Konno (Transportation), and Asst. Prof. T. Yasuhira (Industry).
>
> The work of the committee was to gather necessary statistics and data to explain the "Effect of the Strategic Bombing of our Wartime Economy" in regard to the productive life of the nation.
>
> Secondly, we conducted hearings to learn the opinions of well-informed officials and also those of the people who experienced the most terrible bombing. Such ministries as the Commerce and Industry Ministry, Agriculture and Forestry Ministry, Transportation Ministry and Communications Board, and manufacturing companies such as Mitsubishi Heavy Industrial Inc., Nippon Steel Pipe Producing Inc, Fuji Electrical Machinery Co., Ltd., Tokyo Shibaura Denki K.K., Ishikawajima Shipbuilding, Inc. "Seikosha" Optical and Precise Machine Maker, supplied us with necessary statistics and suggestive opinion.[26]

The substance of the report, charts, figures, tables of various sort occupies some 40 pages. Their content is summarized as follows: (1) Effects of the ocean blockade by the Allied forces; (2) Strategic bombing by B-29s, along with attacks by medium and small sized planes; (3) Effect of the strategic bombing on daily economic life; (4) Effect of strategic bombing on the people's fighting morale. At the end of the last summary section, these statisticians are clear about what happened: "Though there were many different views, the majority of leaders entirely lost heart to continue hostilities. *Particularly, the debut of atomic bombs in the Pacific theater was decisive.*" (Italics supplied)[27]

There are errors of fact in Nitze's "all the facts" report, and serious omissions. Some of them were pointed out by Robert Butow in his 1954 book, *Japan's Decision to Surrender.* One is a serious failure to deal with the revolt of units of the army after the surrender decision became known. USSBS says nothing of the attempted coup d'etat by Inaba and five other junior military officers on the evening of August 14–15, the night before the emperor's surrender rescript was broadcast. This is an amazing omission. Butow devotes a sixteen-page chapter to the insurrection.[28] The Pacific War Research Society's *Japan's Longest Day* is primarily about that specific event.[29] One can understand its omission from *Japan's Struggle* only by assuming that the attempted coup demonstrates such a fanatical resistance to surrender that Nitze's counterfactual becomes unbelievable.

Even as late as 14 August, dissident forces seized the Imperial Compound, assassinated the commander of the Imperial Guards, Lt. Gen. Mori Takeshi, attempted to block the emperor's broadcast, attempted to assassinate Premier Suzuki, and burned Suzuki's residence when they could not find him. There were other rebellions even after the emperor's broadcast.[30] Surrender, in August 1945, barely came off. It was not just around the corner absent Hiroshima, Nagasaki, and a rumored third atomic bomb due on Tokyo.

In addition to ignoring the final convulsion, *Japan's Struggle* contains errors that more time, greater care, and less bias would have prevented. All the errors reinforce the early surrender hypothesis. *Japan's Struggle* says that when Tojo fell and Koiso replaced him in July 1944, "Koiso received an Imperial admonition to give Japan's situation a 'fundamental reconsideration' looking to the termination of the war." Butow refutes this.[31] *Japan's Struggle* states that "The emperor on his own initiative in February 1945 had a series of interviews with the senior statesmen whose consensus was that Japan faced certain defeat and should seek peace at once." Grand Chamberlain Fujita's notes, taken at these interviews, show these claims to be false.[32]

Japan's Struggle says that Prince Konoye told the Survey that he had secret instructions from the emperor in July 1945 to negotiate through the Russians for "peace at any price." No such statement appears in the transcripts of the Konoye interviews, and the testimony of Foreign Minister Togo contradicts it.[33] *Japan's Struggle* states that in April 1945 when Suzuki was made prime minister, the emperor told him to make peace at any price, and that this was known to all members of his cabinet. This is wholly false.[34]

These errors appeared in USSBS reports despite the fact that the Survey had obtained access to the top secret ULTRA decrypts. D'Olier made a big show of obtaining these materials so USSBS could know everything there was to know about the surrender. D'Olier's letter to Truman of 10 May 1946 read:

> You will recall from our recent meeting that one of the Survey's important studies reconstructs the discussions and negotiations in Japan which led to its unconditional surrender, in order to establish more factually and clearly the factors affecting that decision.
>
> Completion of this study requires that we have access to ULTRA information now in the State, War and Navy Departments. Especially important is certain material bearing on the period from April through August 1945, which would be made available on your authorization.
>
> It is therefore requested that the Secretaries of State, War and Navy receive your approval to make this material available to me or my designated representative.[35]

Presidential Assistant Edwin Locke advised Truman the next day to grant the request and Truman agreed.

Many ULTRA and MAGIC decrypts were declassified in 1960, but accounts based on the 1960 release are misleading. Full release of these materials was not made until 1980. In 1946, however, *a presidential order had given the entire lot to USSBS.* There can be no justification for USSBS failing to include such stunning and significant items as SRH-084, a record of talks between Hirota Koki, an ex-premier, and Soviet Ambassador Malik about Soviet-Japanese relations. These talks are represented by anti-Truman writers as indicating that Japan was ready to concede defeat, and seek Soviet help in arranging a surrender. Instead, ULTRA reveals in the summary provided by Pacific Strategic Intelligence Section:

> At their last conference that same evening (14 June 1945), Hirota stated: "Japan will increase her naval strength in the future, and that, together with the Russian Army, would make a force unequalled in the world. In this connection, Japan would like to have Russia provide her with oil, in return for which Japan would provide rubber, tin, lead, tungsten and other commodities from the south (transport would be up to the Russians)." Malik replied that Russia had no oil to spare but that he would study the proposal. In conclusion, Hirota stated that Japan hoped for an early peace, but "the reply was that, since Russia was not a belligerent in the East, His Excellency Mr. Hirota must be well aware that peace there did not depend on Russia."[36]

This was a Nitzean "peace feeler"? More like a breathing space to prepare for the next war.

Subsequent decrypts show Japan becoming increasingly worried about the invasion of Kyushu she expects to take place soon, and trying to get the Soviets to mediate a cease fire, even if a joint empire with the Russians is not in the cards. The proposal of the emperor to send Prince Konoye to Moscow is covered in these decrypts, as is Japanese Ambassador Sato's standard answer from Moscow: Forget it, you've got to accept unconditional surrender. Foreign Minister Togo responds inevitably that the situation is urgent, Sato must see Molotov; but Togo never uses the word surrender. Togo admits several times that his government cannot even agree on what terms it would suggest for a cease fire.

Finally, near the end of the series, after Japan had announced her intention to surrender, on the day before the emperor's radio speech, ULTRA intercepted this belligerent telegram from General Okamura, commander, Japanese Army in China:

> Even if the present prerogatives of the emperor are recognized, who will guarantee this if we disarm and demobilize? The limitation of our sovereignty to the home islands only will reduce us to the time when the race of Yamato was thirty million people. The existence of seventy million people absolutely requires that we have Formosa, Korea, and (South Manchuria?). Such a disgrace as the surrender of several million troops without fighting is not paralleled in the world's military history, and it is absolutely impossible to submit to the unconditional surrender of a million picked troops in perfectly healthy shape, to the Chungking forces of defeated China . . ."[37]

The next day, the emperor spoke. The day after that, Okamura yielded to an imperial emissary and ordered a cease fire.

To get a fix on what the USSBS investigators should have gleaned from the riches at their disposal, we must go to the only comprehensive treatment of ULTRA, from a scholar fluent in Japanese, conversant with Japanese sources, and sophisticated in the ways in which military commanders use intelligence. Edward Drea's *MacArthur's ULTRA: Codebreaking and the War Against Japan, 1942–1945,* is an analysis of how Pacific commanders reacted to the flow of translated Japanese messages.[38] In some cases, these commanders, including MacArthur, used them to obtain advantage, in others they were disbelieving and walked into avoidable disaster. Drea's book was published in 1992, in good time for the curators in the National Air and Space Museum fiasco of 1995 to improve their limited understanding of Japan's decision to surrender. Drea's chapter 8, "ULTRA As Seer: Uncovering Japanese Plans for Homeland Defense, June–August 1945," tells us much about the subject USSBS had so perverted a half-century earlier:

> ULTRA was the only reliable means to assess the scope of the Japanese defenses and perhaps to gauge the enemy's determination to fight to the bitter end. ULTRA unlocked one Japanese secret after another for the Allies, and this otherwise unobtainable intelligence had significant implications even though the Allies did not have to invade Japan. For that reason, an examination of ULTRA's role in the spring and summer of 1945 is more than an exercise in antiquarian curiosity. Decision makers like General Marshall who were at the highest levels in Washington read ULTRA and voiced apprehension as it revealed the massive reinforcement effort on Kyushu. The ULTRA-shaped perception based on deciphered military communications superseded the MAGIC decryptions indicating that Japan's Foreign Ministry was seeking to end the war. ULTRA was a central factor in the decision to drop the atomic bomb on Japanese cities, one heretofore not fully incorporated into the historical record. . . .
>
> One strongly argued view holds that because Japan was already defeated the needless and senseless atomic destruction of humanity was done for political ends. Such arguments . . . ignore the military side of the process. ULTRA-derived knowledge of the massive buildup for a gigantic battle on Kyushu did influence American policymakers and strategists. To ignore that factor assumes that the Japanese were defeated and, more importantly, that they were prepared to surrender before the atomic bomb was dropped. ULTRA did portray a Japan in extremity, but it also showed that its military leaders were blind to defeat and were bending all remaining national energy to smash an invasion of their divine islands.[39]

Whatever praise Nitze gave his crew for being a fast-moving, hard-hitting organization loses its luster when the total output is scrutinized for coherence and consistency. Not only is there an unbridgeable gap between the early surrender conclusion and the raw material on which it is presumably based; there is an embarrassing failure of the Survey to decide what did bring Japan's capitulation. If indeed the civilian USSBS directorate was neutral as between the claims of Army Air Forces and Navy, surely D'Olier or Nitze would have settled the matter and forced all reports to conform to the director's conclusion. This did not happen.

David MacIsaac's *Strategic Bombing in World War Two* addresses "The Great Anderson-Navy War," which is the title of one of his sections. This "war" was an ugly, unremitting, high-stakes battle over the future organization and funding of the American military.[40] Ultimately it led to a decision by D'Olier to allow Major General Orvil Anderson to publish, over the objections of Paul Nitze, an inflammatory report claiming that air forces deserved all credit for winning in the Pacific; the navy and army are ignored. Gentile says of the report in question, "Anderson's pamphlet-like report, with its blatant Air Force parochialism . . . reflected accurately the overall partiality—not impartiality—of the Strategic Bombing Survey toward air power and an independent air force."[41]

Gentile offers the best summary analysis of the USSBS total effort:

> This is the dilemma that emerges from the pages of the Pacific Survey reports: How to claim the decisiveness of conventional air power when there was evidence pointing to the conclusion that a large part of AAF's campaign, while important, was not the crucial factor in Japan's defeat? The devastating effects of the antishipping campaign and of conventional strategic bombing forced the Japanese leadership to realize that defeat was inevitable. But there is a difference between the realization of defeat and the political acceptance of surrender. Here is where the atom bomb enters into the equation. If read as a collective whole, the Pacific Survey reports implicitly suggest that the atom bomb was the sufficient cause that transformed the realization of defeat into surrender, thus contradicting the early surrender counterfactual.[42]

⤜ ⤜ ⤜

Who was Paul Nitze, and why was he so determined to have his organization proclaim a massive falsehood? The simple answer is that he was a proud man who was set on getting back at the JCS for rejecting, in the summer of 1945, his formula for securing surrender by strategic bombing alone with no invasion.

There are three major public sources of information about Nitze; his autobiography, *From Hiroshima to Glasnost: At the Center of Decision;* Strobe Talbott's *The Master of the Game;* and David Callahan's *Dangerous Capabilities.*[43]

Nitze was a brilliant, ambitious, somewhat self-righteous public servant whose boast that he had served every president from Franklin Roosevelt to Ronald Reagan was warranted. The son of an accomplished scholar of romance languages and literature at the University of Chicago, Nitze enjoyed regular visits to Europe and dinner table conversations with a variety of experts. He notes in his memoir that in the sixth grade, he role-played Walter Rathenau, the German foreign minister in Rathenau's plea against the Treaty of Versailles. And at home, in the summer of 1919, "My father's academic colleagues discussed the terms of the Treaty of Versailles at length that summer, and none of them, as far as I could tell, believed in its wisdom. They were, in my estimation, as distinguished a group of scholars as had ever been brought together, but it was evident that they were powerless to influence events. It was then, at the age of twelve, that I decided when I grew up I wanted to be in positions where I could participate in world events and be close to the levers of influence."[44]

After attending the University of Chicago elementary and high schools, and two years at Hotchkiss in Connecticut, he went to Harvard to study economics. There followed a job in the accounting office of a Chicago firm, and a trip to Europe in 1928–1929 with a commission to report on business conditions there. On return, he was hired by Clarence Dillon's investment banking firm in New York, just before the Crash of 1929. In the Dillon, Reed office, Nitze writes, "I worked with some of the most distinguished men on Wall Street and rubbed shoulders with some of its biggest crooks. It was a useful education to be exposed as a young man to the barons and wizards of high finance. The experience left me with little awe of the great and perhaps with excessive confidence in my own abilities and judgment."[45]

He remained at Dillon, Reed, with a year off to study sociology at Harvard, and a brief period running his own company, until 1940. During the year at Harvard, he was influenced by George S. Pettee, a political scientist who believed that Nazis and Bolsheviks were equally odious. James Forrestal was also at Dillon Reed, and Nitze introduced Pettee's ideas to Forrestal. Nitze does not mention Pettee in his memoirs, but he told Talbott that he had given Forrestal a copy of Pettee's book, and "It was his first systematic exposure to the theoretical approach to the problem of communism." Talbott concludes, "His relationship with Forrestal remained close, not least because they shared a conviction that, even at the outset of the struggle against Nazism, the world faced at least as great a danger from Bolshevism."[46]

Talbott also notes that, at the onset of war, Nitze strongly supported America First, the isolationist movement that was part anti-British, part pro-German. America First had many adherents, but

> Nitze's case was especially troublesome. His pessimism about the decline of the West, his outright admiration for the "damned impressive" side of what he had seen of the Third Reich, and his conversational pugnacity all led him to make statements before America's entry into the war that caused him trouble afterward. On top of all that, there was his German background. For years afterward he had to fend off accusations that he had gone beyond being just another America Firster. An FBI file that appeared in a background check on Nitze in 1960 contained both the charge and the defense: "In 1940, Vincent Astor, New York Financier, advised that Nitze, at a small dinner party, said he would rather see America under the dictatorship of Hitler than under the British Empire if either alternative became necessary. James Forrestal, former Secretary of Defense . . . stated he was positive Nitze did not mean to be pro-German but meant that he knew Germany was well organized and could not be easily defeated."[47]

When war broke out in 1939, Forrestal went to Washington as an administrative assistant to Roosevelt. In June 1940, Forrestal lured Nitze there too. For most of the rest of his life, Nitze worked inside the beltway, either serving or opposing the administration in power. Years later, in an unkind cut, William Castle, a retired high-ranking state department official, commented in his diary when Nitze's name had come up; Nitze was then director of State's Policy Planning Staff. "Nitze, who has taken Kennan's place, is a New York banker who knows nothing of foreign affairs but is thrilled to be running the U.S. Government. When a group of them were talking in the Department the other day Max [Bishop] heard Nitze say that the people had no right to complain about taxes as there was a reserve of two hundred billion dollars at least which could be drained off by the Government . . ."[48]

Thrilled to be running policy planning at State Nitze was indeed. Ignorant of foreign affairs he was not.

Nitze worked for Forrestal until Forrestal went to be Under Secretary of the Navy; then Nitze assisted William Draper and Lewis Hershey in working out a selective service law to accommodate the coming rearmament. In 1941, he worked for Nelson Rockefeller in Inter-American Affairs, then for the Board of Economic Warfare. Here Nitze acquired a dislike of the left-leaning politics of Henry Wallace. Then there was service in the Foreign Economic Administration, from which Nitze resigned in 1944 to join USSBS.

The powerful anti-Soviet bias that Nitze first acquired at Harvard was at full strength by the time the war ended, and it lasted until the 1990's when the Soviet was no more. In 1944, Nitze saw the army's point system for determining eligibility for discharge as a communist plot: "that came from agents of influence. That was a poisonous system. The *Stars & Stripes* I think was infiltrated by communists."[49] Nitze didn't really want to demobilize at the end of the war; the Western world was in the greatest peril ever. In 1946, Nitze tried to get city planner Robert Moses to require every new building in New York City to have a large enough bomb shelter to hold all its occupants. On reading Stalin's election eve speech to a Soviet party rally in 1946, Nitze called it "a delayed declaration of war against the United States."[50]

This powerful ideology explains how Nitze found it easy to disregard the massive testimony in USSBS files showing that Japanese leaders believed that without the atomic bombs, and perhaps Soviet entry, Japan would have fought on into 1946. It also explains how he could ignore, or refuse to read, the ULTRA decrypts provided by the president, proving that every ounce of Japanese energy was going into plans for the final battle of the homeland.

But there was additional incentive for him to downgrade the influence of the atom. The JCS and the president, while apparently agreeing to his recommendation in the 1945 targeting deliberations to concentrate on bombing transportation, had rejected his advice to use chemical defoliants on the rice crop, thus accelerating starvation.[51] Worse, the JCS kept the OLYMPIC invasion on the schedule, as if the air forces had not already won the war. Nitze's reference in his memoirs to these slights at the hands of JCS barely conceals his resentment.[52]

There was a belief among some of Nitze's subordinates at USSBS that part of Nitze's motivation for downgrading the role of the atom was his ambition to be the first secretary of the United States Air Force, sure to be created after the war. The fliers were aiming at a seventy-group air force. Atomic bombs were seen as an obstacle to this level of air strength. If one bomb carried by one plane could wipe out a city the size of Hiroshima, what need for seventy groups? Their fliers would be out of business.[53]

Whatever his motives, Nitze was the primary author of the USSBS *Summary Report (Pacific War)*. He complained that he "had to write every word of the damn document," and the early surrender hypothesis was in the preliminary draft of 12 March 1946 much as it appeared in the published report of July.[54]

When asked by President Truman in the fall of 1949 to render an opinion on whether the United States should build the Super or H-bomb, Nitze first consulted Oppenheimer, whose doubts about the project Nitze found "disjointed"; then Edward Teller, who "knew his subject so well that he was able to explain why this thing would work in just two hours time." A year later, it developed that Teller had been wrong; yet "With little or no knowledge of physics, Nitze thought that he had followed Teller's calculations, and that those calculations had proved the Super's feasibility."[55]

In 1950, after Truman had decided to approve development of H-bombs, he instructed Secretary of State Acheson and Secretary of Defense Johnson to appoint a committee to review the U.S. defense posture in light of Soviet capability for atomic weapons. Nitze was made chairman, and the committee consisted of state and defense mid- to high-level officers.[56] Once more, Nitze went into the assignment with his mind made up. He went through the motions of consultation, held meetings and listened to experts, then wrote up a clarion call to triple the defense budget. In April 1950, he submitted what was the 68th paper endorsed by the National Security Council, hence NSC-68, to Acheson; this was widely regarded as the blueprint for the cold war.

Right off, in the first section, we hear the tocsin: "The issues that face us are momentous, involving the fulfillment or destruction not only of this Republic but of civilization itself. They are issues which will not await our deliberations."[57] Odd, since Nitze's crew deliberated for three months, then the president deliberated for another five months, and only as the shock of the Korean War took hold was the document formally accepted. It was, really, a theological production, talking about the "more perfection union" which could be had with a "firm reliance on the protection of Divine Providence, we mutually pledge to each other our lives, our fortunes, and our sacred honor."[58]

According to NSC-68, the Soviet Union was implacably committed to destroying any free society, negotiations were useless, and by 1954, the Soviet Union would have sufficient nuclear weapons to launch a crippling surprise attack on the United States.

Once again, the best evidence presented to Nitze's investigators contradicted his own convictions. The only Soviet experts consulted, Charles Bohlen and Llewellyn Thompson, and George Kennan who was not exactly consulted but made his views known, said the Soviet Union was not committed to world conquest as Hitler had been, that Stalin's prime objectives were maintaining Soviet internal control and protecting Russia's borders, and that while the Soviet Union would move into attractive power vacuums, they would not start a major war. Bohlen was adamant that American nuclear monopoly had not affected Soviet policy at all. A half dozen consultants agreed with Bohlen. Once again, as with USSBS, the dissident opinion was ignored, and Nitze told Secretary Acheson when he delivered this call to arms on 6 April 1950, "The conclusions and recommendations have found general support. The comments reveal no need to alter these in any major way, but it is suggested that you might wish to make the comment attached as Appendix I in forwarding them to the President."[59] (This was to emphasize exploiting U.S. Technology.) Nitze did not, in this document, say he had "all the facts," he simply failed to include Bohlen's vigorous disagreement.

Callahan observes of NSC-68 that "In better times it was a framework that might have been ridiculed as a doomsayer's delusion. But with the cold war at its height, Nitze's approach was destined to alter history."[60]

Nitze spent the rest of his life attempting to alter history. His colleague Galbraith wrote that Nitze's alterations were always in the direction of increased armament, especially by "studying the theory and practice of aerial destruction, emerging in the end as a devout practitioner of the arm."[61] Whether in or out of government, he was a player. He wrote the report of the Gaither Commission, to which Ike responded, "You can't have this kind of war. There aren't enough bulldozers to scrape the bodies off the streets."[62] In 1956, Nitze wrote an article for *Foreign Affairs* claiming that it *was* possible to win a nuclear war.[63]

In 1976, Nitze helped organize the Committee on the Present Danger, to do the same job that NSC-68 had been intended for seventeen years earlier. Shortly after that, he objected to the nomination of Paul Warnke as chief arms negotiator, and actually told the Senate that he, Nitze, thought he was a better American than Warnke, because Warnke was soft on defense. This hurt Nitze considerably. During the Vietnam War, he was reluctant to increase American forces there because this weakened America for the "main show," opposing the USSR. He thumped the table in one confrontation and told his colleagues, "It's us against the Soviets. Either we get them first, or they get us first."[64]

Was there a more belligerent hawk in the annals of the cold war? It's hard to identify one. The irony of Nitze producing the foundation document of the left-wing opponents of Truman's bomb decision is difficult to overlook. One observes when reading these bomb critics — and the most anti-Truman of them cites the USSBS early surrender counterfactual 17 times in one book — that Nitze is never named as the author. It is always merely "an official report."[65]

☙ ☙ ☙

Official Narrative #2, as I label it, may not have aroused much interest among the public when it came out, but it penetrated the consciousness of every disputant on the subject of the mission of *Enola Gay* since. Robert Butow challenged several of its claims. Barton Bernstein noted that some of the Survey's analyses were troubling, and that they ignored some issues. William L. O'Neill said that USSBS had no basis for the early surrender claim.[66] These skeptics went unheeded.

The USSBS report was part of the stimulus that brought forth Henry Stimson's 1947 *Harper's* article, "The Decision to Use the Atomic Bomb," and in his memoirs published in 1948, Stimson wondered if he should have pressed harder to modify unconditional surrender.[67] Joseph Grew, before the USSBS report came out, wrote that Stimson had "been splendid throughout it all," and that together (Stimson and Grew) they had gotten Japan to surrender and saved many American lives. After reading the USSBS report, Grew did an about face, claiming that surrender could have come shortly after the May bombings if surrender terms had been modified. In letters to friends, Grew began to use almost scatological terms to describe Stimson.[68]

USSBS was the major source for the Blackett book dealt with extensively in chapter four. In 1958, Paul Kecskemeti's *Strategic Surrender* cites the Nitze claim.[69] Howard Zinn wrote an essay in 1962 castigating use of the bomb, based largely on the USSBS report.[70] Gar Alperovitz accepted USSBS as gospel truth when he wrote his influential *Atomic Diplomacy: Hiroshima and Potsdam*, but he does not identify Nitze as the author.[71] Herbert Feis, Truman supporter, who had access to classified documents for his two books on the end of the Pacific war, was influenced by Nitze and waffles on whether the war could have been ended earlier.[72] It would be tedious to list all the works on the decision to drop the bomb that cite USSBS. As chapter 6 will show, even in 1995 the National Air and Space Museum curators could not conceive of a text for the *Enola Gay* exhibit that failed to depend on USSBS.

The gullibility of the American historical community in accepting Nitze's work as a legitimate source for understanding the ending of the Pacific war is difficult to understand. The report has "caution" written all over it. How many millions of hours are spent in the archives by ambitious graduate students and assistant professors checking out the minute details of some insignificant activity by a third secretary of embassy somewhere? But for half a century, nobody analyzed the most consequential work on the atomic bomb decision.

The first critical analysis of *Japan's Struggle to End the War* was published by this author in the *Pacific Historical Review* of May 1995.[73] It was followed by a less critical but still revealing article by Barton Bernstein in the *Journal of Strategic Studies,* June 1995.[74] A third, heavily critical study of USSBS bias by Gian Peri Gentile, a student of Bernstein, came in the February 1997 *Pacific Historical Review.*[75] Gentile also has an excellent article showing how the "impartial" civilian directors of the USSBS were actually making the case for an independent air force, in the October 2000 *Journal of Military History.*[76] Gentile's full analysis was published by New York University Press in December 2000.[77] No refutation of these studies is in sight; Nitze is caught in flagrante delicto.

Does this mean that the anti-Truman polemicists will in future bow to this modern scholarly research, and give up citing USSBS as proof that Japan was ready to surrender? Not at all. Gentile takes the measure of the situation here: "The Survey's published reports, unfortunately, have taken on the mystique of being the 'biblical' truth about strategic bombing in World War II." And biblical truth always trumps mere scholarship. Too many reputations have been built on the case against Harry Truman, just as James Conant feared would happen.

3

STIMSON'S DEFENSE

Patterson called me up to say that General Hines of the Veterans Bureau has made a very reckless statement to the effect that as soon as Germany was defeated we were going to withdraw 250,000 men every month or something like that—some prodigious statement—from the Army. That of course will be a terrific boomerang both against us on the floor in regard to the Service Law and also in raising false hopes among the soldiers who are sure to be disappointed.
Stimson Diary, 28 FEBRUARY 1945[1]

An 1888 graduate of Yale, then of Harvard Law, Henry Stimson was well fitted for success in both private life and public service. Membership in the New York law firm at which Elihu Root was senior partner drew Stimson into diplomatic circles; friendship with Theodore Roosevelt brought him an invitation to serve as U.S. attorney for the Southern District of New York, a post he occupied from 1906 to 1909.

Stimson continued to be active in public life. He was Secretary of War under President William Howard Taft, served as a colonel of artillery in World War I (and preferred, all his life, to be called "Colonel"), was Governor General of the Philippines in 1928, and became President Herbert Hoover's Secretary of State the next year. In 1931, the Japanese launched the invasion of Manchuria that rankled the United States with repercussions leading to war. Stimson firmly opposed Japanese aggression; nonrecognition of territory seized by force of arms has been known since 1931 as the Stimson Doctrine. Stimson served Hoover well; American foreign relations were tidier than domestic affairs when Franklin D. Roosevelt replaced Hoover in 1933.

For the first seven years of Roosevelt's administration, Stimson generally opposed the president, objecting particularly to Roosevelt's plan to pack the Supreme Court. But in the area of foreign affairs, Stimson firmly and vocally endorsed Roosevelt's policies: encouraging free trade, opposing rapidly expanding German and Japanese militarism, and strengthening American military forces. When Britain and France caved in to Hitler at Munich and war broke out in Europe, Roosevelt asked the life-long conservative Republican, aged seventy-two, to take another tour of duty as secretary of war. Stimson thought it his responsibility to oblige.

Stimson was in many ways an unwarlike secretary. Despite his patrician background, his empathy with ordinary servicemen was extraordinary. He frequently visited the wounded in military hospitals. He was easily the least bloodthirsty and vengeful of our World War II leaders. He objected to the indiscriminate bombing of cities, especially the destruction of Dresden, but he was unable to turn off the carnage from the air. His one significant victory in this arena was demanding that Kyoto be taken off the list for bombing in Japan, making this stick in face of furious objections from the military targeters. Almost alone, he advocated sharing the secret of the atom with the Soviet Union, fighting a long but losing battle with those who even in 1945 were looking forward to the struggle that we know as the "Cold War."

One would not know it from the negative picture of Stimson in the writings of opponents of use of the bombs, but he was the most eloquent of those who believed the United States had to get along with Russia. On 2 April 1945, after a talk with George Marshall and former Secretary of State Stettinius on how "we simply cannot allow a rift to come between the two nations without endangering the entire peace of the world," Stimson wrote in his diary:

> Marshall told me he had anticipated these troubles and thought they would be pretty bad and irritating but thought that we must put up with them. I told Stettinius that in retrospect Russia had been very good to us on the large issues. She had kept her word and carried out her engagements. We must remember that she has not learned the amenities of diplomatic intercourse and we must expect bad language from her. I told him of my talk with Marshall and told him I had also had a conference during the day with a couple of officers, Captain Patrick A. Teel and Lt. James J. Hannon, who had escaped through Poland into Russia and then had traveled southwesterly through Poland and Czechoslovakia into Hungary, and finally been picked up by General Eaker. These two boys were loud in their praise of the basic kindness of the Russian troops.[2]

To the very end of his tenure in the government, Stimson sought to manage relations with the Soviet Union so as to minimize their suspicion of American intentions.

From January through April 1945, Stimson's main concern, as revealed in his diary, was the alarming shortage of fighting men. He wrote on 15 January 1945:

> A long meeting in the General's office (Marshall) with the Operations and Intelligence Staff. Matters are getting better in the salient, the Germans seem to be on the run; and on the eastern flank the Russians are putting in some good licks with their great new offensive. It seems funny that in such a situation I should be distressed by our successes and our good fortune. But the true fact is that these things are going to make it more difficult than it would have been to get the necessary legislation through our Congress which we had in view at the time when everybody was scared. Just as soon as the news of these victories comes, everybody wants to put on his coat and stop working including Congress. The result was that I have been spending my day trying to get pushed ahead in regard to what we are trying to get out of Congress in the way of a National Service Act before we get any more successes.[3]

Almost every other day there is some worry expressed about the draft bill, or about a shortage of troops. Toward the end of February, his awareness of the scope of the problems changes: "I had a long talk with Marshall on the coming campaign against Japan. It is a new problem for me. I have never studied it or thought it over in the way that I had over the war in Europe and I wanted very much to find out what the staff were doing. So Marshall gave me a long chat about it. I have been a little worried about the prospect of using any more of our masses of troops in fighting on the land of China. I rather don't think the country would stand for it, and I told Marshall so."[4] The Veterans Bureau made an unapproved announcement that as soon as Germany surrendered, about 250,000 men would be discharged every month; Stimson wrestled with this on 28 February. It was immediately denied, both for fear of what Congress would do, and to avoid raising false hopes among the troops.

Beginning in March, Stimson writes less about manpower needs and more about S-1: the Manhattan Project. Clearly he is counting on a successful bomb to save bloodshed. Gradually he sees the boost the bomb might give to political relations with the Soviet Union, though this aspect never displaces the hope for avoidance of battle deaths. He notes the memo from Herbert Hoover on ending the Pacific war, saying only that it was "very interesting, rather dramatic and radical."[5] Talks with his staff on the new bomb were almost unceasing. Later criticism maintaining that the bomb decision had been made "thoughtlessly, by default" overlook not only meetings of the Interim Committee established to make certain decisions about atomic bombs, but the lengthy and continual discussions by Stimson, Truman, Marshall, and the War Department staff.[6] By my count, between 5 March and the Hiroshima bombing on 6 August, Stimson recorded face-to-face discussions about the bomb with Assistant Secretary of War Harvey Bundy on thirty-two separate occasions; with his assistant George Harrison on twenty-six occasions; with Truman at least fourteen times; with Marshall twelve times (this is only the count of times he is with Marshall and indicates the specific subject discussed), and with his assistant John McCloy eight times. The Interim Committee discussions were simply the capstone of a long process. There were also several meetings with British representatives.

By 19 June, in a discussion of the desirability of avoiding a fight to the finish, Stimson mentions the "last chance warning" to be given Japan before an actual landing on the home islands. General Marshall suggested "an additional sanction to our warning in the shape of an entry by the Russians into the war. That would certainly coordinate all the threats possible to Japan."[7] Stimson realized later that the last thing the United States could do would be to tell Japan that the Russians were about to attack, and this proposal was dropped; but clearly the atom, conventional bombing, specification of benefits to Japan if she surrendered, and continued blockade, all are viewed not as alternatives, but as a cumulative process. As for Stimson's generous but mistaken belief that we could benefit by retreating from unconditional surrender, guaranteeing the emperor, Dower's objection is compelling: there would have been no reform.[8]

But if Stimson was wrong about retreating from unconditional surrender, he was everlastingly right about avoidance of a punitive peace. His thoughts on this matter as of 2 July 1945:

> I regard these two subjects, viz.: the effort to shorten the Japanese war by a surrender and the proper handling of Germany so as not to create such harshness in seeking vengeance as to make it impossible to lay the foundations of a new Germany which will be a proper member of the family of nations, as two of the largest and most important problems that I have had since I have been here. In the first one I have to meet and overcome the zeal of the soldier, and in the second the zeal of the Jewish American statesmen seeking vengeance [a reference to Henry Morgenthau and Bernard Baruch]. And in both cases I have to meet the feeling of war passion and hysteria which seizes hold of a nation like ours in the prosecution of such a bitter war. The President has so far struck me as a man who is trying hard to keep his balance.[9]

One does not find such views acknowledged in the picture of Stimson given by the followers of Nitze. Nor does one find the full picture of his memo for the president, "Proposed Program for Japan," dated 2 July 1945. This is a five-page development of Stimson's thought that he says Truman appeared to agree with, but did not carry out. It covers preparations for Olympic; the horrors of actually carrying it out on the hostile terrain of Kyushu; the belief that if we land in Japan the die will be cast for "an even more bitter finish fight than in Germany"; and the advantages of a warning to Japan of the destruction to come if she does not surrender.[10] He then lists the military and moral advantages of the United States, and says that Japan is not wholly governed by fanatics, but possesses "enough liberal leaders" for reconstruction after surrender. He lists the conditions that the United States should tell Japan will be imposed: precisely those incorporated in the Potsdam Declaration, except Stimson included "we do not exclude a constitutional monarchy under her present dynasty." The latter Truman rejected, largely on the advice of James Byrnes. Stimson concludes this memo with "Our own bombing should be confined to military objectives as far as possible."

We then follow Stimson as he goes to Potsdam, observes "Soviet repression" in Berlin, receives and passes on the report of the Alamogordo atomic test that so "pepped up" the president, demands again that Kyoto not be bombed, says we don't need the Russians in the war now, and returns to Washington.[11]

From then until the surrender, he wrestles with how much information about the atom to publish, wonders what effect the two bombs will have (and decides there won't be any for awhile so plans a nine-day vacation that has to be canceled). He regrets Byrnes's refusal to consider any approach to Stalin about sharing bomb secrets, defends vigorously the proposal for universal military training, notes that the only way to make a man trustworthy is to trust him (this apropos dealing with the Soviet Union). He gives a sermonette at his club in the Adirondacks when he does finally get a vacation. His sermonette is devoted to the "spirit of relief at the ending of the terrible war" and "we have been compelled to invent and unleash forces of terrific destructiveness"; only the spirit of Christianity can prevent another war which will "end our civilization."[12] Taking the totality of the diary it is hard to understand the attacks on Stimson as a self-serving liar, a racist imperialist, and a willing perpetrator of unnecessary destruction. The charge that he approved the atomic bombings in order to intimidate the Soviets is ludicrous.[13]

❧ ❧ ❧

But then came *The Article*. "The Decision to Use the Atomic Bomb," in *Harper's Magazine* for February 1947, was not Stimson's idea. James B. Conant, president of Harvard and one of the prominent scientists involved in the Manhattan Project, prevailed upon Stimson to write this account. Conant believed that an impressive U.S. atomic arsenal could induce the Soviet Union to join an international atomic control structure, and he felt that attacks on the World War II atomic bomb decision deflected attention from that pressing agenda. And of course he was sensitive to the charge that the whole enterprise of which he had been a part was morally corrupt. Whether Conant realized that the USSBS "bomb was not necessary" official evaluation was far more potent over the long haul than the moral absolutist objection is not clear, but he did note USSBS reports, assumed they were honest and well-grounded, even if only "Monday morning quarterbacking."[14]

On 23 September 1946 Conant wrote Harvey Bundy that criticism of the bomb decision "is bound to have a great deal of influence on the next generation. The type of person who goes into teaching, particularly school teaching, will be influenced a great deal by this type of argument . . . a small minority, if it represents the type of person who is both sentimental and verbally minded and in contact with our youth, may result in a distortion of history."[15] Conant's rhetorical analysis is faulty here. It was not the moral sentimentalists who damaged the Truman-Stimson narrative, it was the gullibles who were susceptible to the preemptive "all the facts" claim of Nitze's "official" survey.

Adding to the challenge of the churches and the report signed by Conant's friend Reinhold Niebuhr, there came on 31 August a skillful narrative about the bombing of Hiroshima written by John Hersey, which appeared in *The New Yorker*. The issue sold out immediately. Subsequently published as a book, *Hiroshima* became a runaway best seller. Thereafter, as one commentator put it, that one bombing "inspired more debate than the rest of the war's destruction put together. It was as if all the other recent massacres could be set aside and the entire moral problem of modern war could be concentrated in this one question."[16]

Hersey did what no one else had done: he converted the Japanese enemy, previously thought by most Americans to be an "undifferentiated subhuman mass," into recognizable human beings. Modeled on Thornton Wilder's *Bridge of San Luis Rey*, the narrative betrayed little emotion; it simply described what had happened to the town and six survivors. Technical details were few; those that were included were drawn from the USSBS findings. Like the Bombing Survey's report, *Hiroshima* passed itself off as an unbiased account.

Hersey was an unlikely author for a sympathetic treatment of the Japanese. During the war, he had been as appalled over Japanese actions as any of his fellow correspondents. His account of the battle on Guadalcanal, *Into the Valley*, accepts the nonracist explanation for why American soldiers despised the Japanese: they were treacherous on the battlefield. They used "white surrender flags to suck us into traps." His article "Kamikaze," in the 30 July 1945 issue of *Life*, is openly contemptuous. Tokyo radio had exhorted the entire Japanese empire of 100 million men, women, and children "to become a great suicide unit," and Premier Suzuki promised "victory" even if "no Japanese still is alive to enjoy it." Such absurdity was a symptom of societal degeneracy. Hersey acknowledged that individual acts of self-sacrifice have their place in wars, but "The Japanese have done something no other nation in the world would be capable of doing. They have systematized suicide; they have nationalized a morbid, sickly act."[17]

It is interesting to muse about the course of the "blame game" had Hersey devoted his talents to telling an equally elaborate and sympathetic story of six victims of Japan's Rape of Manila in 1944, or of her lethal treatment of slave laborers who built the Burma-Siam railway, or of Unit 731's biological warfare against the Chinese. Even the story of six innocent American sailors maimed at Pearl Harbor would have cast the question about culpability in a different light.

The atomic bomb victims probably drew Hersey's attention because their incineration was the most spectacular event of that deadly war, but Japanese depredations killed far more people, most in horrible ways. United Nations figures indicate ten million Chinese dead at Japanese hands, four million Dutch East Indians, a million and a half Bengalis, a million Vietnamese, etc., but in no case, of course, was there such a single, instantaneous apocalypse.[18] And, thus, there was no comparable explosion in international consciousness. Postwar American eagerness to build Japan up as the Pacific bastion of our frantic anti-Soviet policy encouraged amnesia about the Japanese Empire's many millions of victims. Hersey's book put the stamp on Hiroshima as *the* atrocity of the war.

Then on top of all this, Norman Cousins came out with his anti-bomb writings. Cousins's turnabout was the last straw for Conant. It propelled him into activism.

As Barton Bernstein puts it, Conant thought he and his colleagues had to seize "the contested terrain of early nuclear history."[19] Conant believed that America had a world-historical mission. There must be no more slipping back into isolationism. For Conant, there was only one person whose stature and knowledge was equal to the task of defending the mission of *Enola Gay*. That person was Henry Stimson.

Stimson was then retired to his Long Island estate. During the summer of 1946, the seventy-eight-year-old statesman was working on his memoirs with the assistance of McGeorge Bundy, son of Stimson's wartime aide Harvey Bundy. Prodded by Conant, friends of Stimson prevailed on him to undertake a defense of the decision to drop the bombs. Bundy did most of the writing, and his drafts were critiqued by Conant, General Groves, and others. Conant insisted that the article be a "mere recital of the facts." It should not advocate the decision, merely explain it, and it should not argue against those who had publicly opposed the decision.

When "The Decision to Use the Atomic Bomb" appeared in *Harper's,* it carried a note saying that anyone was free to reprint it because of its "exceptional public importance." The *New York Times* quickly approved: "As Mr. Stimson shows . . . [the reasoning behind the decision] was grim but irrefutable. The Japanese had been gravely weakened, but they were still determined to fight to the death . . . though they had sent out peace feelers through Russia, they still counted on posing as victors and keeping much of the areas they had conquered . . . It would cost at least a million American—and many more Japanese—casualties, and a war lasting to the latter part of 1946, to beat them to their knees."[20] The *Washington Post's* editors ran the *Harper's* article in full but were less convinced that Stimson had presented the whole story. Referring to the USSBS conclusion that Japan was about to surrender, a *Post* editorial hinted that Stimson might have been mistaken about the Japanese will to fight to the death. Nonetheless, the article was commended as a "powerful apologia."[21]

So what about this article later drew the wrath of Nitzeans and detractors of Truman? Primarily, its tone of certainty. In the first paragraph, Stimson writes "No single individual can hope to know exactly what took place in the minds of all of those who had a share in these events, but what follows is an exact description of our thoughts and actions as I find them in the records and in my clear recollection." Of course, Stimson could not produce an *exact* description of his thoughts and actions over a period of five years. Even his extensive diary records only a fraction of his thoughts and activities. This was an exaggeration.

It was seized on by Gar Alperovitz, whose six chapters in 1995 on Stimson's omissions and misrepresentations ("clearly conscious decisions were made to mislead the American people") constitute the most elaborate attack on Stimson.[22] This is doubly unfortunate. In his first book of 1965, Alperovitz thinks well enough of Stimson to dedicate his *Atomic Diplomacy: Hiroshima and Potsdam* "For My Daughter Kari and in Memory of a Great American Conservative, Henry L. Stimson."[23] That Great American Conservative did gild the lily in claiming he had an exact description, but this foible is far from being as offensive as the claim Alperovitz accepts as gospel truth, Nitze's "On the basis of all the facts." Nitze claimed more for his official narrative than Stimson did; both went too far.

Nitzeans object to the Stimson claim that the Interim Committee, appointed by Truman to consider the use of atomic bombs, had done an adequate job. Stimson writes that the Interim Committee unanimously adopted three recommendations: "(1) the bomb should be used against Japan as soon as possible. (2) It should be used on a dual target—that is, a military installation or war plant surrounded by or adjacent to houses or other buildings most susceptible to damage, and (3) It should be used without prior warning (of the nature of the weapon). In reaching these conclusions, the Interim Committee carefully considered such alternatives as a detailed advance warning or a demonstration in some uninhabited area. Both of these suggestions were dismissed as impractical."[24] Stimson explained that the Committee had good reasons; nothing could have been more disastrous for American morale, or as encouraging for Japan's, as the failure of a much-hyped new weapon, and the Manhattan engineers could give no guarantees. One type of bomb needed to be tested; the other, which was to be detonated with a new kind of fuse, had not yet been dropped from a plane. Moreover, even if a demonstration drop were successful, the Japanese could have kept knowledge of it from their people. All these things were considered by the Interim Committee.

Furthermore, said Stimson, "The possible atomic weapon was considered to be as legitimate as any other of the deadly explosive weapons of modern war." Stimson also stressed his responsibility to the people. Americans were sick of the war and eager to bring their boys back home. If people learned that a potentially warending weapon had not been used, Stimson could not, he declared, have "looked my countrymen in the face."[25]

More serious than the charge of exaggeration was the accusation that Stimson had misrepresented the options available in August 1945. He seemed to pose the dilemma as a simple choice between using the bomb and invading Kyushu as scheduled on 1 November. Stimson's critics claimed there were other options, and that the administration *knew* there were other options: (1) modifying surrender terms to allow continuation of the emperor (2) waiting for Soviet entry into the war, or (3) tightening the naval blockade and continued conventional bombing until thousands starved and the rubble bounced.[26]

All these "options" assume the truth of the foundation text on which Nitzeans depend. Neither USSBS nor any other source offers credible evidence that guaranteeing the emperor would have brought capitulation. The opinions of Joseph Grew, Admiral Halsey, Admiral Ellis Zacharias, and other Americans as to what the Japanese would accept as sufficient to get them to quit the war are wholly suspect. MAGIC and ULTRA decrypts make abundantly clear that the modifications of unconditional surrender necessary to secure the agreement of Minister of War Anami and his fellow militarists, even after Hiroshima, included not just retaining the emperor, but avoiding occupation, disarming themselves, and conducting their own war crimes trials. No American government could have agreed to these. There was no option here. There was a strong likelihood that any softening of peace terms would be interpreted as war weariness and lead to stronger Japanese efforts to extract concessions, which if granted would vitiate the bottom-line objective of destroying Japanese militarism.[27]

Of course, Stimson himself had recommended guaranteeing the emperor before the bombs were used in the hope that the concession might help the Japanese who favored ending the war to triumph over the militarists, and he so stated in his *Harper's* article. Ultimately, however, he succumbed to the better wisdom of George Marshall and the menacing message of the decrypts: *these people really wanted to destroy the first wave of an American invasion,* and then they could obtain significant concessions.

As to Soviet entry, due in mid-August, USSBS files and subsequent interrogations of Japanese leaders show some support for the belief that Soviet entry did contribute to surrender, but this is only because it was coupled with the shock of the atom. Alperovitz makes much of a 30 April 1946 report by Col. R. F. Ennis of the War Department Operations Division, which concludes, "The war would almost certainly have terminated when Russia entered the war against Japan."[28] Ennis offers a ludicrous account of Japanese deliberations in August 1945; he misdates Prime Minister Suzuki's concession to surrender, writes of cabinet meetings that did not take place, misidentifies the messengers who took bad news to the emperor, and confuses Suzuki's activities with those of Privy Seal Kido. There is no warrant for the Ennis Report whatsoever. When, in 1998, the most knowledgeable Japanese scholar of the end of the war, Sadao Asada, wrote what will be the definitive account of Japan's decision-making in *The Pacific Historical Review,* he is quite clear that Soviet entry was not the shock that made a difference:

> Because the Soviet entry came on the heels of the Hiroshima bomb, it is hard to separate the impacts of the two events. The foregoing analysis, however, would suggest the primacy of the Hiroshima bomb; the Soviet entry, coming as it did when the bomb had already shaken Japan's ruling elite, served as a confirmation and coup de grace.
>
> From a political and diplomatic viewpoint the Soviet entry was indeed a serious blow to Japan; it dashed the last hope of Soviet peace mediation. But it did not come as a total surprise, which the atomic bomb assuredly was. After all, the Soviet invasion of Manchuria gave them an *indirect* shock, whereas the use of the atomic bomb on their homeland gave them the *direct* threat of the atomic extinction of the Japanese people (Italics in original).[29]

Then Stimson detractors claim that continued bombing and blockade would have brought Japan to surrender in a short time. Whether this would have been a morally superior way to extract surrender will be discussed in chapter seven. Nitze and most that follow him seem to prefer it. They do not, however, address the agonies of death by starvation, nor do they address the probability that Japan would have surrendered due to starvation anytime soon.

Given the unrelenting determination of Japan's controllers, its military, to fight on through the first invasion wave, the argument that starvation would soon lead to surrender has little credibility. Certainly the Japanese food supply was low, and malnutrition was evident by August 1945, but history urged caution. Of course, Japan would surrender sometime, but when? Hundreds of Japanese soldiers on isolated Pacific islands starved rather than surrender. The best discussion of Japanese nutrition levels is in Thomas R. H. Havens, *Valley of Darkness*. He notes that in 1945 the Japanese people "took in just 1,793 calories a day . . . yet even then the amount of protein people were eating held up reasonably well." And by way of summary, "To the very end people managed to find food, however sparse or untasty."[30]

Further observation about the food situation comes from Yoshida Shigeru, prime minister 1946–1947. Food was short in 1946, he says, "Here again, however, the American Occupation forces were most helpful, enabling us to tide over the worst periods with the aid of imported food . . . and also the food stored in different parts of the country during the war—stocks that most fortunately proved to be far more abundant than was expected."[31] A similar observation is made by Herbert Passin, a member of the occupation: "During the last year or so of the war, the Japanese military had stored away several years' supply of food, clothing, raw materials, equipment, and funds in its arsenals, caves, and other hiding places."[32] It was this hoarded supply that led to the scandals agitating John Dower: "With the 'hoarded goods scandal,' structural corruption was established as one foundation stone of the postwar political economy. The materials looted by men of position and privilege were obviously of enormous value. They were, after all, being stockpiled to supply a gigantic home army for a protracted 'decisive battle.'"[33]

Surrender by starvation is an iffy business here. There is no warrant for castigating Stimson; starvation would have taken many months.

The final charge leveled at Stimson is that he grossly exaggerated the cost in American lives of mounting an invasion, thus making the bomb more palatable. Stimson calculated this at "over a million casualties, to American forces alone." Alperovitz calls this Stimson's "most enduring single obfuscation" and asks, "Where did Stimson and Bundy get their 'over a million' estimate? We do not know."[34] We do know at least one, and probably two sources, discussed in chapter one. Alperovitz further claims that Stimson's figure "has no basis in the planning documents." What planning documents? The documents organized by the casualty-shy United States Army before the horrendous Japanese reinforcements showed up in ULTRA decrypts? It stands to reason that a secretary of war who had been advised by the military that Germany would surrender in 1944 (which did not happen) and that MacArthur would recapture Leyte in 45 days with four divisions (it took three months and nine divisions) would be skeptical of low-end estimates put out by those same generals.

Stimson is criticized for not airing his fundamental disagreements with James Byrnes over how to deal with the Soviet Union over the atom. This would have been a juicy morsel for the political gossip mills. Would it have contributed to any worthwhile purpose? Bernstein has suggested that Stimson should not have claimed to be sole author of the *Harper's* article.[35] Was the public seriously misled due to the contributions to the article made by Harrison, Conant, Bundy? Perhaps, but this is not one of the great watersheds of the cold war. The unconscionable misleading of the public occurred not with Stimson's defense of the 1945 bombing decisions, but with the top secret classification and denial to the public of the apocalyptic rhetoric with which Paul Nitze in 1950 steered the United States into the obscene nuclear overkill called for by NSC-68. Picking at Stimson for a flawed article in 1947 seems trivial when compared with the madness that descended in mid-century.

The Stimson article *was* flawed. Stimson framed the issue falsely. Truman did not confront a *choice* between dropping atomic bombs on Japan and launching a costly invasion. He confronted the necessity of using every legitimate means available to end a global war—not one means as opposed to another, not invasion or bomb, not waiting for Soviet intervention or blockade/starvation, not continued conventional bombing or atomic bombs. It was simply not an either/or situation.

Explicitly backing down from unconditional surrender was not a viable option; it would have strengthened the Japanese military rather than the peace forces, and would have jeopardized the reconstruction of Japan after the war. Use of poison gas to flush Japanese soldiers out of the ubiquitous caves was considered, but that was not a legitimate course. Destroying the Japanese rice crop was advocated by several military figures, but this would have been a far worse tragedy.[36] The atom was perceived as an advanced and legitimate development in explosives. No well-placed American official questioned the legitimacy of the atomic weapon, notwithstanding Eisenhower's later (false) claim to have done so.[37]

Stimson's framing of the issue—the atom versus invasion—created the impression that the American high command knew that either of these alternatives would end the war. They did not. Marshall at one point thought that the atomic bomb coupled with invasion would end the war, but he did not know when. Truman, euphoric after Alamogordo, boasted "Believe Japs will fold up before Russia comes in. I am sure they will before Manhattan appears over their homeland."[38] ULTRA intercepts soon quashed his optimism, a condition to which Stimson never succumbed.

Stimson's "just the facts" narrative did win a skirmish in the contest to seize control of early nuclear history, but there is no invulnerable narrative. Opponents can always devise a contrary narrative, and shifting public attitudes can create new audiences sympathetic to it. Until the country became disillusioned with government during the Vietnam War, Stimson's narrative held the field. Some surprising people bolstered Stimson in this endeavor. Eisenhower delivered a eulogy for Stimson at the Century Club in New York, 6 April 1950: "In the war I had the very great good fortune of reporting to the War Department and to two of the greatest men who have ever come to my attention—Secretary Stimson and George Marshall . . . His leadership of the Army in World War II was wonderful. I met him in December of 1941 and from that day onward he has for me meant the man who yields not one second to such enemies as defeat, flattery, favor-seeking, or any kind of thing, except truth and honesty, and the meaning of our great country. . ."[39]

And W. A. Higinbotham, executive secretary of the Federation of American Scientists, having not yet made up his mind about *Enola Gay,* wrote Stimson on 24 February 1947, "I feel that you have done a fine public service in publishing the article in *Harper's*. Many people have criticized the decision about dropping the bomb. This is easy to do in retrospect. Your article will help all reasonable men to a clearer understanding of the issues. We cannot help being impressed by the thinking which took place among your group so long before the war was over. I feel that we have added little since then. I hope that people . . . concentrate on what we have to do to follow through and get world control."[40]

Despite Stimson's tone of certainty, both Stimson and Bundy, shaken by the even greater certainty of Nitze's "all the facts," had second thoughts, and wondered later if perhaps the Japanese *had* been ready to fold, in which case the U.S. might have guaranteed the emperor and ended the war even earlier.[41] So the USSBS poison got to them too. It was already in the collective memory stream.

Barton Bernstein, right about many things, was wrong about the impact of Stimson's article, and about the scene in which it was embedded. Bernstein says Stimson's article "helped to block a probing dialogue, among plain citizens and foreign policy analysts too, about why the bombs were dropped, whether their use was ethically justified, and what role the bomb's use and America's related policy had on the Cold War."[42] The only worthwhile probing dialogue was the one on the ethics of strategic bombing, which Stimson did not block. It continued to flourish, and it will never be settled. Bernstein went on to say that Stimson's article "would become a rich area of dispute and controversy in the mid-1960s and afterward. . . ." The area of dispute and controversy was not exactly a *rich* one. It was a morass of polemic polluted at the source by Paul Nitze.

4

BLACKETT'S ATTACK

The second reason [why the U.S. is likely to use atomic weapons against the U.S.S.R.] is that American opinion, both military and civilian, in marked contrast with Russian, seems to have accepted the use of mass destruction as a normal operation of war.

P. M. S. BLACKETT, IN *Fear, War and the Bomb*[1]

Patrick Maynard Stuart Blackett was a British physicist and political activist. His narrative of the atomic bomb decision adopts in toto the USSBS narrative, crafting on to it the analysis of American motives that made his book almost as important as the foundation USSBS text itself; and his narrative became the dominant account of Truman's motives in Japan. Blackett's book, *Military and Political Consequences of Atomic Energy* was published in Britain in 1948, then slightly revised to eliminate the cruder anti-American sentiments and published in New York in 1949 under the title *Fear, War and the Bomb*. A translation was published in Japan in 1951.

This book was important because as a Nobel Prize winner in physics, Blackett carried great prestige, especially in Japan. It gave the greatest visibility to the thesis that Truman dropped the bomb in order to intimidate the Russians, and Blackett's key text, "we may conclude that the dropping of the atomic bombs was not so much the last military act of the second world war, as the first major operation of the cold war with Russia now in progress," became part of the argument for every important anti-Truman writer since.[2] By introducing the cold war theme, Blackett gave the Japanese the perfect warrant for portraying themselves as victims of American belligerence.

Blackett was a scientist of stature, and of all the principals in the Hiroshima debate, the only one who was clearly a genius. In the discussion that follows, however, I will differ with Blackett on his analyses of the American bomb decision, and on his exoneration of the Soviet nuclear program.

On the maternal side of his family, P. M. S. Blackett had ties with the Royal Navy.[3] Born in London in 1897, he attended a local school, then at age thirteen entered Osborne Naval College, and went from there to the Royal Naval College at Dartmouth. In World War I he saw action in the battles of the Falkland Islands and Jutland. After the war, he resigned from the navy to study math and physics at the Cavendish Laboratory of Cambridge University. In 1921 he earned a degree, took up a fellowship at Magdalene College Cambridge, and continued working in the Cavendish under Sir Ernest Rutherford. Blackett was assigned to take photographs of ionized particles in a cloud chamber; with 23,000 scrupulously made photographs, he found eight forked tracks showing disintegration of the nitrogen atom. He was launched on a spectacular career in physics.

In 1933 Blackett moved to Birkbeck College in London, and in 1937 to a professorship in physics at the University of Manchester. By then Britain was beginning to sense the menace of Hitler, and Blackett began a career as a defense intellectual. He pushed the development of radar, contributed to the design of the Mark 14 bombsight, was instrumental in devising operational research with amazing achievements in protecting Atlantic convoys, and was a member of the early British atomic committee (Maud Committee).

It was in this latter capacity that Blackett's disposition to dissent from group decisions came to the fore. The Maud Committee held that Britain could produce an atomic bomb by 1943 at a modest cost; Blackett disagreed, saying the Americans should be brought in on the project. In this case his judgment was sound, and was acted on. He was also right that Royal Air Force planes should primarily support the Atlantic convoys, not bomb German towns and cities. After the war, when he bought into Nitze's beliefs that atomic bombs were not the Absolute Weapon, and said Britain should not begin a program to build her own nuclear weapons, his opinion led to his exclusion from government circles for a decade. Only in 1962 when Harold Wilson became Prime Minister was Blackett again given important posts.

In 1953 Blackett moved to Imperial College, London, was elected to the Royal Society, made president of that body in 1956, and in the words of Sir Bernard Lovell, his biographer, he was "richly endowed with many distinctions."

The affinity of the pro-Soviet Blackett for the bitterly anti-Soviet Nitze is as difficult to understand as the reliance of late twentieth-century peaceniks on a text of the bellicose Nitze. Nitze and Blackett met when Nitze was in England in 1944 working on USSBS investigations of the European war. How much Nitze's attitude toward area bombing was influenced by Blackett is unknown. When I interviewed Nitze in January 1994, he said "I knew Blackett, knew him well. I thought he was a pro-Communist fellow-traveler."[4] Despite their acquaintance, there are no letters to or from Nitze listed in the inventories of Blackett's papers at the Royal Society in London, and no letters to or from Blackett in Nitze's papers at the Library of Congress.

Blackett was clearly enamored of Nitze's work on the Pacific war, and of the multi-authored USSBS reports from Europe. About the role of strategic bombing in the war against Germany, where Blackett was an authority, Blackett and USSBS saw eye-to-eye, and it is hard to fault them. The bombing of cities did not demoralize the Germans nor damage their military machine until 1944, when heavy bombing seriously interfered with transportation, especially after the Normandy landings. The tonnage dropped before 1944, with terrible loss of Allied fliers, was wasted. Blackett was eloquent about this; in 1961, reviewing Sir Charles Snow's *Science and Government,* Blackett wrote:

> About 500,000 German men, women and children were killed, but in the whole bombing offensive 160,000 U.S. and British airmen, the best young men of both countries, were lost. German war production went on rising steadily until it reached its peak in August, 1944. At this time the Allies were already in Paris and the Russian armies were well into Poland. German civilian morale did not crack . . . If the Allied air effort had been used more intelligently, if more aircraft had been supplied for the Battle of the Atlantic and to support the land fighting in Africa and later in France, if the bombing of Germany had been carried out with the attrition of the enemy defenses in mind rather than the razing of cities to the ground, I believe the war could have been won a half a year or even a year earlier.[5]

In regard to the Pacific, where Blackett had no first-hand information, he appears to have been mesmerized by Nitze's "all the facts" claim. Blackett says several times that the USSBS early surrender counterfactual is convincing. He also agreed with Nitze that atomic bombs were not the Absolute Weapon, that an efficient air raid shelter system built by "presently known techniques" could reduce casualties "to one-twentieth or less of the casualties that would be suffered were these techniques not employed. . . ."[6]

Differing from the defense intellectuals then cropping up on the other side of the Atlantic, Blackett holds "The most important deduction that must inevitably be drawn from this analysis is that any future war in which America and Russia are the chief contestants—and this clearly is the only major war which needs serious consideration—would certainly not be decided by atomic bombing alone. On the contrary, a long-drawn-out and bitter struggle over much of Europe and Asia, involving million-strong land armies, vast military casualties and widespread civil war, would be inevitable."[7]

On minor material claims, Blackett accepted uncritically the false USSBS story that Konoye's aborted "peace mission" to Moscow had "private instructions from the emperor to secure peace at any price. . . ."[8] Blackett is less to be faulted here than Nitze, since the latter had access to ULTRA, which disproved this canard.

All the above Nitze-compatible claims are in Blackett's chapter ten, which chapter was thought by anti-Truman activists to be still worth reprinting in 1998.[9] Blackett does not, of course, confine himself to USSBS texts. One claim he makes is from the Washington correspondent of the *London Times* who wrote on 8 August 1945: "The decision to use the new weapon was apparently taken quite recently and amounted to a reversal of previous policy. A correspondent in the *Baltimore Sun,* writing from an authority which seems unimpeachable, says that, until early in June, the president and military leaders were in agreement that this weapon should not be used, but a reversal of this High Command policy was made within the last sixty, and, possibly, the last thirty, days."[10] The *Sun's* authority must have been hallucinating, since there was *never* an agreement not to use the bomb.

Blackett discusses the timing of the atomic bombs. Why so early, when the U.S. knew the Soviet Union was going to come into the war in August, and knew that this would be a blow to the Japanese? Blackett's counterfactual reasoning is plausible: "Since the next major United States move was not to be made until November 1, clearly there was nothing in the Allied plan of campaign to make urgent the dropping of the first bomb on August 6 rather than at any time in the next two months."[11] Blackett does not comprehend that the controlling factor was not just the casualty fears, but the escalating war weariness. So he goes on to say: "If the saving of American lives had been the main objective, surely the bombs would have been held back until (a) it was certain that the Japanese peace proposals made through Russia were not acceptable, and (b) the Russian offensive, which had for months been part of the Allied strategic plan, and which Americans had previously demanded, had run its course."[12]

Plausible, but false. (a) ULTRA showed beyond a shadow of a doubt that the Japanese were very far from having *any* peace plans to suggest to the Russians, and (b) ULTRA also showed that waiting for the Russian offensive to "run its course" would take quite a while. Drea tells how it stood: not only did Japan expect Soviet entry, the Japanese military expected the Russians to penetrate Manchuria. Tokyo's orders to the Kwantung Army dated 30 May 1945 directed Japanese units to "conduct a delaying action designed to exhaust the Soviet invaders."[13] Japanese troops would slowly withdraw to the rugged terrain near the Korean border, where they could conduct a "protracted defense" for six months. This delaying action would give the defenders of the homeland enough time to smash the first wave of the expected American invasion, at which time a cease fire favorable to Japan would be negotiated. Blackett may not have known this, but his training as a scientist should have cautioned him against speculating in the wild blue yonder. Or even from depending on the good, gray *New York Times.* He quotes from the issue of 15 August 1945:

> Russia's entry into the Japanese war was the decisive factor in speeding its end and would have been so, even if no atomic bombs had been dropped, is the opinion of Major General Claire Chennault, who arrived home en route via Germany. The

founder of the American Volunteer Group (Flying Tigers) and former Air Force Commander in China said that the Soviet armies had been alert for the invasion of Manchuria as far back as VE day. He added that their swift stroke completed the circle around Japan that brought the nation to its knees.[14]

But Claire Chennault was no more prescient about when the Japanese would surrender than he was about the prospects of Chiang Kai-shek defeating Mao's communists in the looming Chinese Civil War.[15] Chennault had not read ULTRA either.

Rounding the narrative of American truculence and ineptitude in his chapter ten, Blackett cites the Franck Report. James Franck was a prominent member of the Metallurgical Lab at the University of Chicago, where the first chain reaction was staged. Franck chaired a committee on Social and Political Implications of the prospective bomb. His committee first met on 4 June 1945, and had a report ready by 11 June. The Franck Report became the most prominent artifact of the Chicago scientists' beliefs and concerns, and a sacred text of the antinuclear movement. One needs to analyze this text carefully to understand where the scientists were coming from, and where they sought to guide their considerable following.[16]

The report begins with the claim that "nuclear power is fraught with infinitely greater dangers than were all the inventions of the past." These dangers, and the threat of nuclear weapons to the United States, can be avoided only by an international authority controlling all nuclear developments. The United States cannot depend on maintaining such a lead in nuclear arms that no one will dare attack us for fear of retaliation; too many other nations know the fundamental facts of nuclear power, and the United States cannot control the raw materials needed to make weapons. Because of the great advantage in a future war of first use of such weapons, we cannot be safe from sudden attack even if we have a massive lead.

This part of the Franck Report contradicts Blackett's belief, which is that the Soviet Union will not stage a sneak attack on the United States, nor will the United States attack the Soviet Union. No matter, Blackett goes on to the next item: the Pacific war, and here the Franck Report begins to disintegrate. "Some officials," says Franck, want "to use them [atomic bombs] without warning on an appropriately selected object in Japan. It is doubtful whether the first available bombs, of comparatively low efficiency and small size, will be sufficient to break the will or ability of Japan to resist, especially given the fact that the major cities like Tokyo, Nagoya, Osaka, and Kobe already will largely have been reduced to ashes by the slower process of ordinary aerial bombing."[17] What were they saying here? Were they saying, "This bomb is not so powerful after all"? Then how can its use be as provocative as the report claims: "Russia, and even allied countries which bear less mistrust of our ways and intentions, as well as neutral countries may be deeply shocked. It may be very difficult to persuade the world that a nation which was capable of secretly preparing and suddenly releasing a weapon as indiscriminate as the [German] rocket bomb and a million times more destructive, is to be trusted in its proclaimed desire of having such weapons abolished by international agreement."

At this stage of the argument, two, and only two, alternative possibilities are presented: (1) it is possible to create international agreement on a total prevention of nuclear war, or (2) effective international control is impossible. Franck and his members obviously lean to the first. But somewhat obtusely, having already told us that dropping the bomb on Japan might not have much effect, they now shift to telling us that "the military advantages and the saving of American lives achieved by the sudden use of atomic bombs against Japan may be outweighed by the ensuing loss of confidence and by a wave of horror and repulsion sweeping over the rest of the world and perhaps even dividing public opinion at home." Therefore, we should have a demonstration in the desert or on a barren island; then, when we obliterate a Japanese city (but will a low efficiency bomb really obliterate anything?) there will be no "wave of horror and repulsion."[18]

If it is hard to see how Blackett has endorsed all this, yet more puzzling recommendations are to come in the Franck Report. Atomic weapons have been compared to poison gas, which cannot be used because of public opinion. Now we read that after a demonstration, and an "ultimatum to Japan to surrender or at least to evacuate certain regions as an alternative to their total destruction," we might just bomb them. "This may sound fantastic," says the report, "but in nuclear weapons we have something entirely new in order of magnitude of destructive power. . . ."[19] No, not fantastic, just confusing; will military use on a Japanese city shock them into surrender or not?

Now the second alternative comes into focus. Perhaps effective international control is impossible. On this view, "early use of nuclear bombs against Japan becomes even more doubtful—quite independently of any humanitarian considerations. If an international agreement is not concluded immediately after the first demonstration, this will mean a flying start toward an unlimited arms race. If this race is inevitable, we have every reason to delay its beginning as long as possible *in order to increase our headstart still further*" [italics added].[20] What would be more likely to induce "a flying start toward an unlimited armaments race" than increasing our lead as fast as we can?

Of course all this argument takes place in an intelligence vacuum. The race was already on. Stalin ratcheted it up several notches the minute he knew the United States had a bomb, even though it had not yet been used.

There follows a technical discussion of "stages of production" of nuclear weapons. The United States had reached only the first stage, but was on the threshold of the second:

> This stage probably requires no elaborate plans and may provide us in about five or six years with a really substantial stockpile of atomic bombs. Thus it is to our interest to delay the beginning of the armaments race at least until the successful termination of this second stage. The benefit to the nation, and the *saving of American lives in the future,* achieved by renouncing an early demonstration of nuclear bombs and letting the other nations come into the race only reluctantly, on the basis of guesswork and without definite knowledge that "the thing does work," may far outweigh the advantages to be gained by the immediate use of the first and comparatively inefficient bombs in the war against Japan [italics added].[21]

Which nations did the Franck Committee think would "come into the race only reluctantly"?

The concluding sections of this document, about "Methods of International Control" were dead right about one thing: the decision on use of the first atomic bombs "should not be left to military tacticians alone."

So on the basis of inferences from a faulty USSBS, and a confusing Franck Report, Blackett is sure that the mission of *Enola Gay* was the first major operation of the cold war. Is his status as a Nobel Prize-winning physicist sufficient warrant for us to take this muddled version of the Nitze narrative seriously?

◡ ◡ ◡

The British press and public took the 1948 version of his book *very* seriously. The climate there was ripe for an anti-American blast, especially from a prominent scientist who had just been beatified by the Swedish Nobel people. The Labour Government of Clement Attlee had been rebuffed by the Truman administration on nuclear cooperation, and the British Government had decided to establish its own atomic weapons program. Blackett had been almost alone in opposing that decision.

Comments on Blackett's book began even before it was in bookstores. The *New Statesman and Nation* on 16 October 1948 carried a letter to the editor anticipating Blackett's defense of the Soviet position on international control of the atom; Blackett, the writer said, went too far in his defense of the Soviet Union. After all, the Russians had "made it plain that the acceptance of their [plan] would not be followed by their agreement to inspection and control of atomic activities. This negative attitude, coupled with insistence on the continuation of the veto in atomic affairs, stultified all progress."[22] Blackett's politics were showing, this letter said.

The same issue of *New Statesman and Nation,* however, carried a rave review by Philip Morrison, an American physicist who had worked on the Manhattan Project and was then a professor at Cornell University. Morrison was not against atomic weapons, largely on the basis of the "fascinating and valuable data of the United States Strategic Bombing Survey," which were "drawn upon heavily" by Blackett. Morrison was "moved to look up the documents of the Survey themselves and found them even more interesting and valuable than Professor Blackett's use led me to suspect."[23] And Blackett was *right* about everything: Truman dropped the bomb to stymie the Russians, the American plan for international control (Baruch Plan) is unworkable but, "Blackett's book has been intemperately and even officially attacked in spite of its moderate and reasoned air and its by no means extreme conclusions."

Intemperance was almost the tone of Lord Cherwell's article in the *Daily Telegraph* of 9 December 1948. Blackett had everything wrong. Strategic bombing is not ineffective; German bombing of London was not a reprisal for British attacks on German cities; atomic bombs add greatly to the power of nations; the Japanese were not prepared to surrender before the atom; Truman was not simply trying to keep the Russians from getting credit for Japan's surrender, etc. Worse: "M. Vyshinsky and his supporters have apparently been greatly heartened by Blackett's' book. In one speech at the United Nations, *Vyshinsky quoted his book some ten times.*" (Italics supplied.)[24]

Naturally some reviews were temperate, such as the *Times Literary Supplement* anonymous review of 19 February 1949. The reviewer bought much of what Blackett contended, but "he so overstated his case . . . that it is difficult to give it the attention it merits."[25]

Controversy sells books; Blackett's was a great commercial success in Britain. He and his publisher, however, were anxious to tap the lucrative market across the Atlantic. His difficulty in getting an American publisher helps explain why it was not until the great disillusionment of the Vietnam War era that an anti-Truman case could be sold in America.

A Mr. Slater of Turnstile Press in London wrote Blackett at Manchester on 26 October 1948. "We are experiencing difficulty in effecting a sale in America and think you ought to know that so far we have had refusals from Macmillan, Scribners, and Knopf with all of whom we have good connections. . . . I believe you mentioned an American publisher you had once approached yourself but had turned the book down. If this is so, I should be glad to know his name. We hope to place the book shortly but we are rather anxious because of the time taken up so far. Have you any objection to publication by a firm called Boni and Gaer?"[26]

Blackett answered immediately. "The publisher I approached was Harcourt Brace, in the person of Mr. Reynal. He read the book and decided against taking it. . . . I have no objection to the firm Boni and Gaer. Originally we tried to get it done by a less political publisher, but if all the respectable firms have turned it down there will be no other course open."[27]

But there was another course open, a gift from the Gods. A letter from Paul Eriksson of John Day Company in New York to Turnstile Press in London on 5 November 1948 relates, "In your letter of October 20th to Mr. Walsh you mentioned Mr. Blackett's book on atomic energy and shortly thereafter we began trying to find out something about it. No one had heard of the book and until today when our press was full of Mr. Blackett's being awarded the Nobel Prize no one seemed to know much about him. Our editorial faces are a bit red at not having followed up your suggestion immediately on October 24th when your letter was received. But then, you did not tell us Mr. Blackett was to come into such fame!"[28]

It was too late. When Turnstile Press wrote Blackett on 24 November, the *Enola Gay* controversy had taken a new turn. Said Wilson of Turnstile,

> I have got more good news for you. After a great deal of toil, midnight oil and transatlantic telephoning, we have sold your book to America on, I think, very favorable terms and, it appears to us, in a way in which we are getting the best of both worlds, in that we are going to achieve mass circulation and, at the same time, have a really good imprint on the book. McGraw Hill has agreed to do the trade edition and the book will probably be sold for $3.50. We had previously fixed with Book Find Club . . . Aswell of McGraw is deeply impressed with the book and believes that it is vitally

important to get as many of his fellow countrymen to read it as possible . . . He raised the question as to whether it would not be valuable to get a preface by someone well known to the American public. For instance, he says it might be possible to get a preface from Einstein. [It wasn't] I suppose you have no objection to this?[29]

On the same date, Michael Hodson of Turnstile wrote Blackett reporting on the "corrections" to be made in the American edition. These were minor, mostly softening insults to American diplomacy, correcting a confusion in Blackett's text of Ernest Oppenheimer (who was wrongly quoted) with J. Robert Oppenheimer who was the correct source, and verifying the new title.[30] After this publication moved rapidly.

On 25 January 1949 Wilson wrote Blackett again, passing on a suggestion that Blackett reject an invitation from *The Churchman* to visit America; were Blackett to come, it should be under "scientific auspices," rather than those of an obscure periodical. Then: "I hope you like the dust cover of the book. I think it is very attractive; the initial print is going to be 50,000 copies and that they are spending a lot of money advertising the book."[31]

On 4 February, ten days before official publication date, Edward C. Aswell of McGraw-Hill wrote Blackett what appears to be the most enthusiastic encomium he ever got from the United States:

> "It seemed to me now . . . that I ought to write you a direct word simply to express not only my personal pride but that of the McGraw-Hill organization over the fact that this book is to come out under our imprint. I am no physicist and am in no position to stand in judgment upon the soundness of your thesis. I can only say that as a layman, I not only read your book most carefully and with intense interest, but that it has done more to clarify for me the problems of atomic energy than anything else I have ever read. I suspect that many of my fellow Americans will share this view.
>
> It seems a foregone conclusion that the book will arouse considerable interest over here and probably may even stir up controversy. It will probably be attacked and some of the attacks will be silly. But already I know that it will be warmly championed. You will be pleased to know that your book will be given a leading review in our most important literary medium, the *New York Times* book supplement, in its issue of February 13. I have not yet seen an advance copy of this review, but it is by Walter Kaempffert, the Science Editor of the *New York Times*, and I am told that its point of [view] toward the book is favorable.[32]

Not quite. Kaempffert wrote that Blackett's book usefully toned down the wilder assertions of doomsday about the new force, "But he goes too far. The physicists are thinking not so much of atomic bombs that are dropped on the cities of a country in the course of several years, but of more or less simultaneous, overwhelming attacks in a night, a week, a fortnight—a period too short for rapid recovery. . . . In spite of its drawbacks this is an important book because the controversy it stirred up in England may be duplicated here and because it presents the Russian point of view which Americans would do well to understand. Professor

Blackett proves one thing he did not set out to demonstrate: that because a man is a success in physics it does not follow that he is qualified to elucidate political issues that perplex able and honest statesmen."[33]

While Americans were adjusting to Blackett's heresy, a fascinating offer came to Blackett from the Hollywood Film Division of the National Council of the Arts, Sciences and Professions (NCASP), seeking to "carry forward the program developed by the Cultural and Scientific Conference on World Peace held at the Waldorf Hotel in 1949."[34] Paul Jarrico, acting for this group sought Blackett's cooperation for a movie to be made on the basis of his book. This was not to be a commercial venture; the NCASP wanted the film to show to students, clubs, and any group interested in peace. It is difficult to imagine exactly how this would have developed, but NCASP promised a plethora of high-powered talent to bring it off: Adrian Scott, Edward Dmytryk, Ben Barzman, Albert Maltz, Ben Maddow, Ivan Moffat, Rod Geiger, and presumably Jarrico himself.

The film proposal was put to Blackett on 4 May 1949. His final response, on 16 June 1949 to Hodson of Turnstile, was negative: "The more I think about it the less can I see any satisfactory film being made of it. I am, therefore, much relieved at not having the prospect of having to bother about the whole business."[35]

The letter Blackett wrote Hodson on that date also revealed an unexpected development. "I am sorry that McGraw-Hill is disappointed with the way the book is going in America. I do not feel very interested myself now in how it sells. I think it has had a useful effect and possibly even done some real good. In a sense one of the themes of the book is that people should not worry about the atomic bomb for the time being and, consequently, [it] logically follows that they need not read the book. I think the short period predictions in the book have come true—now I am interested to see whether my long period predictions in the book e.g. three or four years time, are likely to be wrong or not."[36]

Before looking at Blackett's record in predicting, let us consider why this controversial book had such a short period in the limelight. Nineteen forty-nine was a year of great shocks to the American polity. The Chinese Nationalists, representatives in Asia of a bitter-end anti-Communist element in American politics, lost their war against Mao's communists. Beijing fell, Shanghai fell, Chiang Kai-shek resigned as president, then moved all his entourage to Taiwan while Mao announced Beijing as the new capital of the People's Republic of China.

Cardinal Mindszenty was sentenced to life in Hungary. The NATO Pact was signed, and went into effect in August. What could have been more upsetting to lingering midwest isolationism than this? The Berlin blockade festered until May. Was any shock, ever, save perhaps Pearl Harbor, more traumatic than the announcement in September that the Soviets had exploded an atomic device? Subversion was everywhere; the Hiss trial dragged on. In October, fourteen Communist Party leaders were convicted in Federal Court of advocating overthrow of the government. Mao went to Moscow for—what else? Plotting the destruction of the United States of America. Whatever brilliant analysis there may have been in

Blackett's *Fear, War and the Bomb,* it could not compete with events parading across the daily papers. The chronology in Thomas Parrish's *Cold War Encyclopedia* lists 44 significant events for 1949.[37]

⚍ ⚍ ⚍

Did Blackett have it right, with his blind acceptance of Nitze? The person who knew him best during the war and immediate postwar years, Sir Bernard Lovell, co-founder of the Jodrell Bank Radio Astronomy Observatory, is the best authority on this. Lovell wrote Blackett's biography in the Royal Society series, admiring but not sycophantish. In 1953, Blackett left Manchester for London, while Lovell remained at the Manchester-associated Jodrell Bank; they remained in touch, but the distance gave Lovell a new perspective. Lovell writes that his association with Blackett was closest during 1945–1947, when "Blackett more or less lived in the home which my wife and I had established when we returned to Manchester in the summer of 1945."[38]

Lovell is sure Blackett met Nitze between the autumn of 1944, when Nitze came to Europe as a member of the strategic bombing team, and Nitze's recall to Washington in 1945. Lovell comments,

> If that is correct, then Nitze's views on the effects of strategic bombing during the European War could have been powerfully influenced by Blackett. He violently opposed the bombing campaign but I fear this was influenced by the antagonism of himself and Tizard to Churchill and Cherwell (see for example p. 64 of my Royal Society memoir). I can well imagine the effect he could have had on Nitze at that time. He was always absolutely certain that his own opinions were correct and tended to dismiss abruptly anyone who differed. In fact, I can only remember one occasion when he acknowledged that he was wrong. That is over the question of the nature of the penetrating cosmic rays. It required the combined weekend assault of Heisenberg and Bhabha to convince him that a new particle was involved and that the energy loss theory was correct . . . Blackett badly underestimated the time scale for the Soviet development of the atomic bomb (and of delivery by ballistic missiles). Blackett was with me at Jodrell in August 1949 when the news that the Soviets had tested an atomic bomb was released. He had given strict instructions to his secretary that he was not to be disturbed. However, in the middle of our conversation around one of our embryonic telescopes he was urgently summoned to the telephone. I recall both his irritation at the summons and his amazement at the news of the test, which was then conveyed to him.[39]

Blackett's views were received in the United States with the expected range of opinion: pacifists were neutral (they wanted no nuclear weapons whatever, and Blackett tolerated the Soviet arsenal because of American belligerence); left-wingers whose main bias was to skewer Truman and Stimson loved him; analysts not clearly identified with any ideological position gave him credit for puncturing some stereotypes, while recognizing his eccentricities.

Philip Morrison, whose ultimate rejection of the Truman-Stimson narrative was total, has been quoted earlier: Blackett was a prophet crying in the wilderness. Edward Shils, writing as a conservative, was blunt on the opposite side: "Blackett writes from the Stalinist standpoint . . . a master of artful and intelligent distortion, and his extraordinary analytical powers placed in the services of his strong political prejudices and aided by his schematic and overly rationalistic conception of human motives, especially the motives of politicians, produces a picture which frequently bears little resemblance to reality."[40] Here Shils himself gets taken in; he follows this with "His most significant and powerful arguments, based on the data of the U.S. Strategic Bombing Survey, are not, however, conclusive." One may be pardoned for some confusion here; if the arguments were significant and powerful, why were they not conclusive? Shils had no way of knowing that neither Blackett's, nor Nitze's, arguments were based on the *data* of USSBS, rather on Nitze's pre-investigation conclusion.

Dean Louis N. Ridenour, writing in *World Politics* and *Scientific American,* gives as evenhanded and sober an assessment as I have found in American reviews. After six pages of favorable commentary, he gets to the negatives:

> To say, as Blackett does, that long-range bombers cannot be decisive, and that the atomic bomb changes nothing, is to assert that the war economy of a nation is of no value to that nation in a war. Reduced to these basic terms, Blackett's military contentions are preposterous. . . . The usual reason given in the United States for the timing of the use of the first atomic bombs is that they were not ready any earlier. The usual reason for the nature of their use is that a dramatic demonstration of the bomb's power was felt to be necessary to convince the enemy of its effectiveness, as promptly as could be done. We have all this on the solemn public testimony of the men responsible for the decisions. Blackett brushes it aside; he does not even summarize these arguments as meriting serious attention. The closest that he comes to them is what he calls the "Roman Holiday" theory; that, having spent two billion public dollars on a weapon, the American people were entitled to the bloodiest possible demonstration of its effectiveness. He states that many Americans espouse this view; I know one who does not. . . . Altogether, Blackett's book appears to be an elaborate and lengthy defense of a set of fixed ideas held at the start. J. B. S. Haldane, one of Blackett's colleagues in the British left, has said of him, "He has a mind which seems to be much happier with real things, which he can count and measure, than with the more abstract forms. . . . What is more, he finds the things he is looking for." Haldane's remark, made in an altogether different context, is particularly apt as a description of the way in which the ideas and arguments of Blackett's book must have been arrived at.[41]

In the world of the 1990s, the best assessment of Blackett's credibility comes from science historian Mary Jo Nye. Her study "A Physicist in the Corridors of Power: P. M. S. Blackett's Opposition to Atomic Weapons Following the War" paints Blackett as maturing his opinions during the fifties and sixties, becoming more acceptable to colleagues and statesmen with the passage of time.[42] His views on the immorality of destroying cities came to overshadow his early defenses of

Soviet policy, and his claim that nuclear weapons had not made conventional arms obsolete were ultimately borne out. However, "it was land wars in Korea and Indo-china that made the point, not his original arguments." Nye also offers a careful study, "What price politics? Scientists and Political Controversy," which considers the political careers of Blackett and Linus Pauling, both Nobelists, both at some time anathema to their governments.[43]

Blackett was the outside examiner brought to Cambridge from London in 1963 for Gar Alperovitz's Ph.D. degree. Blackett's work has generally disappeared from the dialogue; Alperovitz caught the wave of 1960s disillusionment, and is still going strong.

Thus the basic parameters of the argument over *Enola Gay* were set with Blackett's publication in 1948. Truman and Stimson had said the motive for the decision was to save American lives and end the war speedily; the bomb was simply "the least abhorrent choice." Nitze had claimed that it was an unnecessary choice, and Blackett said that Truman had lied, that the decision was really to achieve an advantage over the Soviet Union in the cold war. These were still the issues half a century later.

5

COLD WAR, KOREA, VIETNAM

The "ashes of death" that rained down [on the Japanese tuna trawler Lucky Dragon] on March 1, 1954, formed part of the antinuclear mantle in which Japan wrapped itself. The thermonuclear accident revealed the Japanese people's anguish and anger at being three-time victims of nuclear weapons.
ROGER DINGMAN, *Alliance in Crisis*[1]

By 1948, two incompatible narratives about the Mission of *Enola Gay* circulated among those Americans who attended to such things: the Truman-Stimson version, and the Nitze-Blackett version. The first had majority support; the second was supported by an unlikely combination of right wing Soviet-haters and mostly religious pacifists. The controversy never became a big issue with the public until the fiftieth anniversary of the end of the war, in 1995, when the National Air and Space Museum staged an exhibit of the plane. By then, intervening events and two widely read attacks on Truman began to change public opinion. By 1971, only 64% of Americans supported Truman; in 1985 this was down to 55%, and it went slightly lower by 1995.[2] This chapter will attempt to track the growth of the anti-Truman, anti-bomb opinion.

Fifty years later, almost everyone in the United States has forgotten that many of the ten percent who opposed the bomb decision from the beginning did so not because they thought it immoral, but because they were in a sense pro-Japanese, despite Pearl Harbor. These conservatives bought into the Japanese claim that the Greater East Asian War had been necessary to frustrate Communist influence in

Asia. Pearl Harbor need not have happened; the United States had threatened Japan's lifeline to raw materials in Southeast Asia, and demanded withdrawal of Japanese colonists in Manchuria. Such conservatives were willing to overlook what most Americans called war crimes; these were simply things that happened in the bitterness of combat.

One of the heroes to the Air and Space curators (and other anti-Truman writers) in 1995 was John J. McCloy, who, the curators note in the *Enola Gay* script, opposed dropping the bomb without a specific warning to Japan. Michael Schaller has an analysis of McCloy's posture. McCloy was one of those who "persuaded the administration that in Japan, as in Germany, the United States required a 'bulwark against the U.S.S.R. and communism.'"[3] Consequently when McCloy made a visit to Tokyo in February 1946, he

> expressed fear that liberal reforms would drive Japan "further left." Tampering with the economy or the government structure would cause "emotional upset and political unrest." McCloy thought the United States had "little to gain and much to lose" by indicting Hirohito or abolishing the emperor system. He also denounced the trial of war criminals as a "total fiasco." It made little sense to assess guilt, McCloy argued, because "most Japanese look alike in more ways than one."

All this was in a memo to General George Lincoln, chief Army planner; it was one of the last official acts by McCloy before he left the government for a brief period.[4] It certainly establishes him as a cold warrior; it does little for his credentials as an opponent of nuclear weapons.

But liberal reform was precisely what the Allies had demanded in the Potsdam Declaration, and what MacArthur was carrying out. The instructions to MacArthur read:

> There must be eliminated for all time the authority and influence of those who have deceived and misled the people of Japan into embarking on world conquest, for we insist that a new order of peace, security and justice will be impossible until irresponsible militarism is driven from the world. . . . We do not intend that the Japanese shall be enslaved as a race or destroyed as a nation, but stern justice shall be meted out to all war criminals, including those who have visited cruelties upon our prisoners.[5]

War crimes trials were something new under the sun. A precedent was being set in Nuremberg, but conditions in the Pacific were different, and no one knew quite how this process would play out until it was over. McCloy was just one of the more prominent officials to object to the International Military Tribunal for the Far East. Brigadier General Elliott Thorpe, an intelligence specialist on MacArthur's staff, had responsibility for the emperor's physical security and for compiling the early lists of political figures to be tried. He did his job, picking a list of indictees credible enough to satisfy the demands of the most punitive of his colleagues; but as John Dower notes, Thorpe thought the trials were an act of revenge: "we wanted blood, and by God, we had blood."[6]

Brigadier General Bonner Fellers, a hard-right ideologue in MacArthur's office, had as his primary assignment protecting Hirohito from prosecution. This involved private interrogations of about forty Japanese war leaders, and Herbert Bix says Feller's activities "placed all the major war criminal suspects on alert as to GHQ's specific concerns, and allowed them to coordinate their stories so that the emperor would be spared from indictment."[7] In addition to the direct channel through MacArthur's office, the Strategic Bombing Survey interviews gave the protectors of Hirohito an avenue to exonerate the emperor; Kido, Yonai, Suzuki, Sakomizu and the other top officials, while candid in relating Japan's intentions to fight on, were careful to "use their interrogations to shape official American perceptions of Hirohito's role in ending the war."[8]

There were some monumental misjudgments. Hirota Koki was convicted on flimsy evidence.[9] Dower notes glaring absences from the indicted list: "No heads of the dreaded Kempeitai (military police) were indicted; no leaders of ultranationalistic secret societies; no industrialists . . . The forced mobilization of Korean and Formosan colonial subjects was not pursued as a crime against humanity nor was the enslavement of several hundred thousand young non-Japanese who were forced to serve as 'comfort women' providing sexual services to the imperial forces."[10] But the worst omission was of General Ishii who operated the Unit 731 chemical and biological warfare (CBW) factory; his experiments and the use of his products against thousands of Chinese were overlooked in exchange for the data about CBW warfare he had accumulated. Ishii was brought to the United States to be debriefed; he returned to Japan for a long and comfortable life.[11] After the "reverse course" in 1948, when the U.S. stopped trying to democratize Japan and instead began preparing that country as an ally in the cold war, dozens of officials who should have been on trial, and some who were actually convicted, were pardoned and permitted to resume high posts in a resurgent Japan.[12]

Tojo and five other generals were sentenced to death and hanged. The emperor was exonerated. This left most of the nation able to see themselves as victims of evil militarists and evil atomic bombs. Dower observes that "as the Cold War intensified and the occupiers came to identify newly Communist China as the archenemy, it became an integral part of American policy to discourage recollection of Japan's atrocities . . . [the few] sensitive responses to revelation of the hands-on horrors perpetuated by the emperor's men, fragile and fragmented to begin with, never developed into a truly widespread popular acknowledgement of Japan as victimizer rather than victim."[13]

This reassessment of Japanese guilt, and promotion of Japan from hated enemy to collaborator in blocking Soviet advances, was given a major boost by George Kennan. Kennan's prime concern was Soviet influence in Europe, but as head of the Department of State Policy Planning Staff in the fall of 1947, he was confronted with the long-range prospect in Asia. Howard Schonberger tells the story of how Kennan, consulting with Joseph Grew, Harry F. Kern of *Newsweek*, Eugene Dooman and Joseph Ballantine who had worked with Grew, Herbert

Hoover, and various industrialists, became convinced that MacArthur was pushing reform in Japan much too far. Kern was the spearhead of the American Council on Japan (ACJ), a group of Japanophiles determined to cancel the Japanese reforms. ACJ put out a report calling for reversing course in Japan, ignoring the latest directive to MacArthur (FEC-230), which, Schonberger says, Kennan

> no doubt had read, [and] argued that FEC-230 would lead to "economic disaster, inflation, unbalanced budgets resulting in near anarchy, which would be precisely what the Communists want." He told MacArthur not to feel bound by the Potsdam Declaration, which "made no provision for the security of the Japanese islands from aggression, overt or concealed, from outside." In short, Kennan impressed MacArthur with the broad views of the Japan Lobby and Washington policy makers that economic recovery should be made the prime objective of United States policy in Japan.[14]

Two years later, when Kennan turned dovish, his objections to the H-bomb decision and NSC-68 were not accepted. On the reverse course in Japan in 1948, he had full Washington backing. MacArthur was forced to ignore FEC-230, and Japan began the rapid climb to industrial predominance that startled the world. Kennan never regretted his advice here. He says in his memoirs, "I consider my part in bringing about this change to have been, after the Marshall Plan, the most significant constructive contribution I was ever to make in government."[15] Kennan's intervention in favor of promoting Japan probably did more to reverse the image of Japan as villain, and allow her to pose as victim, than all the propaganda of *Newsweek,* Grew, and the American Council on Japan.

Kennan may have let go of the Asian problem after this, but the friends of Grew, Dooman, Kern, and the ACJ went on to spark the attacks of McCarthy and McCarran against China hands John Carter Vincent, Owen Lattimore, T. A. Bisson, and other unwary souls who had demonized the emperor and opposed the reverse course of 1948. Vincent was fired; Lattimore avoided a conviction for perjury engineered by McCarran only through the intervention of a courageous judge.[16]

The repercussions of the Tokyo War Crimes Trials were noticed only after Truman-bashing became acceptable in the 1960s. The Indian justice on the court, Radhabinod Pal, blasted the trial in terms that have been resurrected by many anti-Truman partisans. Dower analyzes Pal's position:

> "It would be pertinent to recall to our memory that the majority of the interests claimed by the Western Prosecuting Powers in the Eastern Hemisphere including China," he [Pal] observed in speaking of Japan's takeover of Manchuria, "were acquired by such aggressive methods" as the Japanese were accused of employing. He also commented, with no little sarcasm, on the ways in which the positive rhetoric of imperialism and colonialism of the Europeans and Americans [changed] when associated with Japan: "As a program of aggrandizement of a nation we do not like, we may deny to it the terms like "manifest destiny," "the protection of vital interests," "national honor" or a term coined on the footing of "the white man's burden," and may give it the name of "aggressive aggrandizement" pure and simple.[17]

The Indian justice took palpable pleasure in suggesting the hypocrisy of the victor's case. He quoted England's prestigious Royal Institute of International Affairs at some length, for example, on how the Japanese had followed the precedents of European imperialism, sometimes "with almost pedantic exactitude."

So much was to be expected of an Indian suffering under British rule when given a platform to criticize the power he and his people sought to shake off. What followed cut to the bone and still appears when the mission of *Enola Gay* comes under attack. Dower again:

> Against the Americans, the most predictable accusation of double standards rested on the argument that the terror bombing of Japanese cities, and the use of the atomic bombs in particular, were also crimes against humanity. Justice Pal made this argument with a notorious statement that the German Kaiser Wilhelm II had conveyed to the Hapsburg emperor Franz Joseph in World War I ("Everything must be put to fire and sword; men, women and children and old men must be slaughtered and not a tree or house be left standing"); he introduced this statement into his dissenting opinion: "In the Pacific war under our consideration, if there was anything approaching what is indicated in the above letter of the German emperor, it is the decision coming from the allied powers to use the atom bomb. . . . It would be sufficient for my present purpose to say that if any indiscriminate destruction of civilian life and property is still illegitimate in warfare, then in the Pacific war, this decision to use the atom bomb is the only near approach to the directives of the German emperor during the first world war and of the Nazi leaders during the second world war."[18]

No more pointed attack on Truman exists in the literature. That it came from a bitter British subject does not lessen its bite. But the answer came from Justice Jaranilla of the Philippines. Jaranilla wrote in his opinion, "If a means is justified by an end, the use of the atomic bomb was justified, for it brought Japan to her knees and ended the horrible war. If the war had gone on longer, without the use of the atomic bomb, how many more thousands and thousands of helpless men, women and children would have needlessly died and suffered, and how much more destruction and devastation, hardly reparable, would have been wrought?"[19] Dower notes that this exchange "defines the parameters of the controversy over the use of the bomb that persisted through the decades that followed." True. What Jaranilla did not present, because it was classified and unavailable, was the solid evidence gathered by Nitze's USSBS interrogators, ignored by all the disputants until 1995, that the war would have continued to slaughter the innocent civilians of Asia and the Pacific probably into 1946 *absent the atomic bomb.*

～ ～ ～

Efforts to isolate one event as the key cause of the cold war and the arms race that it spawned, such as Martin Sherwin's in his 1973 book the subtitle of which is *Hiroshima and the Origins of the Arms Race,* are futile.[20] Those who focus narrowly on 1945 decisions in the White House overlook a long history of American opposition to Communism, whether theoretical or as represented in the Soviet Union. Some authorities believe the cold war got its start with the 1917 revolution in Russia, when the United States intervened in an effort to overturn that revolution. Peter Filene, George Herring, Ralph Levering, and George Sirgiovanni have all discussed events of the World War II period that contributed to the cold war that followed.[21] After the war, there was no end of challenges and provocations: Soviet armies in Iran, Soviet control of Poland and Eastern Europe, Soviet demands for privileges in Manchuria, communist insurgency in Greece, Stalins' 1946 election speech, the Berlin blockade, the Gouzenko spy case in Canada, and so on. These all contributed to the cold war and the Arms Race.

Nothing, however, was as consequential as the series of shocks to American complacency in 1949 and 1950. At the end of these shocks, Japan was a highly valued ally in the most dangerous struggle the U.S. ever faced, or so it was believed. How could we have been so stupid as to drop atomic weapons on her?

In 1949, China fell to Mao's communists. This was an intolerable blow to the Republican Party and to American Protestantism.[22] One wing of the Republican Party had always put "Asia first." World War II in Asia was the Republicans' war, commanded by a great Republican general who had presidential ambitions. The Democrats had made Europe their first priority. Roosevelt wanted to give it the bulk of attention and supplies. Democrats had emphasized a war against Hitler which many Republican leaders felt we had no business prosecuting, since Germany was the prime bulwark against the true menace to America: Russia. It is easy today to forget the pro-Germanism of substantial segments of the Republican Party in the 1930s—a pro-Germanism based upon the belief that Hitler was the last great chance to prevent the Bolshevization of the whole of Western civilization.

As for religion, China was the largest single theater of American missionary enterprise. In 1936, there were at least 6,059 Protestant missionaries in China, each of them with a built-in constituency back home, sponsoring churches to which they reported regularly on sabbatical. Henry Luce was the most powerful missionary tribune. He was born in China of a Christian missionary and developed a lifelong attachment to the cause served by his father. In the Luce theology, which all of his publishing empire served until his death, missions and righteousness, Republican politics, Chiang and Americanism were all bound together and inseparable. In China, the communists won something more important than a military struggle; they won a theological battle, the battle for men's souls.[23]

When China joined the Enemy in 1949, the importance of a friendly Japan increased dramatically.

Then there was the Soviet bomb in 1949. The physicists had said that Soviet science was capable of building it, and most of them said it would not take more than five years, whether or not they had vital information from Klaus Fuchs, Julius Rosenberg, or other spies; but most Americans did not believe that a country that couldn't even supply its people with pencils and toilet paper would achieve mastery of the atom. In retrospect, this derogation of Russia is one of the least understandable American beliefs of the postwar period. What did we think Soviet armies had used to defeat the Germans at Kursk and Stalingrad? We now know that they had better tanks, and better aircraft, in quantity. But we were not ready for *Joe-1* (the Soviet bomb). The shock was immense.

The trauma continued in 1950. On 14 January, the People's Republic of China seized U.S. Consular property, and Ho Chi Minh declared the Democratic Republic of Vietnam. On 21 January Alger Hiss was convicted of perjury; if this mandarin could be a traitor, what was still safe? On 2 February Klaus Fuchs was arrested for atomic espionage. On 9 February Joseph McCarthy began his crusade with a speech to the Republican women of Wheeling. The Sino-Soviet Treaty was signed 14 February. These disasters, some minor but many major, continued to the end of the year. The year 1950 was the point of no return in the cold war, with the strongest incentives for exacerbating the arms race. By my count, seventy-six such events occurred during the year. At the end of it:

- the United States was at war with North Korea and the People's Republic of China.
- Japan was our most important staging area and a major supplier.
- Truman had hinted at using nuclear weapons.
- Father Edmund Walsh, vice president of Georgetown University called for a preventive war against the Soviet Union.
- New York Governor Dewey asked for total national mobilization, with 35% of our productive capacity going to defense.
- And on 18 December, Pacific skiers organized as defense guerrillas to defend the western mountain passes against communist invasion.[24]

Two happenings of 1950 were particularly salient for Japanese-American relations. Both of them involved Paul Nitze.

When the Soviet atomic bomb was announced, the administration was confronted with deciding what United States atomic policy was to be. Most had given up hope of effective international control. Most believed that the U.S. should continue to maintain an atomic capability; but at what level? Should an effort be made to develop fusion bombs, thousands of times more powerful than the elementary fission bombs dropped on Hiroshima and Nagasaki? Edward Teller and some hard-line cold warriors had been arguing for the Super, as it was called, since the beginning of the Manhattan Project. Agitation for precisely that development now increased.

Truman asked the secretaries of State and Defense to advise him on whether to undertake the advanced bomb. There are many good accounts of the H-bomb decision. Most of them believe that this decision, like the decision to drop the earlier bombs on Hiroshima and Nagasaki, was overdetermined—political forces too powerful to resist were pressing for it, and Truman himself was inclined to take no chances. In the final decision meeting with Truman on 31 January 1950, a committee consisting of David Lilienthal, chairman of the Atomic Energy Commission; Secretary of State Dean Acheson; and Secretary of Defense Louis Johnson reported to Truman. Acheson and Johnson were strongly for the H-bomb. Only Lilienthal had reservations about going ahead. Truman asked "Can the Russians do it?" and when the answer was "Yes," the president made up his mind, not listening to Lilienthal's doubts.[25] The meeting took, according to Lilienthal's journal, only seven minutes.

It is not clear how important Acheson's advisers, Nitze and Kennan, were in advising the secretary of state in what to do about the H-bomb. Nitze claims that he and Gordon Arneson were the state department advisers; Barton Bernstein, on the basis of a letter from Oppenheimer to Kennan, believes that Kennan was also formally in the process.[26] In either case, Nitze, after listening to both Oppie and Teller (as noted in chapter two) supported the Super; Kennan wrote in his memoirs that the report he submitted to Acheson on 20 January 1950 was one of the most important he ever wrote. He published his memoirs in 1967, and the paper he wrote was still classified and unavailable even to him. He summarizes it as his memory dictated. The bulk of it was a request to get straight about whether we really wished to see atomic weapons abolished; if so, we *could* achieve some agreement with the Russians. He thought current policy was set on obtaining and using such weapons, and his conclusion was a plea:

> as earnest and eloquent as I was capable of making it—that before we decide to proceed with the development of the hydrogen bomb thus committing ourselves and the world to an indefinite escalation and expensiveness of atomic weapons, we reexamine once more, in the most serious and solemn way, the whole principle of the "first use" of nuclear weapons or any other of the weapons of mass destruction; and I made it as clear as any language at my command could make it that . . . my voice would be cast most decisively in favor of the abandonment of the principle altogether. I described in words something along the lines of the following what I thought should be our public posture: We deplore the existence of all weapons of indiscriminate mass destruction. We regret that we were ever obliged to make use of one. We hope never to have to do so again. We do not propose ever to do so, unless we are forced to do so by the use of such weapons against us. Meanwhile, we remain prepared . . . to accept a certain risk for ourselves, in order to achieve international agreement on their removal from international arsenals; for we can think of nothing more dangerous than a continued international competition in their development.[27]

Kennan thinks Truman never saw this. Acheson thought it naive. Public hatred of the new enemy was too strong; Truman announced the decision the same day he made it. Peter Galison and Barton Bernstein note "The announcement was so popular that many in the House of Representatives greeted it with cheers. A public opinion poll . . . indicated great support (73 versus 18 percent)."[28]

There is no point dumping on Nitze, Acheson, Teller, or Truman for this outcome. The arms race had been on from 1943, when Stalin heard about Los Alamos and ordered the same for the Soviet. There is point, however, in arguing that had this 1950 decision not been made, and had it not been reinforced by the closely following NSC-68, the arms of the world could not have reached the absurd levels of destructiveness that they reached. The arsenals of the two superpowers could have crested at a level far below the obscene overkill capacity of the last quarter of the twentieth century.

We did not need the Super. Even as hardheaded an analyst as David Alan Rosenberg wrote "In retrospect, it is clear that there was merit in the arguments of critics of American atomic strategy and policy during this period. Many of the objections voiced by naval officers to strategic bombing were confirmed in the Harmon Report and appear valid today. As opponents of the H-bomb pointed out, moreover, the JCS could not immediately identify a military role for the new weapon or demonstrate that it was a practical concept in view of limited resources and technical difficulties."[29] Subsequent events have proved that the weapon was unusable, and that the hysteria driving the United States was a weakness that only someone with the will and stature of a Churchill could conceivably have muted. We had no Churchill.

Then there was NSC-68. It is universally billed as the blueprint for the cold war, but it is not. It is an impassioned statement of the *need* for such a blueprint. And while the decision to build the H-bomb was made with dispatch and finality, the companion event, construction of NSC-68, was messy and never had complete closure. On both of these operations, Kennan and Nitze opposed each other; on both of them, Kennan was on the side of the angels. While Nitze was just one important participant in the H-bomb decision, he was *the* force that rammed through NSC-68 against strong opposition.[30]

Due to the continuing secrecy imposed on NSC-68, many documents about its construction were still classified top secret in 1999. Few historians realize that George Kennan, the "Father of Containment," and the principal force in rebuilding Japan as an American outpost, became alarmed at the excesses of the Truman policies, especially the doomsday rhetoric of NSC-68. The best account of Kennan's progress from apparent hawk to dovish restraint is John Lewis Gaddis's *Strategies of Containment*.[31]

In the Long Telegram and the "X" article in *Foreign Affairs,* Kennan warned the U.S. that the Soviet Union was quite different from other European nations.[32] He recommended firm and vigilant dealing with the Soviets. They believed that there could be no security for themselves unless American power was countered and probably broken. But there was no panic in Kennan's posture. Soviet power "does not take unnecessary risks . . . it can easily withdraw . . . when strong resistance is encountered . . . Gauged against the Western World as a whole, Soviets are still far the weaker force. . . . We must see that our public is educated to realities of Russian situation. . . . I am convinced that there would be far less hysterical anti-Sovietism in our country today if realities of this situation were better understood by our people." And the success of the Soviet system was not yet finally proven.

The "X" article, done at the request of Secretary of Defense James Forrestal, was a bit more pessimistic than the Long Telegram, but it too lacked the apocalyptic fearsomeness of NSC-68.[33] So did NSC-20/1, the overview of U.S. Policy that Kennan supervised in August 1948 as head of State's Policy Planning Staff (PPS). There was no alarmism in NSC-20/1, which held that the Soviet was increasing its bombing capabilities, and by 1955 it would be able to launch air attacks on the United States; but it could not invade, the Soviets were not on their way to San Francisco, they had no timetable for world conquest. We did not have to oppose every move the Soviets made, only those that directly threatened American interests. And we were not losing the cold war.[34]

NSC-68 threw all these modifications out the window. Kennan had resigned from government, wanting to take up a scholarly post at Princeton's Institute for Advanced Study. Nitze became director of PPS in January 1950, just in time to get the assignment to "undertake a reexamination of our objectives in peace and war and of the effect of these objectives on our strategic plans, in the light of the probable fission bomb capability and possible thermonuclear bomb capability of the Soviet Union."[35] Truman called for this study at the time he approved the H-bomb program. He assigned it to the secretaries of State and Defense, with Acheson to take the lead. Acheson delegated State's role to Nitze. There were four defense members and four from PPS, and two representatives of NSC. They began work on 8 February 1950, just as Kennan was leaving for a tour of Latin America. Before he left, Kennan drafted an eight-page memorandum reviewing "U.S. foreign policy in its entirely." This circulated among the NSC staff, but Nitze kept it from Acheson.[36] The Kennan memo shows what NSC-68 would have looked like had Kennan rather than Nitze been in charge.

If Nitze was anti-Soviet after studying at Harvard, exposure to James Forrestal and Averell Harriman had turned him into a fanatic. He was obligated to bring consultants before his committee, he had to circulate early drafts to fifteen second-level state department officials and the full NSC. (There are various apparently unsolicited comments in the files.) But in the end, as with the USSBS investigations in Japan, it was Nitze who selected what was to be counted or acknowledged. As noted previously, in his letter to Acheson of 6 April 1950, enclosing the first draft of NSC-68, Nitze said "The conclusions and recommendations have found general support. The comments reveal no need to alter these in any major way."[37]

Nitze could claim on this operation to have some data supporting his alarmism: Assistant Secretary of State for United Nations Affairs John D. Hickerson had indeed been generally approving. There is no way he could claim the responses of Llewellyn Thompson, Russian scholar and an officer in European affairs; George W. Perkins, assistant secretary for European affairs; Willard Thorpe, assistant secretary for economic affairs; and Charles E. Bohlen, Soviet specialist then serving as U.S. minister in Paris were anything but hostile. Bohlen, who for two more years fought Nitze on the basic assumptions of NSC-68, was particularly critical. Nitze was simply wrong to claim that the Soviet Union had a plan similar to Hitler's to conquer the world, and to claim that the main Soviet concern was to destroy the United States.[38]

Nitze's document was so extreme that Harry Truman, who was by then a committed cold warrior, sent it back to the NSC with the charge that another committee should specify more precisely what programs were called for and how much they would cost.[39] Scholars generally agree that had North Korea not invaded

South Korea in June, convincing most of the government (though not Kennan and Bohlen) that the Russians had now shown their intention of crossing national borders to extend their empire, nothing would have come of it, except a modest program for more nuclear weapons. Nitze's tocsin prohibited negotiations with Russia, claimed that the Soviet Union would have the power and probably the will to attack the U.S. by 1954 (the date was moved up to 1952 after the Korean War broke out), and endorsed what came to be known as "rollback"—forcing the Soviets out of territories that they had gained control over during and after World War II. (Eisenhower, despite the rhetoric of his trigger-happy Secretary of State John Foster Dulles, cancelled the rollback doctrine.) Finally, after the Chinese Communists had trashed the U.S. Eighth Army in Korea, Truman signed off on NSC-68/3 and defense expenditures were tripled. Nitze won at least a partial victory on this front, but nowhere near as complete as his legerdemain with USSBS.

NSC-68 appears nowhere in the discourse of the major anti-Truman writers. Just dropping the bombs on Hiroshima and Nagasaki gave us the overkill arms race.

∾ ∾ ∾

If there were no other event of the early postwar years that was seen by both Japanese and many Americans as authorizing Japanese victimage, the H-bomb test series BRAVO on 1 March 1954 did the job. This was one of the first publicly-exposed imbecilities of the U.S. Atomic Energy Commission, a bureaucracy that attracted public skepticism even before Kennedy, Johnson and Nixon stumbled into the Vietnamese nightmare. Forget the fact that nowhere in the world was there a target appropriate for a fifteen-megaton bomb. How many times over did we want to kill the inhabitants of Moscow? Or was it Beijing? Or was Edward Teller simply off on an ego trip, to prove that the U.S. could make a bigger bang than Sakharov? Whatever pathology afflicted the AEC (or—if you feel kindly toward Lewis Strauss, chairman of the AEC, from July 1953 to June 1958—afflicted the military, who were in favor of bigger bombs) the execution of this particular atrocity (BRAVO) could have been handled with more couth. If one wants to understand why so many intelligent and well-educated Japanese do not trust the United States, and believe that the *Enola Gay* was on an evil mission, one need only read Roger Dingman's sober and meticulously crafted narrative of what happened near Bikini Atoll on this date.[40]

The technicians made their calculations. Wind patterns, expected fallout, and other dangers were considered, and several islands in the area were evacuated. Ships were warned not to be within an area of 50,000 square miles around Eniwetok.

There was, however, a Japanese tuna trawler, the *Lucky Dragon*, eighty-five miles east-northeast of Bikini. This was well outside the proscribed area. However, it was not outside the area where capricious nature sent an upper-level wind that day. And the force of the explosion exceeded what the scientists had predicted. Radioactive debris (Bikini ash, as it came to be known in Japan) fell on the *Lucky Dragon* and its twenty-three crew members. One of them saw a dazzling light in the west, and seven minutes afterward they felt the shock wave from BRAVO. Suspecting they had been near an atomic test, they shortly thereafter pulled up their nets and headed for their homeport, Yaizu.

One might, perhaps, forgive the scientists who miscalculated the risks involved in BRAVO. Perhaps one can forgive Truman, who first decided that the United States should build H-bombs; and Eisenhower, for testing the creature in the sensitive Pacific area, where two A-bombs had already been dropped on Asians. What cannot be forgiven is the lying and stonewalling that followed. Unfortunately, the chairman of the Atomic Energy Commission was Lewis Strauss, whose talents included the ability to make money selling shoes, selling stocks, and selling himself first to James Forrestal, then to Harry Truman, and finally to Dwight Eisenhower. Robert Divine compares Strauss to John Adams: "pompous, shrewd, patriotic, but often mean, petty and unpredictable."[41] He was also a certifiable paranoid; he told James Hagerty, Eisenhower's press secretary, that "the *Lucky Dragon* was not a fishing boat at all—it was a 'Red spy outfit' snooping on the American nuclear tests."[42] Strauss was instrumental in canceling Robert Oppenheimer's security clearance. Altogether, Strauss was the worst conceivable person to handle American relations with the Japanese whom all Asia now perceived as victims of a third nuclear detonation.

All the *Lucky Dragon* crewmembers were sickened and hospitalized. The radioman, who had tasted Bikini ash out of curiosity, died 23 September 1954. The rest lived, but recovery was long, painful, and observed all over the world.[43]

The fish brought in by the *Lucky Dragon* were radioactive and had to be condemned. All fish brought in to Japanese harbors from suspect areas were checked for radioactivity for several months; 683 tuna boats were found to have contaminated fish. The Japanese fishing industry was well organized and politically powerful, employing one million workers. One of its most popular products was now suspect. Thousands of pounds were condemned, and the bottom dropped out of the market. Tokyo's Tsukiji Central Fish Market was closed for the first time since a cholera scare in 1935. For the Japanese media, the tuna panic was more important than the sick fishermen.

Japanese citizens had clearly been victims of an atomic test; this reinforced the 1945 charge that the bombs dropped on Hiroshima and Nagasaki had been mere experiments. The *Lucky Dragon* fishermen had become surrogate guinea pigs for the whole Japanese people. Even if most of the crew lived, it was clear that many of them would not be able to work for a long time, and in Japan, this was a living death. The five most important Japanese newspapers took a common position: this was the third atomic bombing.

Japanese doctors could not know the best treatment for their patients, since they did not know the chemical composition of Bikini ash, and the AEC would not tell them. It had to be kept secret from the Russians. Not only were the fishermen's blood counts dangerously low, their hair fell out and their gums bled, many of them were sterile. (Some recovered, and fathered children.) To demonstrate his contempt for the alarmist Japanese, Merrill Eisenbud, director (without a doctorate or any scientific distinction) of AEC's Health and Safety Laboratory, flew to Japan and visited the *Lucky Dragon* with an armful of instruments. As Ralph Lapp describes it, "The jaunty AEC expert refused to put on gloves, mask or protective clothing and rather horrified some of the Japanese scientists by his nonchalance."[44] They were also put off by his lack of credentials. Meanwhile, in the United States Senator Joseph McCarthy of Wisconsin was tearing the American government apart with charges that the U.S. Army was infiltrated with communists. A. M. Halpern, in a Rand monograph dated 1 September 1954 noted that all this gave final confirmation to Japanese newspapermen of "their conviction that freedom was dead and hysteria reigned in the United States."[45]

On 31 March 1954 Eisenhower directed AEC chairman Strauss to appear at the end of a press conference to read a statement about the BRAVO test and the *Lucky Dragon* mishap. After explaining why search planes had not seen the ship before the test, and how the wind changes were unexpected, Strauss misrepresented what had happened: he claimed none of the Marshall Islanders had been injured, there was no significant contamination of fish, the skin lesions of the fishermen were not due to radioactivity, and the fault for the whole thing lay with the tuna captain—he had entered the proscribed zone.[46] All these things were false. One cannot know whether the chairman of the U.S. AEC lied. His paranoia was intense enough, and the self-protectiveness of his super-secret agency was powerful enough, that he could have believed what he was saying.

No Japanese did, and few Americans. And if the head of America's atomic energy agency could so misrepresent American motives and actions in 1954, *so could America's president have misrepresented the reasons for sending the* Enola Gay *on a bombing mission nine years earlier.*

There was worse. Chairman W. Sterling Cole of the Joint Committee on Atomic Energy of the U.S. Congress suggested publicly that the *Lucky Dragon* might have been a spy ship.

Eisenhower, who was more composed than Strauss, moved to mend relations with Japan, and eventually the United States gave $2 million to the *Lucky Dragon* crew and other claimants. But Japan's honeymoon with her conquerors was over.

Asada notes that "the Bikini incident of 1954 . . . suddenly galvanized the Japanese peace movement into a mass movement against nuclear weapons."[47] Tanaka Yasumasu, in his 1970 study of "Japanese Attitudes Toward Nuclear Arms," says *Lucky Dragon* "literally ignited the fiery resentment and protests against nuclear weapons."[48] Roger Dingman's study shows that the fishermen who did not die recovered reasonable health, and all but three were still living thirty years later: "But the *Lucky Dragon* incident generated fallout that influenced relations between the United States and Japan for decades to come. The 'ashes of death' that rained down on March 1, 1954, formed part of the antinuclear mantle in which Japan wrapped itself."[49]

The Japanese *were* victims of this third atomic explosion, and there was no su-preme emergency to justify it, no horrible war to bring to an end, no stubborn mil-itarists whose determination to fight to the finish had to be overcome. There was only the American atomic-military complex riding on the growing paranoia about the Soviets.

≈ ≈ ≈

Norman Cousins, the wartime hawk, reentered the arena on 9 April 1955 when his *Saturday Review* announced a project to bring "Hiroshima Maidens" to the United States for plastic surgery. Sheila Johnson's account of this endeavor notes its appeal for Americans beginning to question the necessity for the *Enola Gay* mission. The twenty-five women who had been disfigured by the bomb were appropriately lodged with Quaker families, and operated on free of charge at Mt. Sinai Hospital in New York. Cousins regularly reported on their progress, what they studied as their scars healed, when they returned to Japan, their jobs, marriages, and babies. Johnson comments:

> Like Hersey's *Hiroshima,* Cousins's Hiroshima Maidens aroused extraordinary public interest and empathy because, once again, people were able to focus on individu-als. . . . The warmth and family feeling that suffused Cousins's reports of his return visits with the Hiroshima Maidens struck a note of genuine reconciliation and opti-mism during the late 1950s, a time when others harping on Hiroshima were becom-ing increasingly shrill and anti-American in tone. Cousins was not unaware of the trend. In 1955 he commented, "Here and there . . . serious questions are raised about the justification for the dropping of the bomb. [Cousins had raised them himself in 1946!] These questions are not to be confused with charges of Communist propa-gandists who have been attempting since the end of the war to whip up public opin-ion against the U.S. because of the bombing."[50]

Talking with two persons who hosted Hiroshima Maidens has convinced this writer that Johnson has accurately assessed Cousins's motives and results. These hosts were sympathetic with the victims of the bombs, but they were under no il-lusions about the horrors of the war that the bombs ended. Johnson is also percep-tive about some of those who fell victim to the fraud of Nitze and the suspicions of Blackett: "Over the years, there developed a sort of trans-Pacific Hiroshima in-dustry—fueled at various times by American Quakers, pacifists, and leftists, all poking through the same set of ruins. It would be pointless to review here every last product of this industry, primarily because so few had any major national im-pact comparable to that of Hersey's *Hiroshima.*" One must, however, acknowledge that the "Hiroshima industry" struck pay dirt in the 1960s.[51]

That was the time a new phrase crept into the popular jargon: "credibility gap." I was unaware of this phrase in the 1950s, but the groundwork for its potency was laid by General Ike Eisenhower. Later generations of academics have forgotten (or never knew) the shudder that went through intellectual circles when we were confronted with hard, incontrovertible evidence that the president of the United States—*our president*—had told a bald-faced lie about Francis Gary Powers and why he was shot down over the Soviet Union. On 1 May 1960, Powers was piloting a U-2 reconnaissance plane over the Soviet Union. Khrushchev announced that an American plane had been downed. Eisenhower said we never violated Soviet air space; Powers, who was missing, was piloting a weather plane that might have gone off course. The Russians then produced Powers, who had parachuted safely to earth, and confessed his mission. Khrushchev then cancelled the summit meeting scheduled for Paris a few weeks later, and the Eisenhower presidency was tarred with an inept and embarrassing ending.[52]

John F. Kennedy hardly did better; most Americans learned after he got to the White House that he had misrepresented the state of American preparedness with talk of a missile gap in order to win the election. Many also noted his white lie about having a cold during the early part of the Cuban Missile Crisis; and some believed he had lied about the circumstances of the Bay of Pigs invasion.[53]

But Lyndon Johnson was mendacious on a wholly new level. The prevarications during the Dominican Intervention in 1965 were uncovered, dissected, and reported extensively by all the major newspapers. Theodore Draper's *The Dominican Revolt,* probably the best but certainly not the only exposure of the government lies in that event, was hugely popular on American campuses.[54] And when Johnson became embroiled in Vietnam, previous standards of credibility went out the window. He was the president who generated the "credibility gap" phrase. During Johnson's tenure, newsmen attributed much of the blame for government lies to Johnson's personality. He lied not just about important things: the reasons for the Dominican intervention, about the conduct of the war in Vietnam, about the reason for release of aluminum stockpiles in 1966, about Hanoi's willingness to negotiate in 1964. Reporters believed him to have lied about small things: about the speed at which he drove, about whether he had decided to fill a vacant government post, about an ancestor claimed to have died at the Alamo of whom no one could find a record, about the place he claimed he was born. As Charles Roberts of *Newsweek* wrote, "If the president doubts this, then I invite his attention to a few jottings from my notebooks. In them is a compendium of deceptions that makes Dwight Eisenhower with his occasional lapses (the U-2 incident) and John F. Kennedy with his artful dodges (the Bay of Pigs) look like congenital, undeviating truth tellers."[55]

In 1968 the Freedom of Information and Press-Bar Committee of the American Society of Newspaper Editors observed: "All administrations manipulate the news to a greater or lesser extent, all have been known to conceal . . and even lie about important information when it is in their interest to do so. Coping with this is the task of every Washington reporter and the ability to cope with it is what separates the men from the boys. But under LBJ the coping is immeasurably more difficult because official deceit is practiced both when there is reason for it and when there is not."[56]

There is no need to comment on the credibility of subsequent presidents; Nixon was of course no better than Johnson, and it was during the 1960s and

1970s that a climate hospitable to doubts about presidents' truthfulness allowed the fraud of the "official" USSBS, as then developed by anti-Truman writers, to take root.

It was not just presidents who came to be seen as gross prevaricators. The performance of the AEC in the *Lucky Dragon* incident has been described, but this is only the beginning of a long series of mendacities by that agency which attracted visceral hatred from many Americans, a hatred that was easily projected back to the beginnings of that agency, the Manhattan Project. I was one of those moved to antinuclear activism by the arrogance and indifference of the atomic-military-industrial complex. David Lilienthal was an exception, but generally the bosses of AEC, and its successors (Nuclear Regulatory Commission, Energy Research and Development Administration, and Department of Energy), have deserved every bit of criticism they received. There was finally a change under Clinton: Hazel O'Leary appeared to be promoting more openness, and many records of earlier nuclear hazards and accidents were released. The full picture, however, remains one of evasion, misrepresentation, and denial.

One landmark case was of a concerned citizen who was initially a strong supporter of Truman's decision, but after exposure to the panicky anti-Sovietism of the cold war turned against the bomb decision and wrote a book to explain why. Stewart Udall's *The Myths of August* is the most complete account of the factors that created the Japanese-as-victims climate in the United States.[57] Unfortunately, Udall never questioned the Nitzean early surrender claim, never read any Japanese authorities on the reasons for her surrender, and showed no interest (other than acknowledging Butow's book) in the material conditions that brought the bomb's use. Udall is perhaps the only strong writer against the bomb who served as a gunner on B-24s during World War II and supported American conduct of that war to the hilt, but turned against Truman and the bomb when he began work as a lawyer defending people injured by fallout from nuclear tests.

In his description of the sins of AEC and its successors, Udall is right on target. He spent years learning how fallout from testing caused damage to people and animals throughout the Nevada testing range and nearby areas. The AEC kept the lid on all this; Udall's chapter describing their contemptible effort is titled "Big Lies, Big Cover-ups." His descriptions of the sickness and death from exposure to fallout are graphic, and while not as heart-rending as Hersey's descriptions of the Japanese who suffered from the atom, they are compelling enough to justify Udall's case against the secret national security apparatus: "When one cast a critical eye on this inner circle of policy makers it was clear that some advisors were prisoners of their own dogmas, others considered deception a tool of their trade, and still others are busy grinding special axes behind the curtains that shielded them from public scrutiny. In the days ahead this insight colored my attitude toward Walt Rostow, Henry Kissinger, Zbigniew Brzezsinksi, and the godfather of them all, Paul Nitze."[58]

It is sad that an investigator so sedulous in gathering all the relevant data about AEC injuries to his Navajo and sheepherder clients as was Udall never considered the possibility that the foundation of the anti-Truman position to which he now subscribed was written by that same Paul Nitze.

One does not reach judgment against AEC and its successors solely on the testimony of one person. After the Three Mile Island incident, Chernobyl, and other less chilling nuclear accidents, there has been a flood of credible material indicting the testers and nuclear promoters. In the Eisenhower administration, there was an effort to negotiate a nuclear test ban treaty with the Soviet Union. Harold Stassen, as Ike's chief disarmament negotiator, seemed to be making progress. The AEC, backed by the Lawrence Livermore weaponeers and by Edward Teller, was determined to sabotage the whole effort. The AEC position was that a ban could not be enforced; the Soviets would test underground, and such tests could not be detected more than two hundred miles away. Hence a test ban would be detrimental to national security.

To prove this, AEC conducted an underground test at the Nevada site in the fall of 1957. I. F. Stone, a heretic on nuclear weapons as on other topics, noticed inconspicuous news stories saying that this underground test had been detected in Toronto, Rome, and Tokyo. He did not have resources to cable these places for verification, so he did the next best thing: he called the seismologists at the U.S. Coast and Geodetic Survey. These scientists, not beholden to Lewis Strauss or Edward Teller, told Stone their seismographs had picked up the test all over the continent, for instance in Fayetteville, Arkansas, 1,200 miles away and in Fairbanks, Alaska, 2,600 miles away.[59]

The AEC found out that Stone had outflanked them. They phoned him, and admitted he was right. But they did not correct their deceitful press release, and every paper in the country except the *St. Louis Post-Dispatch,* where Stone tipped off a friend, carried the false story. Stassen's efforts were sabotaged; testing went on. We now know that there have been close to 1,000 tests since that time.

One of the most notorious abuses of the secrecy barrier occurred in the case of Dr. Thomas F. Mancuso, epidemiologist with the Graduate School of Public Health at the University of Pittsburgh.[60] In 1965, Mancuso was given an AEC grant to study the health records of workers in American nuclear weapons plants. By 1975, he had completed a study of workers at the Hanford, Washington plant with results showing higher than normal levels of cancer. Just to be sure, he brought the most prominent British epidemiologists, Alice Stewart and George W. Kneale, to Pittsburgh to inspect his calculations. They concurred.

The atomic establishment could not tolerate this outcome. It cast doubt on AEC's claim that radiation had to exceed a certain threshold level to damage human beings. By then AEC had been replaced by the Energy Research and Development Administration; that organization took Mancuso's grant away, denied him further access to Hanford figures, and he was forced to give up his studies. They could not touch Alice Stewart, however; she regularly visited the United States, and maintained that Mancuso had been right. Finally in 1990, as principal investigator for the Three Mile Island Public Health Fund, she regained access to the Hanford records. Her reanalysis confirmed the Mancuso conclusions, and was accepted by epidemiologists, even some on government payrolls.[61] The government's long struggle to conceal bad news had only reinforced the image of the atomic establishment as a lying bully. How easy it was then to project the image back to 1945.

J. Carson Mark retired in 1973 as head of the theoretical division of the Los Alamos scientific laboratory. He wrote a decade later that during his service, warhead goals had been set in accordance with the beliefs of the most rabid nuclear promoters in Congress, Senators Brien McMahon and Henry M. Jackson, both of whom publicly stated that the United States should possess every nuclear weapon that it could possibly manufacture. As Mark observed, these goals "did not reflect any judgment of what might actually be needed in the event of a war."[62] Such undeniable charges of overkill production tended to legitimate charges of overkill usage levied at the Hiroshima and Nagasaki bombs.

These attacks on the atomic establishment were neither trivial nor ideologically inspired claims. John Gofman, Arthur Tamplin, H. Jack Geiger, George Wald, Daniel Ford; these and other credentialed students of the atom made it clear that what started out as a legitimate effort to preempt a feared development of atomic weapons by Nazi Germany, which effort enabled Stimson and Truman to cut off the Pacific war well before the Japanese leaders were ready to surrender, had degenerated into an uncontrolled and abusive engine of destruction.[63] Udall was not wrong about the atomic establishment that he encountered; he was only wrong about the aims and intentions of the generation of scientists led by J. Robert Oppenheimer at the original Los Alamos. (Excepting Teller and a few other fanatics, of course.)

≈ ≈ ≈

One event of 1951 that did not fully impact Japanese-American relations until much later was the treaty ending the war between Japan and the Western Allies signed in San Francisco in September 1951. Schaller discusses the long search for a way of formally ending the war in his book *The American Occupation of Japan*.[64] The U.S., especially the military, knew that a peace treaty had to be worked out that provided for continued stationing of American forces in our most important Pacific outpost. Given Republican sensibilities about China and the Pacific area, a prominent Republican foreign policy expert, John Foster Dulles, was commissioned to negotiate a treaty. In May 1950 Dulles began talks with the many parties involved.

By September 1951, Dulles had persuaded, coerced, or bludgeoned some fifty nations to attend the signing in San Francisco. Neither the People's Republic of China nor the Chinese Nationalist regime on Taiwan was invited. The Soviet Union attended, but confronted with a rigid agenda and no chance to change the terms of the treaty, refused to sign. The Philippines and India also refused to sign. The Japanese were required to sign a security pact with the United States right after the peace treaty; it guaranteed base rights for American forces after the treaty went into effect. The whole process was heavily weighted in favor of American interests.

Even though the occupation was officially over, and some American troops began to go home, there was no celebrating in Japan at the signing and very little on 28 April 1952 when Japan became technically sovereign. According to Dower, "In a poll conducted shortly afterward, only 41 percent of the people asked if Japan had now become an independent nation answered yes."[65] Their primary fear was that being under the American nuclear umbrella was not safe. The Korean War was going on; if Truman chose to use nuclear weapons against the North Koreans or the Chinese, would not the Soviet Union fulfill treaty obligations to respond against the primary American base?

The unease did not produce a major eruption until the mutual defense treaty came up for renewal in 1960. Historian Nishi Toshio, then a college student, viewed the situation this way:

> Popular sentiment in Japan was overwhelmingly against renewal. Massive street demonstrations, one after another, day after day, kept Japan on the edge of open revolt. University students . . . staged many violent confrontations with the special riot police force. My friends and I joined in massive street demonstrations for we felt that Japan did not need this defense treaty and that the United States was making a convenience of us for the sake of its own hegemony in Asia. We felt that if war started between the United States and the Soviet Union, the Soviets would attack us first, and worse yet, the war would be fought upon our soil. "Yankee, Go Home!" was a slogan spontaneously inspired by Japanese nationalism.[66]

The mutual defense treaty was directly responsible for another major sore: Japanese involvement, as staging area and important supplier, for the American war in Vietnam. Japanese opposition to this was visceral. Michael Schaller's definitive work, *Altered States,* devotes a whole chapter to the war.[67] Thomas R. H. Havens calls the 1965 escalation of that war a "shuddering jolt" to Japan, the "most powerful shock" to the previously favorable opinion of the United States.[68] Despite Hiroshima and Nagasaki, John Hersey, P. M. S. Blackett, *Lucky Dragon,* and the other goads to Japanese views of themselves as victims, in 1964 public opinion polls showed 46% of the public chose the United States as their favorite foreign country. Anguish over Vietnam was probably the most important factor in the decline of this favorable opinion to 18% by 1973.

Japanese objected to the same things about the war that Americans did, but with an acute emphasis on the bombing. More tons of bombs were dropped on Vietnam than on Japan in World War II. The many antiwar demonstrations in Japan were triggered by the bombing. Havens' study, *Fire Across the Sea: The Vietnam War and Japan, 1965–1975,* explains how the antiwar movement built on the antinuclear movement. The conservative government of Sato Eisaku calculated correctly that it could ride out domestic opposition if it supported the United States in Vietnam, but the price was high. When Sato visited Vietnam on 8 October 1967, protesters staged a bloody clash with police at the Tokyo airport; this was "The first violent moment in a vast chain of rallies and demonstrations over foreign policy that drew 18,730,000 participants during the next two-and-a-half years."[69]

The nuclear-powered aircraft carrier *Enterprise* visited Sasebo on 19 January 1968. There was a week of riots, with police clubbing student demonstrators in front of the television cameras. The siege of Khe Sanh, February to April 1968, brought more riots. News of the My Lai massacre reached Japan in November 1969 when Prime Minister Sato was about to leave for Washington. There were five days of demonstrations, and more arrests.

Thus the considerable relief that many Japanese felt when World War II was over, some of them even welcoming the atomic bombs as "the kamikaze that saved Japan," steadily turned to rejection of the conqueror, distrust of American motives, and fear of the threat of total nuclear destruction should war again break out. Japan had been, and was still, a victim of the atom. Many of the postwar events that generated this hostility toward the U.S. were well known abroad; the victimage image took hold in the U.S. too, accelerated by the credibility gap and by what most of the public came to believe was one vast American atrocity in Vietnam.

It was this latter development, the acceptance of the Nitze-Blackett narrative by a large proportion of Americans, and by an overwhelming proportion of academics, that set the stage for the NASM's *Enola Gay* fiasco. So ensconced had the USSBS "official" account become, that by 1994, it was almost the conventional wisdom, and attacks on it by outraged veterans were written off as wholly unwarranted. Most ridiculous of all, the Nitze-Blackett version was viewed as the product of "the most modern scholarly research," when no scholarly research on its core document had been published at all.[70]

Almost all writers on the *Enola Gay* matter were agreed, however, that the Nitze-Blackett narrative achieved ascendancy primarily because of widespread rejection of U.S. government claims about its motivations during the Vietnam War. The migration of Stewart Udall from Truman supporter to Nitzean is paradigmatic of the trajectory of American writers during this period. Vietnam was the final straw. In a chapter titled "Notes on a Journey," Udall tells how as a Johnson administration cabinet officer he gradually came to question the war; how his congressman-brother Morris came out publicly against it; and then the biggest crisis of all in 1969 when "Scott, our second son, deserted the army and sought refuge in Canada."[71] This was the beginning of Udall's journey to a repudiation of the atomic-military establishment of the 1960s, and of the Truman administration that he had once proudly supported.

Barton Bernstein, in his review of the bomb controversy, writes that the atomic diplomacy position of William Appleman Williams "met indifference or hostility until the mid-sixties when opposition to the Vietnam War created sympathy for critical analyses of American foreign policy."[72] Paul Boyer, in an essay "Whose History is it Anyway?" discusses this "post-1965 wave of critical scholarship about the bomb" as being shaped by Vietnam; he reviews the career of Gar Alperovitz, one of the students of William A. Williams, who went on to do a Ph.D. at Cambridge (with P. M. S. Blackett as one of his examiners).[73] Alperovitz's dissertation was published in 1965 as *Atomic Diplomacy: Hiroshima and Potsdam,* and Boyer writes:

That year saw the first major stirrings of an antiwar movement that would soon come to question the official version of the war and the bombing campaign against the North Vietnamese. It was a propitious moment, indeed, to probe the motives that led an earlier American president to call tremendous destructive power down upon an Asian people.

Not surprisingly, the critical reassessment of the A-bomb decision launched by Alperovitz steadily gained ground after 1965 within academia especially among younger scholars, as a succession of events eroded the credibility of public officials and their pronouncements: the optimistic bulletins that flowed from Vietnam as the body bags and the shocking TV images multiplied; the New Left's ideological assault on "the Establishment"; Henry Kissinger's secret bombing of Cambodia. . . .

It must be observed that Alperovitz's "critical assessment" did not include any curiosity about the Nitze-Blackett narrative; this was an "official" account that he found sacrosanct, and continued to hold as authoritative in 1995. Barton Bernstein says, "Alperovitz is Blackett with footnotes."[74]

In 1975, Martin Sherwin's *A World Destroyed: The Atomic Bomb and the Grand Alliance* also found a ready readership. That it, like Alperovitz's successful book avoided the use of any Japanese sources, ignored the work of all Truman biographers, made no reference to the considerable literature on the Soviet atomic program, tapped only the military historians who wrote official histories of the Manhattan Project, adopted without analysis the absolutist position on the morality of the *Enola Gay* mission is not noticed by Boyer.[75] Both these works (Alperovitz and Sherwin) are written in a very narrow ethnocentric focus: what went on in the United States Government (and to some extent, Britain). Within this framework, the realities of war in the Pacific fade into insignificance—until Truman decides to drop the bombs.

A more realistic picture of the controversy over the atom bombing of Japan is given in the many publications of Barton J. Bernstein. He alone of those who question Truman's decision realized that the USSBS case on early surrender was questionable; and he develops modest suspicions of Nitze's position in the 1976 book he edited, *The Atomic Bomb: The Critical Issues:* "At some critical points the Survey's analyses are troubling, for they sometimes overstate positions and ignore or slide over issues."[76] And in his major study for *Political Science Quarterly,* spring 1975, he takes a remarkably nonconfrontational view of the bomb decision.[77]

In the *PSQ* article, he notes the pressure on the Manhattan Project to get the bomb quickly so the war could be ended sooner; states that Truman did not attempt to delay Soviet entry into the war in order to use the bomb (which charge was made by extreme anti-Truman writers); acknowledges that Truman could not risk additional casualties that might be attributed to nonuse of the bomb; disparages calls for guaranteeing the emperor as likely to embolden the Japanese military; classifies the "peace feelers" put out by Japan in July as too feeble to mean much; all of which positions were anathema to hardcore Nitzeans.

Later, in an article of 1987 titled "Ike and Hiroshima: Did He Oppose It?," Bernstein debunks Eisenhower's 1963 claim, "I told Stimson it wasn't necessary to hit them with that awful thing." Systematically, Bernstein marches through the bomb literature, showing how Alperovitz, Teller, Stephen Ambrose, Herbert Feis, Richard Rhodes, and Charles Mee have uncritically and unwisely taken Ike's post-war claim at face value.[78] In 1990, Bernstein criticized Alperovitz and Robert Messer for taking an off-the-cuff statement of Truman as being a considered opinion, when there is much reason to believe that it was casual and not significant.[79] Only in castigating Truman's use of a one million-casualty expectation for the invasion of Japan does Bernstein appear to be injudicious. As chapter one in this book points out, there were many estimates in that range floating around, at least one of which Truman read and initialed.

There were partisans in the argument over the bomb decision who have not been discussed here; they do not appear to have been greatly influential. Events were in the saddle, and rode mankind. Put another way, *nonevents* were more important than the factors conventionally considered to be a part of the ongoing discourse about Truman's decision. Of these, the most significant of all was the total failure of the disputants to inspect the foundation document of all opponents and supporters of the bomb's use, which document was always referred to with the respect due to a revelation from on high, but never attributed to the archhawk who wrote it, Paul Nitze. Nor did the disputants, with minor exceptions, utilize the extensive materials developed by the small but active corps of liberal Japanese historians. The ethnocentrism of the whole American historical establishment was monumental. One can only conclude that all were bowing before the preemptive but fraudulent "On the basis of all the facts . . ."

6

ENOLA GAY AT AIR AND SPACE
Anonymity, Hypocrisy, Ignorance

*I would avoid "revisionist" in or out of quotes, and just go with "some historians . . ."
Revisionism is still a fighting term. Also, I wouldn't mention Alperovitz by name;
Blackett was first to make the argument [that Truman's main motive was to
intimidate the Soviet Union] in 1948. If I were writing this label, I would just say
that most historians argue the military motive was primary and sufficient, but that
the political motive was reinforcing in the decision.*
GREGG HERKEN TO NEUFELD AND CROUCH, 8 DECEMBER 1993[1]

*Even if I think Alperovitz is wrong and tendentious, I refuse to write him out of the
historiography since he has played and continues to play an essential role in
stimulating debate and research.*
MICHAEL NEUFELD TO WAYNE DZWONCHYK, 12 MAY 1994[2]

Martin Harwit took charge of the National Air and Space Museum in August
1987, facing a demand from veterans that he do something about the most glaring
omission of historic aircraft from the museum's displays: *Enola Gay,* the aircraft
that dropped an atomic bomb on Hiroshima and, along with Soviet entry into the
Pacific war and a second bomb on Nagasaki, effectively ended the war.[3]

Enola Gay was under Smithsonian control but housed in inadequate facilities at
Silver Hill, Maryland. It had been neglected for almost a decade. The veterans
wanted the plane completely refurbished and "displayed proudly" in a setting that

would commemorate the heroism of those who won the war, as well as recognize the genius of American technology. In the lingo of memorialists, this means that the veterans wanted a narrative of good triumphant over evil.

Leading the agitation about *Enola Gay* were members of the 509th Composite Group, the U.S. Army Air Force's contingent under Paul Tibbets that had been assigned to prepare an attack with atomic bombs against both Germany and Japan. When it appeared that Germany would surrender before the first bomb was ready, the 509th found itself practicing for early August drops on Hiroshima and Nagasaki.

Members of the 509th founded the *Enola Gay* Restoration Association in the summer of 1984. Partly due to their campaign, NASM began to restore the aircraft in 1985. When Harwit took over NASM in 1987 a display of *Enola Gay* was already top priority. World War II pilots were determined to see the aircraft displayed in top condition before they died; if NASM wouldn't do it, they had many suggestions of museums and airfields where it would be welcomed.

The plane had a bittersweet welcome at NASM. The paper trail establishes that Director Harwit and his chief assistants were convinced:

1. that scholarly research would show using atomic bombs against Japan had been a mistake.
2. that the Japanese would have surrendered soon without them.
3. that had Truman told the Japanese they could keep their emperor, surrender could have come even before the bombs were dropped.
4. that the huge casualties Truman said he had been told to expect if we invaded Japan as scheduled 1 November 1945 were a postwar creation.
5. that racism, revenge, and intimidating the Soviet Union were important and illegitimate motives for Truman's decision.
6. that the obscene nuclear arms race with the Soviet Union was a legacy of the two atomic bombs we dropped, not caused by Soviet determination to have any weapon its adversaries had.
7. and that the veterans who believed the bombs foreclosed an invasion and thus saved their lives were simply ignorant and mistaken.

In short, NASM bought the Nitze-Blackett narrative in toto.

This heavy ideological baggage made it difficult for the NASM team to put together an exhibit that would be true to their own beliefs, and satisfy the veterans. If all these anti-bomb claims were warranted, the *Enola Gay* should be on a junk-heap somewhere, not displayed prominently in a national museum controlled and financed by the United States government.

But the *Enola Gay* was securely under the control of NASM, and Harwit had to produce. To say that what followed generated trouble is to understate the situation. Ultimately, after much expenditure of time and money, the planned exhibit was canceled. There have been many postmortems; here I argue that the exhibit died of anonymity, hypocrisy, and ignorance. No minds were changed.

∽ ∽ ∽

Museum exhibits, like other scholarly efforts, require documentation. Of all the debilities a "scholarly" presentation might suffer, surely the most unusual is anonymity of sources. Most critiques of the often-erroneous products of the CIA and other intelligence services note that one liability of such bureaucratic operations is their anonymity. They are *secret* organizations, and no one person is responsible for false information. Who told Kennedy that the Cubans were ready for revolt when Brigade 4506 landed at the Bay of Pigs? Who was really responsible for the catastrophic U.S.-backed overthrow of Mossadeq in Iran in 1953? Even if one thinks it necessary for national security reasons to keep such CIA findings secret, what possible reason could Harwit have had for hiding the identities of the scholars on whom NASM relied?

Even in everyday arguments, the common challenge "Says who?" requires an answer. Where, as in the *Enola Gay* case, the whole structure of NASM's narrative depends on the claim of the curators to possess "the best scholarly research," the necessity for identifying *whose* research is inescapable, yet nowhere in the text of the exhibit are we told whose research underwrote the narrative.

Two critics of the NASM objected to this violation of scholarly norms. Richard Kurin, director of the Center for Folklife Programs and Cultural Studies at the Smithsonian, speaking at a symposium sponsored by the Smithsonian and the University of Michigan at Ann Arbor 19 April 1995, had harsh words for his colleagues. Their first script on *Enola Gay* had an anonymity that "conveys a sense of disembodied authority we know to be inappropriate."[4] As the editor of the symposium summarized Kurin's presentation, "Kurin thought that a small group of scholars and curators was no longer in sole possession of knowledge; the lived experience of those who flew *Enola Gay* was, he believed, not 'fully and honestly' engaged by the curators."

More sympathetic to the NASM curators, but aware of liabilities in their product, Daniel Seltz, in a monograph of the East Asian studies program at Brown University, December 1996, noted "The Smithsonian also confronted the problem of accountability. The exhibit never cited any of the historians whose theories they had integrated into the script by name. This meant that these historians were not involved in a direct way in defending the findings of their research, and it also grouped scholars with varying perspectives under vague and encompassing phrases such as 'most historians believe.'"[5] We were indeed never told which historians believed what, nor what they based this belief on.

The *Enola Gay* script mentioned a miscellany of people: various U.S. Marines and Army privates who fought in the Pacific; three Japanese kamikaze pilots; Roosevelt, Hitler, Chamberlain, Churchill, Stalin, Truman, Einstein; Gen. Leslie Groves, J. Robert Oppenheimer, Henry Stimson, Joseph Grew; B-29 pilots and crew; survivors of the fire-bombing of Tokyo; the *Los Angeles Times;* Adm. William Leahy, and Dwight Eisenhower. None of these were scholars of the bomb decision, of the Japanese decision to surrender, or of the causes of the cold war nuclear arms race, and certainly none of them were recent. But over and over the curators wrote that "the consensus of historians" says Truman had other ways to end the war, or "recent scholarly research reveals" that Japan was ready to surrender before Hiroshima, or some such weasel phrase. Of course this was not recent at all; it was simply a knee-jerk recitation of what Paul Nitze wrote in 1946.

Thus the NASM curators sought, using what Pamela Walker Laird calls "unattributed presentations, with all the authority of the institution housing them," to gain credibility without specific attribution.[6] But here the institutional authority, that of NASM, was not powerful enough to prevail. And only after the planned exhibit was cancelled did we find out who actually wrote the script.

The limitations of Harwit's peculiar notion of scholarly competence come through clearly in his claims for the quartet who wrote the script. Harwit tells us, "When the Museum sought in 1990 to hire a lead curator for the exhibition of the *Enola Gay* we followed federal procedures and first approached numerous senior American scholars, but none of them were willing or available to take on this complex task. Finding none, we offered the position to Mike Neufeld, a Canadian citizen who clearly had the required credentials."[7] These credentials were training as a social historian, and writing a book on the German V-2 rocket. Neufeld was the lead curator.

Harwit describes Tom Crouch, NASM's aeronautics chief, as "a prolific historian of the early years of flight," which enabled him to "exhibit the impact that the technology has had on life in the twentieth century."[8] Crouch had been at the Smithsonian for many years. He was also a prime writer.

The other two involved in writing the script were junior employees of Crouch's aeronautics department: Thomas Dietz, trained in the navy as an aviation electronics technician, and Joanne Gernstein, who came to the Smithsonian from the Science Discovery Center in Ithaca, and was a doctoral candidate in American studies at George Washington University.[9]

This quartet of scriptwriters obviously lacked the status of experts in any of the relevant fields. Two of them were, and the two junior ones might become, genuine scholars—in some field. No doubt given sufficient time, and making great effort, they could digest the relevant scholarly research on (1) the decision of the Truman administration to drop the bombs; (2) the Pacific war; (3) the decision of the Japanese government to surrender; (4) the origins of the nuclear arms race; and (5) the morality of warfighting. There is no evidence that they did so.

Backing them up were other NASM employees, the most prominent of whom was Gregg Herken, head of NASM's department of space history, and the author of three books on the relations of scientists to government policy. One of these books, *The Winning Weapon: The Atomic Bomb in the Cold War 1945–1950* was directly concerned with the subject of unit V of the proposed exhibit. Herken viewed the Cold War arms race as a direct outcome of Truman's decision to use the bomb against Japan; Truman's decisions "to proceed with the 'Super' and with NSC-68 were properly the culminating events of the policy on the atomic bomb that had begun with the destruction of Hiroshima."[10] Of all the NASM personnel who appear in Harwit's pages, Herken is the only one who claims distinction in a field that might be relevant to this exhibit. Harwit gives no hint as to why Herken was not in charge of *Enola Gay*. Herken's advice during the various critiques was generally apropos, and mostly well informed. Herken's judgment on the place of the atomic bombs in the origins of the cold war is at odds with that of specialists on the Soviet nuclear program, but he did not claim this as a specialty.

The names of the scriptwriters eventually became known to the press and hence to some wider publics, but not the names of the historians whose work they appropriated. Why did Harwit do it this way? The archives give a clue. The curators believed that Gar Alperovitz, the anti-Truman writer whose 1965 polemic against the bomb decision was the most-read document of Nitzean derivation, could not be acknowledged as a source. His conclusions outran his data, he was strident, and most other writers on the subject disagreed with him; NASM would not identify him as a source.

Despite this public distancing from the most prominent exponent of the Nitze-Blackett narrative, NASM files tell us that Alperovitz's beliefs were very much present. On 8 December 1993, Herken wrote the two lead curators about their preliminary draft. In regard to page 39, he wrote "I would avoid 'revisionist,' in or out of quotes, and just go with 'some historians . . . ' Revisionism is still a fighting term. Also, I wouldn't mention Alperovitz by name; Blackett was first to make the argument [that Truman's main motive was to intimidate the Soviet Union] in 1948. If I were writing this label, I would just say that most historians argue the military motive was primary and sufficient, but that the political motive was reinforcing in the decision."[11] So Alperovitz never appeared in print.

The archives, however, tell us that on 21 April 1994, when Neufeld was pressed by a group of military historians who had seen the script to provide "some evidence" for its claims, he wrote them:

> In response to comments and criticism made at our recent meeting or in the written comments from Air Force History, I am enclosing three photocopies of secondary sources which provide evidence, I think, for three points: (1) that the Soviet Factor was of some influence in the thinking of Stimson, Byrnes and Truman before and during the Potsdam Conference; (2) that this position is now the consensus among historians, although there is wide disagreement over how significant a factor it was; and (3) that Bernstein and the historians of the "consensus" position on the "decision to drop the bomb" form a separate, middling group from the Alperovitz "revisionists."[12]

Finding this document in the files of the Naval Historical Center, but without the three photocopies of what Neufeld believed to be evidence, I wrote Neufeld on 25 September 1999, asking if he could recall what the photocopies were. He responded that he was sure one of them was from J. Samuel Walker's 1990 article on the historiography of the bomb decision; the others were probably from articles by Martin Sherwin and Barton Bernstein. Neufeld also explained that "the 'consensus' historians on the center and the left had split away from Alperovitz and did not support many of his positions while remaining somewhat skeptical of the atomic bomb decision."[13]

The military historians were not convinced that Alperovitz had been banned from the *Enola Gay* script. Wayne Dzwonchyk, historian in the Office of the Chairman, Joint Chiefs of Staff, wrote Neufeld 28 April 1994. Dzwonchyk believed that the exhibit script contradicted Neufeld's letter. Dzwonchyk observed,

> It cannot be demonstrated that the US conducted any atomic diplomacy at Potsdam. In fact, the interesting thing about the conference is the demanding and aggressive stance taken by the Soviets. To flatten all nuance and state, as the script did, that Truman delayed the conference in order to have the bomb in hand for tough negotiations with the Soviets is pure Alperovitz strategy of a delayed showdown which in its bald form is rejected by Sherwin and Bernstein . . . To reiterate a point I tried to make at our recent meeting, perhaps without sufficient clarity, the script's repeated reference to the Soviet factor and to US desire to "intimidate the Soviet Union," inflated it out of proportion to its actual importance. The bomb would have been dropped on Japan, as Bernstein says, even if the Soviet Union had not existed.[14]

Neufeld responded on 12 May 1994:

> Part of the problem with that section stems from the fact that the script tries to represent the *range* of the debate, and not merely my view of these matters — that is especially the case in the "Historical Controversies" labels, at least as they were in recent drafts of the script. Those labels often use the Alperovitz thesis as a place to start, but end up saying that most scholars reject his one-sided formulations. . . . Even if I think Alperovitz is wrong and tendentious, I refuse to write him out of the historiography since he has played and continues to play an essential role in stimulating debate and research.[15]

In June 1994, Tom Crouch was more positive than Neufeld. M. K. Stone of Philadelphia wrote Crouch protesting the absence of Alperovitz's doctrines from the script as he understood it. Crouch answered with a form letter about the exhibition, which did not engage Stone's complaint. Stone protested in another letter: "I would appreciate receiving a letter that deals with the particular points I mentioned." Crouch tried again, on 28 June: "My apologies. It was a form letter. I can assure you that a clear statement of the Alperovitz thesis and the arguments in its favor are included in the exhibit."[16]

The military historians were also clear about this. Mark Jacobsen, U.S. Marine Corps Command and Staff College historian on the review board for the second version of the script, was censorious primarily about the curators' concealing the Alperovitz doctrine. As he wrote his superior on 18 July 1994,

> The Air and Space Museum is right to discuss the Alperovitz thesis and right to assign it to a controversy sidebar. But like a "bad penny," it keeps coming back. By force of repetition in one form or another, the Smithsonian pounds it into its readers' heads that the US dropped the bomb to influence the Soviet Union. Although the

authors of the Smithsonian script deny their intellectual debt to the oeuvre of Gar Alperovitz, the central contention of his 1964 *Atomic Diplomacy* informed the previous script and survives in several places in this latest version.[17]

So Alperovitz was in, but he was not in. Clearly the curators felt that to acknowledge the reputed leader of American anti-Hiroshima discourse would bring them grief. But why did they not acknowledge Sherwin, Walker, and Bernstein *in the exhibit text?* This question will be addressed in the last section of this chapter.

Perhaps had the NASM been open about their dependence on the small group of anti-Hiroshima writers who had made their reputations as scholars of the bomb decision, the museum would have gotten away with it. Their feeling that Alperovitz's ideas had to be camouflaged is understandable. But the judgment that *complete* anonymity of their sources would enable the institutional authority to prevail miscarried. When the hostility of the veterans was reinforced by the rightward shift of congress, their anonymity did not save them.

～ ～ ～

One of Harwit's first approaches to an *Enola Gay* exhibit came in a 1 November 1988 letter to Ruth Adams of the international security program at the MacArthur Foundation. His projected exhibit was to be entitled "From Guernica to Hiroshima: Strategic Bombing in World War II." The title would change many times, but the concept lasted. He wanted to

> hold a colloquium series on strategic bombing, which would culminate in a retrospective symposium with members [of] the 1946 Strategic Bombing Survey. We plan to videotape the proceedings (and a number of ancillary interviews) in order to document vividly for future generations the ways in which participants such as John Kenneth Galbraith, Paul Nitze, and George Ball came to understand the role and legacy of strategic bombing after more than 40 years of reflection.[18]

Would MacArthur like to sponsor this series?

Apparently Adams's division of the MacArthur Foundation would not, as the subsequent correspondence is with Denise McIntosh of MacArthur's program on peace and international cooperation, which did approve. The proposed series, promised Harwit, would result in published proceedings. There would be open programs at which audience members could ask questions, and there would be closed programs at which outside experts would hold workshop sessions with NASM staff who would produce the resulting exhibit. There would be eight parts to the series, beginning as soon as possible, following the history of strategic bombing chronologically. The preliminary draft outline for this series was six pages single-spaced.[19]

On page four of this prospectus, Harwit anticipated a new thrust for Air and Space. He noted that the museum had been criticized as "largely a giant advertisement for air and space technologies," and that the omission of *Enola Gay* from

NASM exhibits in the face of pressure to display her "can be seen as the first crisis of the new museum." Harwit appealed to the peace-minded at MacArthur with this departure from NASM's past: "The proposed exhibition on Strategic Bombing will deal honestly and forthrightly with what might be called 'the dark side of aviation.' Its centerpiece will be the fully restored *Enola Gay*."

This candid statement of where Harwit intended to take the museum apparently never came to the attention of the Air Force Association and other enemies of the exhibit. "The dark side of aviation" would have made a beautiful sound bite for a vigorous press campaign. And there was more. Appealing no doubt to the MacArthur people, but certainly heretical for the director of a national air and space museum dependent on the largesse of the U.S. government:

> Strategic Bombing presents a classic case of what can happen when military planners place excessive reliance on the supposed infallibility of technology and on doctrines evolved in the absence of empirical evidence. The subject of the efficiency of strategic bombing is a highly controversial one; we may be able to treat this aspect by presenting the most cogent available statements of the opposing positions by the major participants. We should aim at presenting the facts as objectively as possible, drawing no conclusions, but providing enough information for viewers of the exhibition to draw their own.[20]

The mood of the exhibition would be "somber." Text captions would be "understated, letting photographs, artifacts, and participants speak for themselves." Joseph Heller's *Catch 22* and Kurt Vonnegut's *Slaughterhouse 5* (these are somber?) could be used to reveal "the existential absurdity of life in a bomber crew [and] the surreal quality of mass destruction by fire storm. . ." And the capstone evaluation of the success or failure of World War II strategic bombing would be videotaped interviews with those stalwarts of the United States Strategic Bombing Survey, Nitze, Galbraith, and Ball.

A final hint to the MacArthur people that this exhibit would be a real departure from past NASM practice came when Harwit noted that "the *Enola Gay* cannot be exhibited in the present Museum building." Not only was the plane too large to fit there, but "the appropriate mood to be evoked by the strategic bombing exhibit surrounding this airplane would clash with the predominately soaring spirit of aviation which dominates" the other galleries. *Enola Gay* would go to a new museum extension then being planned.[21] The tone of this whole proposal was evangelistic; Harwit was remaking the chauvinistic NASM.

MacArthur made a generous grant, the symposia were duly held. Harwit brags in his 1996 book, *An Exhibit Denied*, "Fifty prominent people were invited. Incredibly, forty-nine responded. I do not remember who declined."[22] Note well *his* designation of the participants: "prominent" people, not scholars, not Pacific war experts, nor Truman biographers, nor specialists in Japan's decision to surrender, nor moralists on warfighting, nor experts on the Soviet decision to build nuclear weapons as fast as possible.

The need for political backing became clear as veterans pressured NASM to speed the restoration and display of *Enola Gay*. As NASM increasingly had to respond to veterans groups, Harwit began to see that presenting the dark side of aviation as it related to this particular airplane would be inflammatory to thousands of Americans.

On the other hand, Japanese sensitivities to a display of *Enola Gay* had to be taken into account. Harwit notes a warning he received from Morihisa Takagi, president of Nippon Television, in November 1988: "The Hiroshima and Nagasaki bombings remain firmly imprinted in the Japanese consciousness, much as the Holocaust does with the Jewish people." Harwit was sensitive to the danger of "precipitating a potentially serious international incident between the United States and Japan."[23] And he wanted to borrow artifacts from the Hiroshima and Nagasaki museums; Japanese goodwill was absolutely essential for this purpose.

The only viable stance for NASM was therefore complete neutrality on the question whether the bomb's use against Japan was justified. There were two sides to this question, and NASM would support neither one—in principle. The exhibit would simply lay out the facts, and let the viewer judge. The artifacts and the accompanying text had to be "balanced." The contentious years at NASM between 1990 and 1995 were one long struggle between the political necessity to develop an exhibit that would *not* bias viewer's opinions, that would be non-judgmental, and the gut instinct of Harwit and his crew to display the dark side of aviation, thus inducing Americans to regret the use of two atomic bombs against Japan.

It is perhaps unnecessary to present the many repetitions of NASM's "we take no sides, we only let the visitors choose" mantra, but some of the rhetoric is surprising. One of the persons Harwit strained to convince of the curator's neutrality was Robert Adams, secretary of the Smithsonian until shortly before the exhibit was to open, and hence Harwit's boss. On 16 April 1993, reporting on a trip to Japan, Harwit wrote Adams,

> We had an opportunity in Hiroshima, last Monday, to talk at length with mayor Takashi Hiraoka, who very clearly voiced the strong sentiments of his city that all atomic weapons must be eliminated, and who wanted to assure himself that our exhibition would not convey a message contrary to that spirit. . . . I told the mayor that the museum was not in a position to make political statements, so that advocacy of the abolition of all nuclear weapons was not a message we would be presenting. The intent of the exhibition was, rather, to make visitors think and come to their own conclusions.[24]

By contrast, when dealing with Japanese whose goodwill he solicited, Harwit had a different story. This in a letter of 18 May 1993 to Akihiro Takahashi, a bomb sufferer then working for the Hiroshima Museum:

> I can well understand the depth of feeling that the exhibition proposed by our museum must evoke in you. . . . I would like to assure you, therefore, that we do not plan

to simply dwell on the Manhattan Project or the technical aspects of the bombing. . . . For most of us in America, the *Enola Gay* is an uncomfortable symbol. It represents a destructive act, which many of us feel to be incompatible with our perceived national character. The *Enola Gay* is a symbol that does not agree with that national characterization. . . .[25]

In early 1994, when he got negative comments on the bias or lack of balance of the script, Harwit sought a second opinion from six NASM employees, most with a military background, and wrote them on 26 April 1994, "Whatever the origin of these differences, the Museum must be certain that the exhibition we mount is indeed balanced. I am therefore asking you to serve on an independent Tiger Team, once more, specifically to look for any signs of imbalance, and to report back to me by Friday, May 13. I regret the short deadline, but the exhibition schedule is tight and corrective action if needed will have to be taken at once."[26] The Tiger Team did report, on 24 May 1994. Their report was devastating.

This was no group of enemies out to get the curators: Brig. Gen. William M. Constantine, USAF (Ret.), volunteer NASM docent and team chairman; Col. Thomas Alison, USAF (Ret.), NASM curator for military aviation; Dr. Gregg Herken, chairman, NASM department of space history; Col. Donald Lopez, USAF (Ret.), former NASM deputy director and senior advisor emeritus; Kenneth Robert, NASM volunteer docent; and Dr. Steven Soter, special assistant to the director of Air and Space. These critics produced 100-plus pages, nineteen of which are negative comments agreed to by the whole group.[27] This Tiger Team does not say, "The script is unbalanced and tendentious because its authors are crusaders against Truman's decision," but one can read this between the lines.

Later criticism by the Air Force Association may have been more prickly, but the Tigers were equally clear: this script would not do. Lopez was typical: the script

reflects the viewpoint of the writer rather than an impartial historical view. The labels are written for the peers of the authors and not for the average museum visitor . . . the imbalance is almost palpable. A visitor, expecting something honoring 50th anniversary of WWII, either a veteran, or with some connection to a veteran, will be appalled. . . . I would leave the exhibit with the strong feeling that Americans are bloodthirsty, racist killers who after beer parties and softball go out and kill as many women and children as possible . . .[28]

Michael Neufeld attended the first meeting of this Tiger Team at Constantine's request. He was troubled by what he heard, and wrote to Harwit and the Tiger Team about it on 25 April 1994.[29] Harwit says Neufeld's was a "thoughtful" response; I read it as defensive and evasive of the Tiger Team's critique. Neufeld refers to the "thirty years of research" that went into the script, which shows that "the decision is debatable on its political and military merits." He then reiterates the anti-Truman litany, determined to change even the Tiger Team's responses. At this stage, it should have been abundantly clear to Harwit that his curators could *talk* about being nonjudgmental, but they were not going to produce a script that achieved this.

Harwit and the curators were constantly responding to hundreds (perhaps thousands—the archives are full of them) of letters inquiring about the exhibit. They usually answered with a form letter. One such went from Tom Crouch to David Blasco of Fort Lauderdale, Florida, on 17 August 1994:

> Thank you for your letter regarding our exhibition, "The Last Act: The Atomic Bomb and the End of World War II." I can assure you that the exhibition, which is scheduled to open in the spring of 1995, will most certainly honor the brave Americans who fought and suffered for their nation during World War II. Moreover, it will identify Japan as the aggressor nation in the Pacific War, and outline the nature of the atrocities committed by the Japanese. At the same time, it will present the reality of the atomic bomb as experienced by the people of Hiroshima and Nagasaki. In short, the presentation will be an honest, balanced treatment that encourages our visitors to think about a crucial turning point in the history of the 20th century.[30]

But it was all in vain. The script was conceived, written, and revised by true believers in the Nitze-Blackett narrative of the bombings. When the big, glaring phrases were removed from the text under prodding from inside and outside NASM, the small, subtle bias remained, through hundreds of hours of conferences with critics. The fifth and final script was perceived, even by some of the initially hostile military historians, as acceptable, but it was too late. The Air Force Association and other groups had gone to Congress, newly under the control of Newt Gingrich and conservative Republicans, who readily believed that *these* curators were basically un-American and could never get it right. The un-American charge was of course false. It was no more un-American to oppose the use of atomic bombs on Japan than it was to oppose the American intervention in Vietnam. But the politics were different. Thousands of survivors of World War II approved of the bomb for ending the war as soon as possible and no adequate warrant for changing their minds came out of NASM. In contrast, almost the whole country regretted Vietnam.

Harwit, the unlucky leader of this attempt to change the collective mind about *Enola Gay*, went through agony. Periodically he had to admit that the effort to be neutral, to create an exhibit that presented balanced facts and let visitors make up their own minds, had failed. The cognitive dissonance must have been tremendous. It shows in his 1996 book. Through the long, detailed narrative, he reinforces his claims to want a balanced, nonjudgmental exhibit, only to be foiled by wayward curators. Thus, on 2 July 1993, in a memo to Tom Crouch about Neufeld's latest draft, he explodes in a memorable chewing-out:

> I am absolutely convinced Mike's new draft, as written, will be rejected out of hand, by the Secretary. . . . The consistent problem with Mike's headings, subheadings, and introductory paragraphs, is that they do not do what the Museum always claims it intends to do: To let visitors judge. Mike appears at each stage to prejudge. . . . His headings consistently emphasize only the most dramatic. A central image in the opening section will show "a small boy taken immediately after the

bombing of Nagasaki." Does one have to add "streaks of blood are visible on his cheek"? Why not let the visitor see for himself what the boy looks like? The opening paragraph again reverts to the form Mike has had all along. The context of Europe and Japan in World War II has been eliminated, after I had painstakingly inserted it at the Secretary's suggestion. The broader picture has been erased. . . . Where is it that the visitor ever has a chance to formulate an independent opinion? Where does a visitor have a chance to see for himself whether the war in the Far East differed from that in Europe, or for that matter from other wars throughout history?[31]

When he wrote his book, Harwit included much of this memo. When he had finished his text and began to wrestle with a preface, however, he appears to have forgotten his earlier pique with his subordinates. In the preface he attacks the new Smithsonian secretary, I. Michael Heyman, who cancelled Harwit's elaborate plans. Harwit says Heyman implies "that a true history of the mission of the *Enola Gay* could not adequately honor the nation's veterans; and that it was more important for America to accept a largely fictitious, comforting story in this commemorative year than to recall a pivotally important twentieth-century event as revealed in trustworthy documents now at hand in the nation's archives."[32] The fancy language did not conceal what Harwit thought of the veterans: "You've got nothing to commemorate. You don't know what went on in the decision centers." But if Harwit really believed this, how could he have castigated Neufeld for saying practically the same thing?

Most of the veterans continued to find that the exhibit demonstrated NASM's evangelical mission to upset their beliefs. Richard Hallion, air force historian, complained to Tom Crouch on 9 August 1994, about Crouch's statement that

> veterans are only concerned with one exhibit unit (the Ground Zero portion of the exhibit) out of five, as if all five sections were equal. But they aren't all equal: the real core of your exhibit is Ground Zero. That's the section about which you stated—in our very first meeting with Martin, Mike, and Herman—"That will rip the visitor's heart out." You may recall that I said at the time, "I hope their hearts will also be ripped out when they see what was happening in the Pacific War on the road to Japan." You are too experienced in museum affairs not to recognize the powerful influence of artifacts, photographs and graphics. They overwhelm words. They cannot be balanced by some minimal text on Japanese aggression.[33]

And Preble Stolz, prominent law professor at the University of California who was furnished a copy of the text when Michael Heyman took over as Smithsonian secretary, found almost nothing but bias: "I think there is a problem. I am not sure I would describe it as a problem of 'balance' or 'fairness.' Rather, what I come away with is a distinct sense that I am being preached at, and that, I think, is wrong." Stolz went on for eleven pages with illustrations of preachiness, which he did not believe was "the business of the Smithsonian."[34]

Lance Morrow, in *Time* magazine, was close to the mark. He had been in Hiroshima, watching school children come out of the Peace Memorial Museum:

Now it is common for Japanese children to practice their English on the *gaijin,* and
. . . a little boy danced up, peered into my face and said brightly, "Murderer! Hello!" I
thought of that Japanese schoolboy in recent months as Washington's Smithsonian
Institution shuffled through one script after another, trying to figure out how to deal
with Hiroshima in a 50th-anniversary exhibition about the end of the war. . . . The
first script for the exhibition, which will display a part of the reassembled *Enola Gay,*
was way left of the mark. It interpreted Hiroshima and Nagasaki in a way that managed to transport a righteous '60s moral stance on Vietnam ("Baby killers!") back in
time to portray the Japanese as more or less innocent victims of American beastliness
and lust for revenge. As if the Japanese had been conquering Asia by Marquis of
Queensbury rules. The curators said to the American public, "Murderer! Hello!"[35]

Tom Crouch saw part of the problem clearly in a memo to Harwit of 21 July
1993. "Do you want to do an exhibition intended to make veterans feel good, or do
you want an exhibition that will lead our visitors to think about the consequences
of the atomic bombing of Japan? Frankly, I don't think we can do both."[36] Given
his assumption that the consequences were all bad, he was right.

Crouch was woefully wrong about one thing. The curators were ill informed
about the consequences of the atomic bombing.

Attempting to change American minds about bombing Hiroshima while you
are pretending to be nonjudgmental is—there is no kinder word for it—hypocrisy.
It was a replay of Genesis 27:22; "And Jacob went near unto Isaac his father; and he
felt him, and said, The voice is Jacob's voice, but the hands are the hands of Esau."
In the final edition of the *Enola Gay* script, perhaps some of the words were words
of neutrality, but the tone was the tone of judgment.

The curators were, however, sensitive enough to the rhetorical bind they were in
to realize that, even though *they* believed that the Nitze-Blackett narrative was the
correct one, the exhibit text could not straightforwardly offer evidential support
for much of that narrative. They therefore adopted the technique of indirect, suggestive, phrasing, common in the discourse of advocates operating in a hostile environment. This technique is exposed famously in Charles S. Maier's *The Unmasterable Past: History, Holocaust, and German National Identity.* Maier shows that

> disguised theses, proposed in a pseudo-interrogative mode . . . travel under false pass-
> ports. This seems to be the case of Nolte's argumentation [that Hitler was only antic-
> ipating Soviet destruction of Germany when he attacked]. . . Nolte, Fest, and Hill-
> gruber argue that the historian who objects is substituting taste for truth, and
> aestheticizing a political argument. But there is a test. A genuine historical question
> will not influence opinion unless it is actually answered. A spurious one is designed to
> sway opinion by virtue of its just being asked.[37]

Asking spurious questions is what the curators did on many of the pressure
points of *Enola Gay* argument. A series of "Historical Controversies" in the text
are phrased as pseudo questions, which the curators dare not answer according to
their foundational documents since this would expose their bias. So they ask,
"Would the bomb have been dropped on the Germans?" "Did the United States

ignore the Japanese Peace Offensive?" (Note in this instance they avoid calling it an offer to surrender, since nowhere in the Togo-Sato decrypts did Togo use the word surrender.) "Would the war have ended sooner if the United States had guaranteed the emperor's position?" "How important was the Soviet factor in the decision to drop the bomb?" "Was a warning or demonstration possible?" (Here they load the question heavily; of course it was possible; the real question was, would it have been effective?) "Was the decision to drop the bomb justified?" On all of these questions the text waffled. On all of them, the massive scholarly research on Japan's decision to surrender would have weighed strongly against the Nitze-Blackett narrative, but as the next section will show, the curators systematically excluded all discourse that did not come from their preferred sources.

Various journalists realized that asking these questions was not legitimate framing of the issues, but they lacked Maier's sophisticated analysis to show why.

⌇ ⌇ ⌇

Whatever blame attaches to anonymity and hypocrisy in the NASM *Enola Gay* fiasco, it does not rise to the level of misfeasance of the museum's claim to have sought and obtained the best modern academic scholarship relevant to the atomic bombings. "Modern scholarly research" was a mantra recited even more than "balance" or "objectivity." Monotonously, vehemently, the museum told supporters and critics alike that it had the latest historical truth about the *Enola Gay* mission: Japan would have surrendered before invasion. Joseph Grew was expert on the Japanese and he said guaranteeing the emperor would have brought surrender in May or June. Soviet entry into the war would have brought surrender. And Truman lied about his motives and about how costly invasion would have been.

Despite all the talk about modern scholarly research, the old Nitze-Blackett narrative had a stranglehold at NASM. It *was* the conventional wisdom. Historians of any stripe who favored Truman-Stimson were by definition not expert, not scholars, not worth seeking out. One might apply Irving Janis's term "groupthink" to the *Enola Gay* curators; or to use Bernstein's analysis in a different case, the anti-Truman devotion (in this case) of the curators "should be understood primarily as a cultural act with political purposes," so that normal search procedures were disregarded.[38]

Harwit sensed the rhetorical potency of the Nitzean narrative, as an "official" report, from the start. His application to the MacArthur Foundation mentioned the USSBS directors twice. The archives show Harwit's major effort to bring in a USSBS director to speak at the museum was to obtain Nitze. When the 1990 symposium series was first set up, Nitze agreed to participate. In a letter to Nitze of 29 June 1990, Tami Davis Biddle, then a fellow in the NASM department of space history, indicates that the "Sifting the Rubble: Strategic Bombing Surveys" program was scheduled for 6 September, to last two hours, beginning at 8:00 P.M. After an introduction by David MacIsaac, Nitze, Ball, Galbraith, Ramsey Potts, and Lord Zuckerman were to follow in that order. Each of the speakers was to have twelve minutes; the texts of all speeches were to be in the volume to be published in 1992 (it was not published). Each speaker was to cover two themes: "(1) your conclusions about the [bombing] campaign right in the aftermath of the war, and (2) your thoughts on the campaign as you reflect on it today, with the benefit of forty-five years' hindsight."[39] It never occurred to NASM that forty-five years reflection might mean forty-five years of additional psychic investment in the validity of the original beliefs.

The next contacts with Nitze were made by Helen C. McMahon, manager of cooperative programs at the Smithsonian; Nitze was to be paid $250, and needed to furnish his social security number, and a brief resume.[40] But something went wrong. On 23 August 1990, Tami Biddle wrote Lord Zuckerman lamenting the fact that Nitze and Ball had withdrawn, for unknown reasons.[41] Ball's absence did not seem to matter; Nitze's mattered very much. Harwit instructed McMahon to film Nitze at a time he found convenient, so that the film could be shown in the Smithsonian Theater the night of 6 September.[42]

McMahon described the difficulties this raised in a memo of 31 July. Their A/V unit did not have the right equipment, renting it would be expensive; they were already over budget. There was no message from Nitze at the 6 September meeting.[43]

Solly Zuckerman did appear, and said things against nuclear weapons that were compatible with NASM attitudes. A similar message would have been unlikely from Paul Nitze. As Nitze's memoirs, and the two critical Nitze biographies reveal, his 1946 derogation of nuclear weapons rapidly morphed into a more belligerent posture. It is hard to find a weapons system that the later Nitze did not like. With the exception of his aberrant "walk in the woods" with Kvitsinskiy, the Soviet representative in the 1983 arms limitation talks, Nitze's activities were as ferociously pro-nuclear as anyone's. If one is to assess impact, surely his fanatical language in NSC-68, that trumpet call to cold war rearmament, where Nitze faced down Kennan, Bohlen, and much of the state department, shows early on his basic "you cannot have too much defense" posture.[44] In 1976, at a crucial juncture when American determination to out-nuke the Soviet was flagging, Nitze helped organize the Committee on the Present Danger. Had he been candid with Harwit in 1990, Harwit might not have been so anxious to have him enter the lists against *Enola Gay*. Paul Boller in a 1983 article has deliciously exposed how the American Left supported the atomic bombings: "Hiroshima and the American left: August, 1945."[45] That today's left, attacking the bombings, looks to rightists such as Nitze and Grew for support is no less ironic.

In every draft of the *Enola Gay* exhibit script, Nitze's "all the facts" early surrender paragraph appears, with only the modest qualifier "Others are less confident that the Japanese rulers would have accepted defeat." This usage was challenged by the veterans. Harwit describes the tussle over the USSBS quotation this way:

> We had extended debates with the Legion about whether a label summarizing the results of the United States Strategic Bombing Survey should be kept. The Legion argued that the survey's claim that Japan was virtually defeated before the dropping of the atomic bomb was postwar propaganda by those who wished to show the power of

conventional bombing and to establish an air force independent of the army. I retorted that the survey had been commissioned by President Roosevelt and had been delivered to President Truman. I saw no reason to accuse men like Paul Nitze, who had played a leading role in overseeing the survey and had later been an advisor to virtually every president of the United States since Roosevelt, of such motives. The label stayed. Months after the exhibition had been canceled, Hugh Dagley cited this particular label as one major reason for the Legion's insistence that the exhibition be canceled.[46]

After the *Journal of American History* published a series reflecting on the canceled *Enola Gay* exhibit in its December 1995 issue, this author wrote a critique of Harwit's dogged defense of Nitze, noting that Harwit could have sent any of his considerable staff to the National Archives and in a week that researcher could have found that Nitze, rather than summarizing the results obtained by USSBS, had ignored them and substituted his pre-investigation beliefs.[47] In answering this criticism, Harwit claimed poverty, and denied the role of original research for the museum in principle:

> The National Air and Space Museum's every statement on the subject made it clear that our aim was always to base our exhibits on the most up-to-date scholarship. We did not have the resources to critically examine primary documents on each and every issue ourselves. Nor, in so important an exhibition to be seen by millions of people, would a national museum have acted responsibly, if we had included new results stemming from our own research before our findings had been adequately vetted.[48]

Of course, this was not just "each and every issue," but a red flag waved before a bull. However, Nitze was to be believed implicitly; the museum said it could not afford to, and it clearly did not want to, check his credibility.

On the financial front, Harwit's statement is hard to credit. With a whole crew of researchers already on the payroll, it would have cost NASM perhaps fifty dollars to ship one of them over to the National Archives for a week. NASM spent many thousands shipping its officials to Japan.

And research? Commonsense would dictate that *the more important the exhibition, the more necessary that the museum verify statements made in "official" government reports*. After all, it was the "official" government report (mostly Stimson's *Harper's* article) that the curators were out to repudiate.

Von Hardesty, chair of NASM's aeronautics department, wrote Harwit on 28 December 1987 reporting on lengthy discussions in his shop, the consensus of which was that an exhibit on strategic bombing was "warmly endorsed and the proposed exhibition of the *Enola Gay* has been opposed for numerous reasons." One reason for opposing *Enola Gay* was that it would upset the restoration schedule. But more important, "who would provide intellectual leadership for such a complex undertaking? . . . Our concept of the exhibit remains vague and ill defined the assumption being that the exhibition would be relatively easy to fashion once we found a place for the *Enola Gay*. The research and preparation for this essential phase of the exhibit should not be underestimated."[49] Hardesty lost that battle.

Harwit is not entirely straightforward about his reasons for not researching USSBS findings. In places, he brags about the care with which *his* researchers vetted a script: "Once a script was drafted, half a dozen to a dozen members of the museum staff independently worked their way through it to verify facts and search for possible errors."[50] It is hard to believe that with Nitze's hypothesis so counterintuitive no one was assigned to check it out.

Here a judgment must be made as to whether museums should do significant research on their own. Otto Mayr, former curator of the National Museum of American History, says "Yes." In "The *Enola Gay* Fiasco: History, Politics, and the Museum," Mayr writes,

> For the defense of its intellectual independence, a museum needs a base that can withstand attack and that is professional, not political. It needs a source of intellectual authority from which to draw fresh information and original interpretation. This source can only be the museum's collections and its own original scholarship on these collections. If a museum merely disseminates the results of conventional academic scholarship, it does so on borrowed authority. The museum will be vulnerable to questions not only about the specific reliability of such secondhand contributions but also about the essential merits of its activity.[51]

One might add, if the borrowed authority contradicts the firm beliefs of almost all of the actors in the arena with which it is dealing—in this case the Pacific war—the "borrowed authority" of a small group of anti-Truman partisans none of whom are authorities on the Pacific war, on the Japanese decision, on the Soviet nuclear program, or on warfighting morality, is clearly not probative.

Some NASM "authorities" were especially vulnerable to challenge. Nitze, for instance, who claimed interrogations of Japanese officials were warrant for his early surrender hypothesis, could easily be proved wrong. Another NASM stalwart, Joseph Grew was not beyond challenge either. He was used in the exhibit text to establish some very doubtful claims, as this in Unit II:

> A key stumbling block to any Japanese surrender was the position of the emperor. To Japanese leaders, the Allied demands for "unconditional surrender" meant a destruction of the whole Japanese political system, including the monarchy. . . . Grew was the last United States Ambassador to Tokyo before the war. Although sympathetic to Japan, he supported stronger diplomatic action in 1940 as a warning against further Japanese aggression. . . . Beginning in May 1945, Grew urged President Truman to make an offer of surrender conditional upon the retention of Emperor Hirohito on the throne. Grew understood the mentality of the Japanese leadership, and he wished to end the war early to minimize Soviet influence in Asia. But Grew was unable to convince Truman and his key advisers . . . In hindsight, it is clear that American and Japanese leaders might have reached an agreement on Japanese surrender, if the United States had made such an offer . . . A question like this can never be settled, but it is possible that there was a lost opportunity to end the war without either atomic bombings or an invasion of Japan, if Grew's advice had been accepted.[52]

Grew's contentions cannot be rejected as surely as Nitze's, but had the curators been willing to read two or three relevant sources, readily available in 1994, they would have known that this line of thinking was also misleading. To begin with, Grew was a Boston mandarin, and mixed only with Japanese elites; he did not understand the Japanese military, or the common people. Had the curators read Nakamura Masanori's *The Japanese Monarchy: Ambassador Joseph Grew and the "Symbol Emperor" System*, published in 1992, they would have known Grew was not a reliable guide to Japanese action.[53] Unconditional surrender did not mean destruction of the whole Japanese political system to many Japanese leaders: Foreign Minister Togo; President of Privy Council Hiranuma; Kase Toshikazu, officer for American affairs in the Japanese Foreign Office; former foreign minister Shigemitsu Mamoru; and others all knew and said before August 1945 that surrender was demanded only of the armed forces. Japan was promised a government of its own choosing once it was demilitarized.[54]

As for the possibility of a pre-Hiroshima surrender if only the emperor were guaranteed, the curators should have read the whole series of MAGIC decrypts; they would then have known that the controlling military demanded not only retention of the emperor, but no foreign-conducted war crimes trials, no extended occupation, no forcible disarmament—and they demanded these things even after the Hiroshima bomb and the emperor's first call to surrender. Only after the Nagasaki bomb, proving that the atom was not a one-shot weapon, did the emperor prevail over Minister of War Anami Korechika. Sadao Asada's definitive analysis of the Japanese surrender decision in *Pacific Historical Review* (November 1998) put the Grew claim to rest.[55] Grew, as one of the earliest heralds of extreme anti-Soviet cold war agitation, was never an appropriate standard-bearer for late twentieth century peaceniks.

∽ ∽ ∽

One abortive effort to get a line on the best modern scholarship began when Harwit contacted Akira Iriye of Harvard, inviting Iriye to come to lunch when he was in Washington; Iriye came, was apparently supportive of Harwit's intentions and agreed to help NASM get in contact with Japanese scholars who were expert on the Pacific war.[56] Iriye didn't have addresses with him, so Harwit wrote for them; Iriye responded on 25 February 1993. Two senior professors who should be contacted were Makoto Iokibe of Kobe University, and Ikuhiko Hata of Takushoku University.[57] This is a slim list; there are many other prominent Japanese students of the end of the Pacific war. Iriye also gave Harwit the names of two junior scholars who had been students of Iriye.

NASM personnel (Harwit, Neufeld, Crouch) subsequently made three trips to Japan. Three of the four scholars recommended by Iriye were apparently not contacted at all. One junior scholar, Keiji Nakatsuji of Hiroshima University, was seen by Harwit, but the contact was so fleeting, or so discouraging, that Harwit does not mention Nakatsuji in his book. The archival records are crowded with names of Japanese who were important to Harwit, and whose opinions about his exhibit he solicited and recorded: journalists, Japanese diplomats, the directors of the Hiroshima and Nagasaki museums, their assistants, and their publicists; Japan Airlines employees; the director of the Radiation Effects Research Foundation; attachés in the American embassy, Tokyo; the mayors of Hiroshima and Nagasaki; a Japanese astrophysicist, and so forth. Crouch seems to have met several Japanese historians, but it is difficult to discern any outcome. Of the nineteen Japanese mentioned in the index of Harwit's book, only Iriye is a historian, and his forte is not Japan's decision to surrender, but the rarefied discussion of similarities between American and Japanese interpretations of Wilsonian idealism in international affairs.

Harwit's contacting Iriye suggests that the research sophistication of his staff left something to be desired. The curators should have known the names of the Pacific war scholars prominent in Japan. At least six university libraries in Washington, D.C., had subscriptions to the *Bulletin of Concerned Asian Scholars, Journal of Japanese Studies, Journal of Asian Studies, Japan Quarterly, Journal of American-East Asian Relations, Pacific Historical Review* and similar periodicals. Any Asian studies bibliographer could have introduced them to the volume edited by Sadao Asada in 1989: *Japan and the World 1853–1952: A Bibliographic Guide to Japanese Scholarship in Foreign Affairs.*[58] This includes a comprehensive description of the scholarship most relevant to the issues in *Enola Gay's* mission. Hosoya Chihiro's introductory chapter alone is essential background for anyone who wants to understand why Japan did what she did. Some of Hosoya's references are to monographs not then available in English; for a fraction of the cost of NASM pilgrimages to Japan they could have been translated.

Also in the Asada volume, Hatana Sumio's chapter, "Japanese Foreign Policy, 1931–1945" could have been the starting place for serious research. Asada and Hatana co-authored a chapter titled "From the Sino-Japanese War to the Pacific War"; they note that Japanese historians tend to accept P. M. S. Blackett's revisionist account of Truman's bomb decision, but they recognize the meager warrant for this judgment. They also display convincing evidence that the Greater East Asian War was Japanese aggression. Neither Harwit's account nor the Smithsonian archives show that any of Harwit's team was aware of this volume. Equally useful for anyone dealing with the Pacific war is the fifteen-volume set, *War in Asia and the Pacific,* edited by Donald S. Detwiler and published by Garland (New York and London) in 1980. For monolingual researchers unable to use the archives in Tokyo, this series is the best substitute. Detwiler's introduction notes that

> On 12 October 1945 . . . the Japanese government—which, unlike that of its German ally, had survived defeat—was ordered to establish "a bureau for investigations concerned with the compilation of sufficient data to obtain a complete historical war record." For this purpose, former Japanese military and naval officers were hired as civilians in the First and Second Demobilization Bureaus, the former Army and Navy sections of Imperial General Headquarters. Working under American direction, they began the compilation . . . of a series of some two hundred studies now on file. . . .[59]

If there had been any urge on the part of NASM curators to question the received wisdom on which they operated, they could have satisfied their curiosity by dipping into the Garland set, particularly the sections headed "Interrogations of Japanese Officials on World War II, Translations of Japanese Documents," and similar titles. This would have been easier than going to the National Archives and sitting in front of microfilm readers.

To deal with the most incendiary paragraph of the NASM exhibition text, however, the curators would have had to read English translations of Japanese historians. This paragraph, in Unit One of the first draft of the text, read (in full context):

> In 1931 the Japanese Army occupied Manchuria; six years later it invaded the rest of China. From 1937 to 1945, the Japanese Empire would be constantly at war.
>
> Japanese expansionism was marked by naked aggression and extreme brutality. The slaughter of tens of thousands of Chinese in Nanking in 1937 shocked the world. Atrocities by Japanese troops included brutal mistreatment of civilians, forced laborers and prisoners of war, and biological experiments on human victims.
>
> In December 1941, Japan attacked U.S. bases at Pearl Harbor, Hawaii, and launched other surprise assaults against Allied territories in the Pacific. Thus began a wider conflict marked by extreme bitterness. For most Americans, this war was fundamentally different than the one waged against Germany and Italy—it was a war of vengeance. For most Japanese, it was a war to defend their unique culture against Western imperialism. As the war approached its end in 1945, it appeared to both sides that it was a fight to the finish.[60]

The curators have it right about the bitterness of the fighting, and about Japanese atrocities. Many Americans did want to avenge Pearl Harbor, the Bataan Death March, the torture and degradation of Allied prisoners, the construction of the Death Railway in Thailand, or the starvation of General Wainwright. But how the war was fought, and why Americans were fighting, were not the points of contention here. Asserting that the Japanese were only fighting for their unique culture could only be done by someone totally ignorant of Japanese scholarship. Once this was in cold print, veterans and American scholars not bonded to the Nitze-Blackett narrative knew that this exhibit was perverse beyond belief. Eliminating this statement from subsequent drafts, with some slight embarrassment showing, did nothing to improve NASM credibility; it merely highlighted the real attitudes, and the ignorance, of the curators.

Geoffrey M. White, prominent Japanologist writing in *Asian Pacific Issues* of July 1995, worries not only about the inaccuracy of the unique culture statement, but about its impact on Japanese chauvinists:

> Citing the line most mentioned by American critics of the script, to the effect that the Japanese saw themselves fighting a war to "protect their unique culture against European imperialism," while the Americans were "fighting a war of vengeance," Japanese scholars worried that such language undercut their own efforts to counter conservative attempts to rationalize wartime aggression. Author Michio Saito wrote in the *Asahi Shimbun,* "I wonder if it is all right for an American to write such a thing. . . . It supports the Greater East Asia War in essence."[61]

Harwit and others attempted to defend the unique culture statement by saying that it was what the Japanese thought, not anything the NASM was claiming to be true. This only makes the absence of any serious scholarly understanding that much more obvious. Saying the media took this out of context is no better. The context in no way justifies the "unique culture" claim.

Iritani Toshio's *Group Psychology of the Japanese in Wartime* came out in 1991, in plenty of time for a curator to read it through before committing himself to paper.[62] It had a distinguished imprimatur, the assistance of the Japan Foundation and the Hoover Institution at Stanford. Iritani has strong moral objections to the atomic bombs, but he makes it abundantly clear that the Japanese people knew they were embarking on military expansionism. They welcomed it, and liked the war (until they started losing it). The Japanese were willing to fight to the last man, woman, and child even when the tide of battle turned against them, regarding themselves as victims only at the end, when they had killed some 20 million of their fellow Asians.

Kitahara Michio, a Japanese psychoanalyst, published his *Children of the Sun: The Japanese and the Outside World* with St. Martin's Press in 1989. At the same time Harwit was beginning his symposia with fifty "experts," Kitahara wrote,

> In 1938, the Japanese Government officially announced the formation of "The New Order in East Asia," in which the elimination of the western imperial powers from East Asia and the elimination of communism were among the stated objectives . . . the principle objectives of this plan . . . were in fact fully implemented—in the Japanese way. The massacres in Korea and China and in Southeast Asia at the hands of the Japanese armed forces were comparable in extent and brutality to the Nazi "holocaust" in Europe. Inasmuch as the Japanese were "superior," rationalization was easy, in the same way that the Nazis justified their actions.[63]

On page 87, explaining why during the American occupation the Japanese were remarkably cooperative with the warriors who had days before faced them in a war without mercy Kitahara says: "The reason seems to be that, in the eyes of the Japanese, there were far fewer atrocities than expected. Those who were familiar with the atrocities committed by the Japanese forces in various parts of Asia during the war were prepared to see similar actions by the soldiers of the Allied Powers." There were so few crimes of any kind during the occupation that despite the two atomic bombs and the destruction of all the big cities many Japanese saw the Americans as saviors.

Ienaga Saburo's *The Pacific War* (1978) was a standard account of that conflict on both sides of the Pacific long before Crouch and Neufeld set pen to paper. Ienaga is a pacifist; he is against atomic bombs; but he waged a twenty-nine-year battle against the Japanese Ministry of Education, which forced him to delete from a high school history book the statement: "World War II brought atrocities on an unprecedented scale, and they were an infamous hallmark of the Japanese military. . . . Here I wish to elaborate on this theme, and show by concrete examples that the Greater East Asian War, which has been glorified as a moral cause, was a dirty war of sadistic cruelty."[64] No one who reads Ienaga could ignore his caustic phrases about Japan's "culture." Harwit's people apparently never read them.

Tsurumi Shunsuke's *An Intellectual History of Wartime Japan* came out from Kegan Paul in 1986. Tsurumi is heavily influenced by the anti-Truman writings of the USSBS, Liddell Hart, and other Hiroshima activists. Harwit would have found support for much of his text in Tsurumi. But he would not have been able to incorporate the line about defending their unique culture. Tsurumi describes how self-defeating Japanese culture was, and how the kamikaze pilots forecast national self-destruction: "The tenet was that even when all the Japanese, including the emperor himself, had perished, that structure would remain. . . . Very few people in Japan doubted this line of reasoning. . . ."[65] National self-destruction does not seem to quite fit the NASM line about defending their unique culture.

Bamba Nobuya, prominent Japanese pacifist scholar, published (with John F. Howes) *Pacifism in Japan* with the University of British Columbia Press in 1978 — plenty of time for NASM curators to locate and use it. This book was cutting-edge scholarship at the time, not superseded since. Bamba had support from the Japanese Ministry of Education, The University of Toronto-York University Joint Centre on Modern East Asia, and a grant from the University of British Columbia. In the concluding chapter, we find this pungent statement:

> According to the Marxist interpretation of imperialistic war, the "people" should have been innocent, but they were not. The Japanese populace did not passively support the nation's military expansion, nor did they back the government simply because they feared the police. On the contrary, most people competed to get front seats on the fascist bandwagon, as the then common saying, "Basu Ni Noriokureruna" (Don't miss the bus) vividly suggests. It was rather the people that agitated for tough diplomacy.[66]

Even more devastating for the NASM account of Japan's war-making is the 1963 *Thought and Behaviour in Modern Japanese Politics* by Maruyama Masao published by Oxford with kudos from seven prestigious Asianists in Britain and the United States. Maruyama's influence endures; the January–March 1997 *Japan Quarterly* devotes a major article to his continuing prominence in Japanese historiography and politics. Maruyama wants to "broaden the perspective of my Marxist contemporaries." This means recognizing not just the class interests but the personal pathologies of Japan's fascist leaders, and by extension of their followers. If there is one book that the curators should have read to further their understanding of that "unique culture" that they so sympathetically presented in Unit Four (Ground Zero) of their text, it is this book. Murayama was blessed with a superb translator—Ivan Morris. The evidence of the Tokyo War Crimes Trials provides much of the grist for his account. He shows how the Japanese wanted war, but were afraid of war. No better distillation of what moved the Japanese state in 1941 can be found than this paragraph of Maruyama's:

> The men in the dock at the Tokyo trials had unquestionably been motivated by a common aspiration: the desire to establish a Greater East Asia Co-Prosperity Sphere, to

build up a new order with the "Eight Corners of the World under One Roof," to proclaim the Imperial way throughout the world. Not one of the defendants ever indicated that he regarded this as a mere quixotic dream. Some of them, it is true, were
inhibited by intellectual scruples from openly voicing their dream, while others,
though firmly believing that the dream would eventually come true, placed the happy
date rather further in the future; and even the most fanatic among them, as they gradually drew near to the windmill, were momentarily daunted by its size when compared with the puny lances in their hands. Yet all of them were driven ahead, as if by
some invisible force. Trembling at the possibility of failure, they still thrust their way
forward with their hands over their eyes.[67]

None of this Japanese research is discernible in the *Enola Gay* text. Its absence
was deplored by Ed Drea, a military historian at home in the Japanese sources, and
the author of two esteemed accounts of the end of the war. Drea was one of the
military historians conscripted by NASM when it became clear that the early drafts
of the exhibit text would not wash. In his report of 13 April 1994, Drea concludes
seven pages of comments with "The story line is an overview of 50 years of American historiography about the bomb. The glaring deficiency is the absence of 50
years of Japanese historiography on the same subject."[68]

Kawahara Toshiaki's *Hirohito and His Times* was published in 1990. Kawahara is
one of the Japanese historians who dared to repeat Hirohito's statement at a press
conference in 1975. "I feel that it was truly regrettable that the atomic bomb was
dropped. But it was in the midst of a war, and however tragic it may have been for
the citizens of Hiroshima, I believe it was unavoidable."[69] This would have produced a bit of "balance" for the script, had anyone at NASM been genuinely interested and assiduous.

Michael Barnhart, professor of history at SUNY Stony Brook and an Asianist
with impeccable credentials, has it right. In the 1997 review of scholarly books on
Japan-U.S. relations in *Journal of American History,* he highlighted the merit of
Japanese contributions, and says,

> An examination of their footnotes reveals how well versed each author is in trans-
> Pacific scholarship and research. Hiwatari found a gold mine in the records of the
> United States State Department's Office of Intelligence Research, for example. Hara
> plumbed the records of the American Embassy and copious American military
> records. Asada reveals intimate familiarity with the papers of Alfred T. Mahan, Theo-
> dore Roosevelt, Charles E. Hughes, Henry C. Lodge, and many others, in addition
> to an encyclopedic grasp of secondary literature by American historians. Now all the
> best work is being done by Japanese.[70]

None, however, was done by the NASM curators, or the Nitzeans on whom
they depended. To understand what a travesty of "modern scholarship" the *Enola
Gay* text is one must read the non-chauvinist, generally liberal Japanese scholars.

Whatever bizarre reason might explain the curator's failure to inspect accounts
of the war by Japanese historians it cannot explain why they chose to ignore the
many competent American Japanologists. Foremost among them would be John

Dower, author of the classic *War Without Mercy* and of the landmark *Embracing Defeat: Japan in the Wake of World War II*. Dower does not support Truman's bomb decision, but he is clear that unconditional surrender was necessary to reconstruct Japan, that the Japanese had probably slaughtered more than 15,000,000 Chinese plus millions of other Asians, that Japan had accumulated massive military stockpiles for a fight to the finish, and that there were no heroes among Japan's old elites, no counterparts to the opponents of Hitler who lost their lives opposing the Nazis.[71] Dower endorsed the final, much revised draft of the *Enola Gay* script; it is a tragedy that he was not intimately involved in the project from the beginning.

The same goes for Carol Gluck, professor of Japanese studies at Columbia; Robert Butow, then still teaching at the University of Washington; Alvin Coox, Japanese scholar/linguist whose many writings on the Japanese decision to surrender and the end of the war continued until his death in November 1999; Michael Barnhart, mentioned above; Norma Field at the University of Chicago; Ed Drea, then of the U.S. Army Center of Military History, now an independent historian, and others. These American scholars of Japan do not endorse the use of nuclear weapons in principle; some of them may feel that even the urgent need to stop the slaughter in the Pacific did not justify Hiroshima and Nagasaki. But any of them would have improved the fatal first script.

In addition to the complex of issues demanding knowledge of Japanese intentions, morale, and the meaning of the feeble "peace feelers," there was a cluster of issues the intelligent discussion of which demanded knowledge about the events of the Pacific war. What were the Japanese defense preparations for the last glorious "battle of the homeland" as revealed in the whole set of ULTRA decrypts? How serious were American problems of morale when troops who had fought in Europe were being sent to the Pacific? From which experts could Harwit and NASM get the best evidence on these topics? Since the most bitter criticisms were likely to come from veterans groups, Harwit's need for tapping the modern scholarly research of Pacific war historians was great. The Nitze-Blackett-Alperovitz-Sherwin axis was not in this category.

Harwit and Crouch knew and claimed to respect Richard H. Kohn, former air force historian and in the 1990s professor and head of the curriculum in peace, war, and defense at the University of North Carolina, Chapel Hill. Had NASM gone outside their clique of Nitzeans, they would have known, and heeded, the American Military Institute 1990 meeting, at which Kohn presided over a plenary session on "World War II Scholarship: Its Present Condition and Future Possibilities."[72] Kohn introduced the four speakers as "four distinguished historians," and indeed they were. One, Stephen E. Ambrose, was about to become the most-read historian in the United States, and was at that time Boyd Professor of History at the University of New Orleans. He was followed by Ronald H. Spector, whose *Eagle Against the Sun* is arguably the best book about the Pacific war by an American. In 1993, when Harwit sorely needed a prestigious war historian, Spector was just up the road from NASM, at George Washington University. Harwit's neglect of Spector has to be called obscurantism. Third, the Kenan Professor of Modern

History at UNC/Chapel Hill, Gerhard L. Weinberg, was about to publish what many believe to be the best one-volume account of World War II. Finally, Sir Michael Howard, former Regius Professor of History at Oxford, and in 1990 the Lovett Professor at Yale, gave his views on World War II scholarship.[73] Howard would be my choice as the greatest living World War II authority, but by the time Harwit might have tapped him, Howard was back at his country place in England. The other three would have been easily available. Harwit was not looking for them.

If the NASM staff had missed this parade of prestigious experts, which was written up in the July 1991 *Journal of Military History,* they should have connected with the announcements in several scholarly journals of a conference on the Pacific war in the spring of 1991 at the Eisenhower Center at the University of New Orleans.[74] Spector and Ambrose were participants in this conference also, and they were joined by seven other knowledgeable historians any one of whom would have graced Harwit's roster. NASM apparently missed the seminal paper on "Racism, the Atomic Bomb, and the Transformation of Japanese-American Relations" by Ambrose and Brian Loring Villa of Ottawa University. Again, none of the New Orleans experts appear in Harwit's narrative.

Of course, there are many other accomplished historians of World War II not featured at these conferences. It would have been easy for the NASM team to read the dozen or so military history journals to see who was regarded as outstanding. An exhibit team dedicated to utilizing the best scholarship would have read their books. Roy E. Appleman, Robert J. C. Butow, Alvin D. Coox, John Costello, Conrad Crane, Roger Dingman, William Craig, John J. Stephan, Michael Sherry, Mark Stoler, Christopher Thorne, all had written on the war to general approbation before 1995. Granted several of these were journalists, hence not kosher in some parts of the academy; but there were enough with sterling academic credentials to triple the credibility of Harwit's "modern expertise" contingent with one or two appointments.

Harwit had an aversion to "military" historians; he sometimes stated that there was an unbridgeable divide between military and academic historians.[75] This may have kept him and his curators from reading journals with "military" in the title, but he could also have explored the range of expertise he needed in the book review sections of *The American Historical Review, Journal of American History,* or the *Pacific Historical Review. The New York Review of Books* would also have stood NASM in good stead.

In the event, the only mainstream military historian of World War II actively consulted by NASM was Richard Kohn—months after the first, inflammatory draft of the text had been written. Harwit had an advisory committee (discussed later) to which drafts of the exhibit text were sent, and two scholars employed by the military were on it, but no leading Pacific war scholar from the academy. Harwit lays some of the blame for his troubles on what he calls the failure of this committee to provide "the substantive critique required." But from Kohn, he got that substantive critique in spades.

Kohn occupied (and occupies) a centrist position in military studies. A former chief of air force history, he is respected as a scholar of American military policy and civil-military relations. He understood NASM's situation and wanted to see the exhibit succeed. In one letter to Tom Crouch, he expostulated "Nothing in *Crossroads* [then the title of the exhibit] should be watered down; my recommendation is for balance, comprehensiveness, accuracy, and as little tendentiousness or moralizing as possible. Damn, Tom, I'm a bleeding heart, in truth, too, and view the people of the Japanese cities in much the same way as you."[76] And at the conclusion of his major critique, written 18 June 1994 to Harwit, Kohn says:

> Martin, I know this might be troublesome. But in my judgment, the stakes are extraordinary. This exhibit is the most important to be mounted in the nation's capital for the next ten years—a decade in which the world will struggle with nuclear proliferation and adjustment to a post–cold war international system. . . . Besides the millions of citizens and influential people, countless national and world leaders will visit the Museum in this decade before you move the airplane and exhibit to Dulles—and probably then, too. This exhibit will be the most graphic, intimate, and personal exposure they will ever have to nuclear weapons and their use (at least we hope!). If there is the least hint of bias, of polemics, or moralizing, of a political agenda, the credibility of the exhibit and the Museum will be lost. The educational value of the exhibit will be lost. The Museum will then have blown the greatest educational opportunity it ever possessed of contributing to world peace.[77]

So what provoked this burst of passion? His critique summarized Harwit's product: "What I'm saying is that your history is bad: unbalanced, skewed, misapplied . . ." There are sixteen pages of critique in the letters I found in the archives. From this accomplished and sympathetic scholar, the indictment of NASM's tendentious script is compelling.

From the 18 June letter to Harwit:

> My overall reaction is to understand more fully the objections of the Air Force Association. . . . The draft I read . . . while extraordinarily good, *is* somewhat unbalanced, political, and moralizing, and needs to be fixed. . . . There is no explanation of what this war was about . . . and particularly the Japanese goals in the war . . . Allied goals and methods in strategic bombing are not very explicitly explained, and given such scholarship as Sherry's book, that is inexcusable; the interpretation here is almost as though the two sides 'fell into it' out of the orgy of destruction. The discussion of the decision to use the bomb, or the causes of its use, comes off as a miasma of historical controversy rather than as a historical event that is the occasion—*indeed the most important historical event.* . . . the discussion of the decision by Japan to surrender is superficial and abrupt, and not at all connected to the bomb, even by sufficient speculation. [Kohn's emphases]
>   The Kurt Vonneguts of the world would like to make Dresden the symbol of the American strategic bombing campaign in Europe, but historians know that it was not. This section needs to matter-of-factly explain what the Americans and British wanted to do, what they did, and why, over the course of the conflict. EG: 122-L2 doesn't really explain LeMay's decision to go low-level incendiary at night. . . . In

other words, the policy, strategy, operational, and tactical context of the decision needs explication, rather than leaving it to the jet stream and the "context" of "racial bitterness" and "hatred" that is implied in the exhibit as a whole. . . . I suggest you and the curators take a look at Brigadier General George A. Lincoln's memorandum to the War Department Historical Office in mid-1946, in the Lincoln Papers at the West Point Library.

I've always thought the casualty argument was simple-minded and lacking in context. The real issue was the campaign, not just the invasion. With Japan prepared to fight all-out indefinitely, and having stockpiled 9,000 aircraft, most for kamikaze use, the casualties would have been just tremendous on *both* sides, and everybody at the time knew it. That should be explained; planners put in numbers because that is necessary for logistical and other reasons, but to argue about them is utterly to miss the point, and that is what scholars have done. The controversy over numbers trivializes the business. If one were to project Iwo Jima and Okinawa onto Japan, the numbers are horrendous—and this whole dispute is in my judgment an embarrassment to the historical profession.[78]

And on the failure of the text to explain the pressures on the government to end the fighting as soon as possible, Kohn observes "This whole discussion has the tone of special pleading and polemics." Again he recommends the Lincoln memorandum as the best evidence for what the government thought it was doing.

Kohn has a suggested addendum for the section of the text headed "A WORLD GONE MAD." "The text is out of date . . . attention should be paid to people like Gaddis and Mearsheimer, who have begun to advance the concept of the 'Long Peace' and the stabilizing effects of nuclear weapons . . . in the future, it may turn out to be thought that nuclear weapons, and perhaps even the atomic bombing, saved what could have been a massive, World War III bloodletting . . . by deterring all sorts of wild plans."

On one of the scripts Kohn critiqued, Gerhard Weinberg also made comments. These, plus the sober and reasonable critiques from the Veterans of Foreign Wars, Retired Officers Association, and the six service historians, produced major changes in the text, but not enough to disguise its basic anti-Truman thrust.[79] Paul Tibbets's comment on the first draft, that it was "a package of insults," might not have applied to the fifth draft. Despite the changes, the Lincoln memo was not used (nor did I find it in the records).

At the height of the public controversy, Gregg Herken suggested staging a public symposium that would demonstrate the museum's probity, and show that "we're not making up an historical controversy, just reporting it." [Of course, Nitze "made up" the basic controversy in the USSBS report of 1946.]

Gregg Herken to Martin Harwit et al., 31 August 1994:

Since the Museum is under attack for siding with "kooks" and "revisionists" on the questions of whether the bomb ended the war and how many American lives were saved, why not show our critics that there is a legitimate debate over these questions by sponsoring a symposium where these issues would be debated. . .

The "dream team" would be:

Paul Fussell on why the bomb was necessary
Bart Bernstein on why a million lives weren't saved
Marty Sherwin on why the bomb wasn't necessary
An AFA spokesperson—Correll?—on the USAF point of view
Richard Rhodes as the moderator
It might be better to do the symposium sooner than later, given the fever pitch in the media.[80]

Had this come off, the "fever" in the media and elsewhere would have been pitched to a new height. Few more explosive combinations are imaginable.

Not only were there rich but unexplored resources that Harwit might have tapped for modern scholarship on Japan's decision to surrender and on the USSBS claim that the bomb was not necessary, but one needs to take a brief look at available scholarship on several domestic issues: Truman's reasons for deciding to use the bomb, whether he "knew" there were alternatives that would have yielded surrender in the summer of 1945, whether the bomb would have been dropped on the Nazis had it been ready in time, whether he "ignored" legitimate Japanese peace feelers, whether his various six-figure estimates for casualties in Olympic were "postwar inventions," and similar matters. The Nitzeans depended on by the NASM curators certainly claimed expertise in these areas. Might their bias have been colored by generational factors, such as their coming of age academically with the Vietnam revulsion and the charismatic draw of William Appleman Williams? Inspecting indices of bias in their findings would take a long monograph; here it is only necessary to note the mainstream Truman scholars, who were not consulted, perhaps not even read, by NASM. It is not unreasonable to claim that for at least the appearance of fairness, NASM should have balanced the anti-Truman stance of the Nitzeans by consulting and incorporating, if not privileging, the work of Bert Cochran, Robert Donovan, Robert Ferrell, Norman Graebner, Alonzo Hamby, Richard Kirkendall, Michael Lacey, David McCullough, and David McLellan. It will not pass muster for NASM to pretend that only Truman's critics have the truth, and that mainstream historians are unworthy of consideration.

This brings us to unit 5 of the *Enola Gay* text, headlined in bold type "THE LEGACY OF HIROSHIMA AND NAGASAKI." In small print underneath, we read "The introduction of nuclear weapons into the world, and their first use at Hiroshima, left powerful legacies beyond the long-term radiation effects on the survivors. For Japan, the United States, and its allies a horrific war was brought to an abrupt end, although at a cost debated to this day; for the world, a nuclear arms race that still threatens unimaginable devastation."[81]

This unit of the script, to some of the curators, was the most important part of the exhibit. Hiroshima and Nagasaki were bad enough, but the uncontrollable proliferation during the cold war—"A WORLD GONE M.A.D." is one NASM heading—was an intolerable legacy.

What did *Enola Gay* contribute to this arms race? Surely the major source of relevant information would be the records and testimony of the American authorities who decided to expand the nuclear arsenal and build H-bombs; and the records and testimony of the Soviet officials involved in their decisions to match or exceed the United States. Such elementary conclusions about necessary research were not made.

For the American decision to build the H-bomb, two of the primary actors were easily available to NASM: Paul Nitze and Edward Teller. Neither was brought in to discuss the H-bomb decision. Bart Bernstein, who wrote an excellent analysis of that decision, was apparently never asked about it.[82] A relevant article by David Alan Rosenberg, also an authority on this, was listed in the suggested readings worked up by the curators to accompany the exhibit, but apparently Rosenberg was never consulted.[83]

Nor was the other party to the "race," the Soviet Union, represented in the list of authorities consulted by NASM. David Holloway of Stanford had written prominent books about the Soviet nuclear arms program; so had Steven Zaloga who was closer to Washington, in Connecticut. Neither was consulted. A young Russian scholar, Vladimir Zubok, located in Washington, D.C., had published on the Soviet nuclear program in 1994; NASM appears not to have heard of him.[84]

Where did they get their take on the escalation of the arms race? From Martin Sherwin, whose *A World Destroyed: Hiroshima and the Origins of the Arms Race,* was the important Nitzean work of the 1970s. Sherwin's ethnocentricity somewhat lessens the value of his analysis. Any monocausal approach to something as complicated as an arms race has to be suspect. By definition, a race involves two parties. The United States built the first two atomic bombs, and used them to shock Japan into surrender. Sherwin follows this narrative in detail. But what was happening with the other party to the race? We know that as soon as the Soviet Union learned from Fuchs and Rosenberg about Manhattan, the arms race was on. Did the mission of *Enola Gay* significantly affect the Soviet program? Yes. How do we know? Not from Sherwin. His one grudging acknowledgment of a Soviet authority was a quotation attributed to Gen. G. K. Zhukov.[85] Stalin wanted to hurry up the Soviet program when he learned from Truman at Potsdam about the new weapon, but the arms race was already underway.

Research based on recent openings of Soviet archives, as summarized by Zubok in 1999 in "Stalin and the Nuclear Age," tells the story:

> Some historians believe that until Hiroshima, Stalin did not appreciate the significance of the bomb. Thomas B. Cochran and Robert Standish Norris argue that Stalin and Beria "in particular" may not have comprehended the significance of the Trinity test. The main argument in favour of this supposition is that Stalin did not sanction the crash atomic program immediately after Truman's announcement: he did so only on 20 August, two weeks after Hiroshima, and more than a month after Trinity. . . . This interpretation, in my view, is based on a misunderstanding of the character and content of Stalin's choices at the time. Hiroshima made a big impression on Stalin, but already at Potsdam, he must have appreciated the significance of the bomb (and his own miscalculation). According to Georgi Zhukov, Stalin said at Potsdam: "I should talk to Kurchatov about the acceleration of our works."[86]

Significantly, this 1999 state-of-the-art Zubok article does not mention Sherwin's accounts of the arms race.

But NASM wanted to highlight the arms race; the curators could have pointed to what was arguably the *most* important consequence of the use of these two bombs: people saw how terrible they were, and they have never been used since. The "inoculation" phenomenon has been widely discussed.[87] Although Truman was tempted to use nuclear weapons when the Eighth Army was all but destroyed in Korea, Nixon contemplated their use in Vietnam, and the Soviets solicited American connivance to use them to destroy the Chinese nuclear installation at Lop Nor in the 1960s, a tradition of nonuse has taken hold. Richard Rhodes, one of Harwit's advisors, mentioned that "Deterrence seems to work at every level except the one unique situation in 1945, when we were the only nation in the world that had a nuclear capacity."[88] And Leo Szilard admitted at one time in his quixotic career (though *this* is not cited by NASM) that only a full wartime deployment could convince the world of their potency.[89] Szilard later changed his mind, but subsequent events bear out his earlier opinion, and a balanced *Enola Gay* exhibit would have included it.

Harwit also had advice from Michael Sherry, author of a prominent anti-airpower book, who encouraged Harwit in a letter of 2 June 1994 to hang tough against the "undue influence that the Air Force Association and others are attempting to exercise."[90] Sherry's advice is to retain the photos and artifacts showing the bomb's effects; not surprising from an opponent of strategic bombing. But there is this startling additional line: taking out the graphics "would deny viewers an important way to understand the non-use of nuclear weapons after World War II." Are we to understand that the inoculation argument is valid? Harwit's answer to Sherry seems elliptical to this reader, but it may be significant that after a substantive response, "I appreciate your understanding of the pressures being exerted on the Museum and our attempts to resist them," Harwit takes a methodological flier: "On quite another matter, I still remember reading your book on air power, when I first came to the Museum seven years ago, and learning a great deal from it. I also remember the talk you gave here some years later, which I thought was particularly interesting, reminding me somewhat of the work of deconstructionists like Culler and Derida [sic], who came at quite different questions from somewhat similar analytic points of view."[91] Anyone who lets Derrida into the zoo of nuclear antagonists has a lot to answer for.

Victor Bond, the physicist M.D. Harwit chose for his advisory committee, told NASM the "Legacy" section was wrong: "I do not believe that it was the Japanese bombings that left us a legacy of a nuclear arms race. It was the building and perfection of atomic weapons, and the cold war that provided this legacy, which very likely would have been present whether or not atomic weapons were dropped on Japan."[92] Harwit was not listening. The Nitze-Blackett contribution to *Enola Gay's* narrative was too firmly fixed in his mind.

The impetus behind the cold war arms race, the question of whether the Soviet threat was ever a warrant for our massive nuclear buildup, continues to produce legitimate controversy. After this manuscript was begun, I received a release from the Chief Attorney's Office, Department of the Army, responding to an FOIA request for materials in Record Group 59, National Archives, originating with the Policy Planning Staff. That office, then (1950) headed by Paul Nitze, had been constructing the clarion call to arms known as NSC-68 as noted in chapter two. Among other documents with which Nitze's group dealt was a "Statement of Mr. Charles E. Bohlen before the Voorhees Group on April 3, 1950." The ways of the bureaucracy, including the declassification bureaucracy, are devious and wonderful; I had thought all the documents applied for in this FOIA request had already been provided. Now the Bohlen statement came.

Why it should have been the last, or at least among the last, of the "secrets" of NSC-68 to be cleared might be inferred from Bohlen's comments. He covers the whole range of defense-related matters: the difference in the meaning of "security" in the United States and Europe, European fears of being "mashed up" if war started before strong U.S. forces were available to defend them, and the fear of France going neutral. His bottom line as I see it: "It is my belief that the Russians are not deterred from fighting now primarily by our stockpile of A-bombs. I have not been able to detect the slightest influence on Russian policy resulting from our possession of the A-bomb."[93] Why did they not attack? Stalin feared our overall economic strength. Bohlen and his counterpart Kennan were holdouts against the alarmism of 1950; his testimony serves in the twenty-first century to challenge part V of the *Enola Gay* script, that the arms race was a legacy of Hiroshima.

A final category of authorities whose work would be vital to this exhibit is the warfighting theorists, or ethicists. After all, the point of the whole exhibit was to ask the question, "Was the decision to drop the bomb justified?" This *has* to include an ethical component. Nevertheless NASM chose to finesse it: let the viewers decide on *this* one at least, after they have been through the emotionally charged galleries. Granted that ethical theory of any sort can be obscure and ethereal; there are still some approaches to the problem that can be adapted to nonphilosophers. One senses from immersion in the paper trail of this exhibit that ethics was not dealt with because the mindset of the curators precluded the very possibility of an intellectual (or moral) justification of the bombing. This was a shortsighted view, as chapter seven will contend. Moralists distinguish between acts of deliberate evil and acts in which evil happens without intent or foreknowledge. Though he denied it, Truman reacted to the carnage in Hiroshima with moral revulsion, and this reaction is widespread and legitimate. These *are* genocidal weapons; they *do* belong in the same category as poison gas and biological warfare. But this was not known before their use. What was known was that the Japanese empire was killing millions of Asians, and that this killing was accelerating as defeat loomed. There was a good case for using a new powerful weapon to bring the war to a close, perhaps even a weapon as horrible as the atom. Fixated on the presumed mendacity of Truman's claim that he was saving the lives of millions of American boys, the continual loss of millions of Asian lives escaped the attention of NASM. It should not have. In the archives is a letter from Dr. Y. C. L. Susan Wu, pleading with Harwit to put the mission of the *Enola Gay* in perspective, which here means acknowledging the horror that Japan created for its conquered territories: "Living under Japanese occupation, I know that early ending of the war stopped the meaningless killings and sufferings of everyone, including the Japanese."[94] It was another message that Harwit did not want to hear.

The most popular work dealing with wartime morality is Michael Walzer's *Just and Unjust Wars*.[95] He condemns use of the atom against Japan. Unfortunately, he is ill informed about the Pacific war, or was when he wrote the book in 1977. In 1995, he had some second thoughts. He was by then prepared to deal with the inoculation argument: "The argument is that the reason nuclear weapons have not been used since 1945 is that they were used then. The bombings did not break down a moral limit or set a precedent for the future, as critics at the time argued they would do. Quite the contrary: nuclear terrorism has, so far, had no copycats. . . . we might describe this outcome as Harry Truman's moral luck: that what he did in 1945, however horrifying at the time turned out to have long-term benefits."[96] Luck? Perhaps, or perhaps Truman knew how catastrophic the Pacific war was for *all* involved, and calculated correctly that extreme means were warranted to end it.

Were one to attempt to package warfighting morality for consumption in the arena of public discourse, there are better sources than Walzer. Sheldon Cohen, in *Arms and Judgment* (1988), is sophisticated but clear.[97] Surely the public viewers of an exhibit designed to make them *think* about the consequences of the flight of *Enola Gay* deserve no less.

As perceived by anti-Truman writers, a righteous, liberal, scholarly account of *Enola Gay*'s mission—that is, the NASM account built on Nitze and Blackett—was challenged and its authors forced to recant.[98] The belief that the challenge was justified, and the recantation proper, has great currency with the generation that came of age by the 1940s. But more than generational viewpoints are involved—there are politics.

NASM curators observed in horror that when disaffected veterans groups began looking for support, they found it in right-wing politicians. The left, which dominates in academia as it did in NASM, found the politicians had better media skills and deeper pockets. To the academy, it was poor but honest scholars versus corrupt and chauvinistic politicians.

When Michael Neufeld at NASM asked Martin Sherwin for permission to refer hostile inquiries to him, Sherwin responded succinctly (11 April 1994): "Absolutely. You may give out my name, and I will tell them that if the display followed their wishes you would be doing mythology rather than history. None of this surprises me. (What possessed the museum to take this on????) The Right is always there at the starting gun, and the Left is invariably late. The fun hasn't even begun."[99] Sherwin was wrong; the "fun" began in 1946.

Neufeld responded belatedly to Sherwin 19 May; he was hired to do the exhibit. He was not enjoying it, and *Time* just did "a trashing of our exhibit disguised as a news story. It's right out of the pages of the Air Force Association magazine . . . It is of course up to you if you want to insert yourself at all into these battles, especially in view of the fact that you thought the exhibit too far to the right already."[100]

By the beginning of 1994, Harwit's repetition of the claim that NASM tapped unimpeachable scholarship began to run into trouble. He concluded that perhaps his in-house crew was not up to staging an exhibit that could be adequately defended against the many historians and veterans who believed that dropping the bombs had ended the war sooner than any alternative and was justified by the outcome. Perhaps it was time to bring in some outside advisors.

He appointed a committee. Its nine members were the "experts," the practitioners of modern research before whom many commentators on the *Enola Gay* affair genuflected. While the authorities whose works were incorporated in the anonymous script remained out of sight, the nine-person advisory committee assumed much of the spotlight. These nine scholars did provide some of the requisite expertise missing from the NASM staff.

Heading the list, Barton Bernstein of Stanford probably rates as the best informed student of the decision making in the American government that led to the bombing of Hiroshima and Nagasaki. Bernstein is not a fanatic, has shown the ability to change his mind when new evidence appears, and has often pointed out the misrepresentations of evidence made by some of the polemicists.[101] He supported the original *Enola Gay* exhibit, writing many long letters to the curators advising them how to handle their press problems. Unfortunately, he did not warn them that his researches into USSBS showed Nitze to be way off base.

Richard Hallion, air force historian, brought his colleague Herman Wolk with him to Harwit's meetings. He and Wolk wrote a three-page critique of the NASM script that Harwit claims is "generally favorable," and at the end of it, Hallion wrote "Again—an impressive job! A bit of 'tweaking' along the lines discussed here, should do the trick. . . . "[102] As I read the text of the Hallion-Wolk commentary, there is much about the script they think unsound. Later, when accused of changing his tune, Hallion said his "impressive job" comment was just to appear helpful. The sum total of the Hallion-NASM interactions in the archives leaves the feeling that there was more bad blood than misunderstanding.

Akira Iriye of Harvard was also a paper member of the committee; he was unable to attend its meetings. He has devoted his scholarly life to improving Japanese-American relations, and his viewpoint needed to be included, as it was through correspondence. Despite his long attention to trans-Pacific affairs, there is some question as to his understanding of the Pacific war. In his most prominent work, *Power and Culture,* Iriye holds that the peace forces in Japan were much stronger than other historians believe, and as John Dower, himself a monumental figure in trans-Pacific scholarship observes, "Iriye's approach to the cultural significance of the war between Japan and the United States is so highly selective that it can be argued he has bent the conventional sense of culture, vague as it may already be, almost beyond recognition. The suggestion that there may have been serious lost opportunities for a peace settlement in 1944 or early 1945 remains almost unbelievable, and the small murmurs about peace which Iriye seizes upon seem as candles set against an inferno of hate."[103] Iriye did not approve the changes made in the first edition of the script; he did not think that the script "made the United States look like the aggressor and Japan as the victim."[104]

Edward Linenthal, prominent student of museums, who wrote on the U.S. Holocaust Memorial Museum brought a keen sense of the dynamics of memorials, and an open mind to the NASM deliberations. He understood, perhaps better than anyone, the intensity of the conflict between heroic and tragic modes of remembrance. Harwit chose well here.[105]

Martin Sherwin of Dartmouth was the most evangelical Nitzean on the committee. His position on the origin of the nuclear arms race has been discussed previously. Here it need only be added that the attack from the veterans and the right-wing politicians enraged him; he warned an audience at the 1995 meeting of the Organization of American Historians that the attack on NASM was part of a widespread attempt to stifle critical inquiry in the United States, and if this attempt were not stopped, it would "wrap itself around the First Amendment like a boa constrictor."[106] Grant the colorful analogy, but even serpents have specialized tastes. This boa constrictor only gorged on U.S. government museums which were spending the people's money in a bad cause. American University was not afraid of his boa constrictor, and its 1995 *Enola Gay* exhibit displayed many of the artifacts and anti-Truman documents of the canceled NASM script with no sign of trouble.[107] Harwit, who was well aware of Sherwin's fanaticism, should have conscripted a mainstream cold war historian to create at least the appearance of balance. This did not happen.

The late Stanley Goldberg was a historian of science and a biographer of Gen. Leslie Groves. He wanted more "interview materials of people who shaped the atomic bomb program." His view was that Truman was constrained by the momentum of the atomic project and could not have canceled the use of the first fruits. His contribution to the committee seems to have been modest.

Victor Bond was a prominent radiation physicist; Harwit named him "to make sure we had properly presented the medical effects suffered by the population exposed to atomic radiation."[108] Harwit got more than he bargained for; Bond dissented from NASM conclusions.

Edwin Bearss, chief historian of the National Park Service, was a wounded and decorated veteran of the assault on Guadalcanal and was involved in the fiftieth anniversary of Pearl Harbor. This was an appropriate background, but his scholarship (fourteen books) relates entirely to Civil War battlefields and national historical sites.

Richard Rhodes, Pulitzer Prize winner for *The Making of the Atomic Bomb*, was soon to publish *Dark Sun* about the hydrogen bomb. His report to Neufeld of 25 February 1994 brought up the "deterrence works" argument, and seven pages of other cogent comments. He begins this report with "I'm sorry our collective comments at the meeting pissed you off, but then you asked for free advice, so you shouldn't have been surprised. And in fact all that back-and-forth was probably helpful, at least to illustrate what the exhibit will face from the critical press. Though perhaps not quite so obtusely as Marty Sherwin's complaints. Whew."[109]

These were the nine Harwit chose. They met only once and without Iriye. Harwit was not happy:

> I was disappointed that most of the committee members concentrated on only one or two topics of current academic research interest, leaving whole portions of the exhibition untouched. Several times during the day I asked the committee to discuss other aspects, but the debate invariably gravitated back to the decision to drop the bomb and the necessity for dropping it. Normally, the expert advisory committees the museum appointed gave us far broader, more dispassionate advice."[110]

Any museum curator venturing into a controversial area would be wise to include advisors known to be hostile toward the museum's dominant opinion. Unlike Lyndon Johnson who kept George Ball around to get a second opinion on Vietnam (which, sadly, LBJ then disregarded), Harwit could not claim that he included a known naysayer in his group. Note, however, that Harwit sought the expertise of these wise men *after the first draft of the exhibit script had been completed.*

With the exception of the Truman administration category, where Bernstein would rank very high, none of them are in the first rank of scholars in the *vital* fields. The Smithsonian could have commandeered the very best for this committee, even if Harwit was unable to get his first choice as project director. He desperately needed the top person in Pacific War history, and Ronald Spector was five minutes away. If Bart Bernstein could have made it from Stanford, so could David Holloway. Iriye was prominent, but not the best person for Japan's decision to surrender; if Harwit could not have persuaded Asada to come from Japan, Robert Butow could have made it from Seattle. An ethicist? This probably never crossed his mind, though there is a prima facie case for one. As the committee divided on the advice it gave, two (Sherman, Iriye) wanted a text at least as anti-Truman as the first draft; the rest wanted improvements. No one, with the possible exception of Rhodes and Linenthal, anticipated the intensity of the storm that was about to break.

A final fix on NASM's claim to have tapped the best modern scholarly research can be had by looking at the "Suggestions for Further Reading" bibliography, draft #2, July 1994, designed to be part of the exhibit catalog which was to be available when the show opened (this catalog was not published).[111] If Harwit's list of consultants is ethnocentric and lacking in top people for the most vital subjects, this bibliography is positively parochial. Among the seventy-six items, there are exactly four Japanese authors, only one of whom has standing as an authority. But two books by Gen. Curtis LeMay are included, as is Fussell's *Thank God for the Atomic Bomb,* and a book of pictures drawn by atomic bomb survivors. A *Time-Life* book is included. Perhaps one should not look for scholarship in a list designed for the non-specialist public, except that the museum had made such a fetish out of it.

~ ~ ~

As an extended historical argument, the atomic bomb decision requires several judgment calls. Bernstein and most of the NASM curators believe that one can legitimately invoke such data as Eisenhower's and Leahy's claims that the bomb had not been necessary, even though those warriors had no adequate foundation for such claims, and even though they were postwar creations. They were, Bernstein says, part of a "rich area of dispute and controversy" and hence need to be considered.[112] He holds it is probative that Ike turned against the bomb, if in retrospect. I do not find this convincing. Of course such statements are part of the historical discourse; however, it is not a "rich area," but has been polluted at the source by the Nitze fraud. And when they are presented as arguments *for* the anti-Truman position, even though they are mistaken (as Bernstein argues Eisenhower's claim to have advised against using the bomb is mistaken), they should have no weight and should not be used.[113] We do not advance the arguments *for* slavery as probative even though they were part of the historical discourse, since we now do not credit them. Yet it is precisely to influence *present* opinion that the NASM text uses such artifacts, not just for purposes of understanding how the argument developed. Ike and his fellow warriors were not credible authorities on Japan's surrender then, and they are not now. There was no "rich" area of dispute and controversy; there was only a long concatenation of error beginning with USSBS.

Which brings us to "Who *are* the best authorities now?" There has been much published since 1994. By all odds the most compelling is Sadao Asada's November 1998 *Pacific Historical Review* article, "The Shock of the Atomic Bomb and Japan's Decision to Surrender—a Reconsideration," which can lay valid claim to be based on "all the facts," as Nitze's hyperbolic boast could not. The flood of materials that became available with the death of Hirohito has now been largely digested by Japanese scholars, of whom Asada is foremost. This article can truly be called a landmark history.

Also of landmark status is John Dower's multiple award-winning *Embracing Defeat* of 1999. This book is a sobering account of the worst features of Japan's empire and of the American occupation, both of which are duly excoriated. Also important is Herbert Bix's, *Hirohito and the Making of Modern Japan*, published in 2000. Richard B. Frank's *Downfall* is a seminal work, though the academy will probably not recognize the merits of a work not done by one of its anointed. Edward Drea's *In the Service of the Emperor*, Yukiko Koshiro's *Trans-Pacific Racisms*, John Lewis Gaddis et al. *Cold War Statesmen Confront the Bomb*, Michael Pearlman's *Warmaking and American Democracy*, Frank Gibney's *Senso*, D. M. Giangreco's *Journal of Military History* and *Pacific Historical Review* casualty studies, Stanley Weintraub's *The Last Great Victory*, and Robert Maddox's *Weapons for Victory* all provide key insights.

There remains the searing insight of Pamela Laird writing on "The Public's Historians" in the July 1998 *Technology and Culture*. She says, "Publicizing proof that decision makers had reasonable alternatives would portray veterans as brave dupes, at best; they could not be heroes, for heroes slaughter civilians only for good cause."[114] Of course the so-called alternatives were not that at all, they were simply other facets of an overall strategy to force Japanese surrender, and were pursued simultaneously. There was only a long acceptance of Nitze's fraud embellished by generations of partisan polemics that never engaged its foundation myth.

Tom Crouch was right. A national government museum could not make a whole generation of veterans out to be dupes even for the sake of argument, and survive the attempt. Edward Linenthal believes that forcing reconciliation on veterans who are not ready, as was tried at Pearl Harbor in 1989, will be oppressive. And when apparent apology was forced on Pacific war veterans by NASM in 1995, it was perceived as oppressive. No individual veteran could know that his life was saved by the bomb, as the invasion might have been called off to wait for a million Japanese to starve, or there might have been no bullet with his name on it. But each veteran knew that the invasion was scheduled, and that the slaughter would be tremendous if it came off. Those truths were worth more than NASM's sloppy "research."

Any account of this argument should show the basic accuracy of what veterans "knew" about the end of the war, and how, far from being "dupes," they were possessed of a significant body of fact. They knew, because they had observed, that (1) Most Japanese would fight to the death rather than surrender; (2) Japanese resistance to American advances grew more intense the closer the fighting got to Japan's home islands; (3) Okinawa proved that outnumbered and undersupplied Japanese troops could decimate attacking Americans; (4) Germany, though more completely devastated than Japan, surrendered only when Allied armies occupied the homeland, and (5) The Potsdam Declaration setting forth reasonable surrender terms was rejected by the Japanese Government. Their accusers, by contrast, offered not facts, but a fraudulent account of Japan's willingness to surrender. In any unbiased historigraphic evaluation, the veterans win hands down.

7

A TRANSNATIONAL NARRATIVE
Recognizing the Claims of Japan's Victims

As Americans, we are genuinely appreciative of you and your staff's efforts in preparing the exhibit of "The Last Act: The Atomic Bomb and the End of World War II." But as Asian-Americans, particularly those of Chinese descent, we feel being ignored and insulted, simply because while in the 14 years of war (1931–1945) between China and Japan, the Japanese had virtually killed over 30 million Chinese, nearly 90 percent of them being innocent civilians, more than the casualties of all our Allies in World War II combined, no Chinese Holocaust which is doubtless worse than that of the Jewish has been planned in your exhibit. Any discussion on war in Asia without due emphasis on the Sino-Japanese War is a distortion of truth and history.

ASTRID PEI TO MARTIN HARWIT 18 SEPTEMBER 1994[1]

Awareness of the death and destruction caused by Nazi Germany is widespread in the United States. Even my college senior students, for whom World War II is a hopelessly distant event despite the best efforts of Tom Brokaw, know about the six million—the number of Jews killed in the Holocaust. Ask them about the damage done by the Japanese empire, and they will know we lost a few thousand sailors at Pearl Harbor, a "whole bunch of Chinese were killed at Nanjing," and some of them have heard of Bataan and the Bridge on the River Kwai. What was the total carnage caused by the Japanese? I have yet to hear a student estimate in seven figures. Yet the conservative scholarly estimate of persons killed by the Japanese, most of them Asians, is 20 million. Why the German awareness, but the Japanese memory hole?

Part of the explanation was discussed in the previous chapter. The onset of the cold war, with the most traumatic events (China going Communist, North Korea attacking the South) involving Japan directly, made Americans conscious of Japan's worth as an ally. This was a powerful engine for amnesia. One of the most remarkable phenomena was the negotiation of national self-images. During the war, both nations portrayed the enemy as inherently inferior. Dower's *War Without Mercy* is still the bible on this. After the war, as Yukiko Koshiro explains in her monograph, *Trans-Pacific Racisms,* the place of ethnic minorities and former colonial subjects was never directly discussed:

> Instead, the Japanese and the Americans collaborated to restore the kind of racial hierarchy that had existed in the days of Japan's colonialism. . . . As the Cold War advanced in Asia, Japan was reappointed as the region's junior leader, and the idea of Pan-Asianism was restored. . . . Thus, Japan was allowed to preserve—and resume under the Cold War sanction of the United States—its presumption of superiority over the Asians. Also, Japan's racist wartime ideology, which had propelled atrocities against Asian soldiers and civilians alike, escaped scrutiny and condemnation. . . . The postwar collaboration was built on a shared racist view of the world, in which both nations assumed a duty to lead the "inferior non-West" nations, a concept in which Japan was an "honorary Western nation."[2]

So we have settled back into our normal assumption of racial superiority, with the Japanese as junior partners.

There were other phenomena that influenced our vivid "memories" of the Holocaust, and our tendency to forget the Pacific destruction. German atrocities had high visibility for Americans; reporters saw the death camps, which were in Central Europe, and were spectacular artifacts. Auschwitz and Buchenwald were simply unforgettable. The Japanese empire had no similar memorial sites; the 434 Japanese prison camps were scattered over a quarter of the globe, and none of them, except possibly Bilibid, was notorious. The Nazis did not significantly cover their tracks; the Japanese biological warfare factories were dismantled before capture, animals infected with experimental toxins turned loose, and most evidence of Lt. Gen. Ishii Shiro's infecting people with plague, cholera, typhoid, anthrax, and glanders was destroyed.[3] On the other hand, Nazi creations from human skin and other atrocities entered the world of well-known artifacts.

No heaps of slaughtered Chinese remained from the 1937 Rape of Nanjing when Americans entered that city in 1945; bones were found aplenty, but did not get the press coverage or generate the stench of Auschwitz. The jungles of Burma yielded plenty of graves of slave laborers who died of beatings, disease, and malnutrition, but few visitors ever saw them. And most of all, the tons of incriminating documents seized by Allied troops as we rushed through a disintegrating Germany were witness positive to what the Nazis had planned and done. Japan had many weeks before Allied troops could physically occupy forward positions, during which time documents were being destroyed by the ton.

Another factor in the American forgetfulness of Japan's crimes as compared with Germany's was the existence of an influential international Jewish constituency to remind the world of what the Germans had done. Japan's victims were dispersed, unorganized, and convulsed with anti-colonial wars and material deprivation beyond belief. Not for fifty years were the tens of thousands of "comfort women" able to confront their oppressors and demand redress, or identify those who had perished in that infamous service.[4] Not until the end of the century did the Koreans, Chinese, Filipinos feel able to demand redress from a resurgent Japan.

The significance of these factors for the moral argument on *Enola Gay* is that they almost totally obscure the price in death and destruction that was being paid, in 1945, for every day the war went on. This was not primarily destruction from major battles, although Iwo Jima and Okinawa were horrendous for both sides. The significant cost of the war came from the death throes of the Japanese empire. The primary Japanese killing field was still China, but every other occupied nation was caught up in the slaughter. Here is where the ethnocentrism of the *Enola Gay* dispute is most debilitating. Both sides were (are) hung up over how many American lives would have been lost had the Kyushu invasion gone forward. In 1945, Truman and his advisors had to attend to prospective American casualties first and foremost; fifty years later, a quite different calculus must be invoked.

For a museum taking a moralistic position on the destruction of Hiroshima and Nagasaki to turn a cold shoulder to the pleas of Chinese telling them that the *great* carnage was not from the two atomic bombs but from the Japanese empire, one must have contempt. Can Harwit and company defend themselves by saying "We knew the war would be over soon, the bomb wasn't necessary, Nitze said so, and that was official," or "Truman could have gotten surrender much earlier by guaranteeing the emperor, Joseph Grew (and Commander Zacharias) said so," when they made no move whatever to conduct a scholarly investigation of the worth of these pronouncements?

Can one quantify this outrage that slipped under the NASM radar screen?

The closest thing to a consensus figure for deaths in the Pacific war, including the original Japanese invasion of China, is twenty million. This is the figure used by Toshio Iritani in *Group Psychology of the Japanese in Wartime* and Seiitsu Tachibana in "The Quest for a Peace Culture: The A-Bomb Survivors Long Struggle and the New Movement for Redressing Foreign Victims of Japan's War."[5] These figures conform to a United Nations survey: *Report of the Working Group for Asia and the Far East,* published by the Economic and Social Council in 1948. This report is a summary, lacking detail. It is a huge number. When one sets out to gather the particulars, it does not seem exaggerated.

One must start somewhere. Try Gavan Daws in his well-received *Prisoners of the Japanese:*

Asia under the Japanese was a charnel house of atrocities. As soon as the war ended, evidence of war crimes began piling up, in mountains. POWs, civilian internees, and Asian natives starved, beaten, tortured, shot, beheaded. The water cure. Electric shock. Cannibalism. Men strung up over open flames or coiled in barbed wire and rolled along the ground, nails torn out, balls burned with cigarettes, dicks cut off and stuffed in mouths. Women dragged naked behind motorcycles, raped and ripped open, babies skewered on bayonets. Cities in China and provinces in the Philippines laid waste, mass murders in the Indies, towns and villages wiped out, all the way to the remotest of small places in the Pacific, the island of Nauru, where the thirty-four sufferers in the leprosy hospital were taken out to sea and drowned, and Ocean Island, where days after the war ended all the native laborers were pushed over a cliff.[6]

Chinese accounts of Japanese mayhem are even more gripping, and a *New York Times* advertisement of 17 June 1994 claims Japanese use of germ warfare on 1,300 occasions in fourteen provinces; this ad was sponsored by the Chinese Alliance for Memorial and Justice. Many Chinese sources claim 30 million were killed in China alone.[7]

John Dower is the only American historian to directly confront the ethnocentricity of casualty studies in the Pacific. He writes:

> Yet now, at a distance, the numbers have a capacity to shock as well as inform; and it is sobering to observe not only how many men, women, and children died in Asia, but also how many of these deaths occurred in the final year of the conflict, after Japan's defeat was already assured. China aside, as many or more individuals died after the outcome of the war was clear as perished while there was still reasonable doubt about how events would unfold. Accurate mortality figures are impossible to obtain, especially for Asian victims of the war (other than the Japanese themselves); and the task becomes next to impossible when civilian deaths are included, extending to "peripheral" victims such as conscript laborers worked to death and ordinary people who died of epidemic diseases as a consequence of the war's ravages. Still, the approximate human toll can be suggested.
>
> It is often stated that close to 55 million people died in World War II. . . . In fact, cumulative estimates of the human cost of the war by Westerners have tended to neglect Asian deaths other than Chinese and Japanese, and to ignore the millions of Asians who fell victim to the economic chaos that accompanied the rise and fall of the mis-named Co-Prosperity Sphere. When the situation in Asia is taken fully into account, the total death count for World War II may be even higher than has previously been appreciated.[8]

I was inclined to accept the 20 million total figure for Asian deaths until two recent studies appeared. R. J. Rummel's *China's Bloody Century,* published in 1991, gives a consolidated figure for war-related deaths in China from July 1937 through August 1945 of 19,605,000, of which 13,283,000 were directly attributable to the Japanese.[9] The principles on which Rummel makes his calculations discount high estimates heavily, and his sources appear to be comprehensive.

The document I find even more disturbing, which led me to adjust the Irokawa/Tachibana figure upward, is *The Rape of Nanking,* by Shi Young and James Yin, 1997. They investigate not just the Nanking massacre, which they persuasively claim killed 369,366 Chinese, but the activities of the Japanese armies en route to Nanking from Shanghai.[10] Their account makes clear that when you add up the thousands of small-scale, isolated incidents—Sungking, Soochow, Changzhou, and on almost to infinity—there was unprovoked killing everywhere Japanese troops went. Young and Yin put the total Chinese deaths from Japanese invasion at 30 million.

One cannot know for sure, but the force of Rummel's and Young-Yin's calculations compels me to scale up my estimate for deaths in all of Asia in the Pacific war to twenty-five million. And this is still a conservative figure.

What this does not include is a factor for the accelerated killing in the last year of the war, Dower's "most deadly" year, or "the killing year." All observers are agreed that the closer the war got to Japan, the more intense the fighting, and the gratuitous killing. The rage of the losing armies mounted; as Laurens van der Post puts it, they were going to "pull down their own sprawling military temple, Samson-like," and destroy their enemies along with themselves.[11] Food became scarcer than ever, especially in China, where the *Ichigo* Offensive in China's rice-producing regions produced "prolonged famine." Malnutrition increased throughout the empire, medicine became even scarcer, and Red Cross supplies rarely reached the intended recipients. Meanwhile, in the Japanese home islands, LeMay geared up for a bombing campaign targeting towns containing nearly 5,400,000 people, to be leveled by the end of October.

It is impossible even to begin to canvass the literature describing the death and destruction of 1942–1945 in the vast area of Southeast Asia and the Pacific. Literature on the Philippines, Indonesia, Malaya, Indochina, and the hundreds of islands all points to accelerating casualties toward the end: Anthony Reid, in a Yale Southeast Asia studies book of 1980, says it for the whole Japanese occupied area. "The last year of the war was a time of unprecedented deprivation for most Indonesians. Many, especially in Java, were simply unable to obtain food and were seen 'waiting for death' along the road."[12] While we cannot know that Olympic would have gone forward, we do know that death was marching inexorably forward all over the Pacific and Asia.

If we take the twenty-five million estimate for deaths in the Japanese-controlled areas for 1937–1945, and assume a constant rate, there were 400,000-plus deaths each month. The only handle we have on how long the war would have lasted absent the atom is the estimates of the Japanese officials, with a majority believing the war would have lasted into 1946. If these officials had it right, unless some miraculous food supply appeared to lessen the starvation rate, two million more people would have died between 15 August and 31 December—*with no major land battles*. If Olympic had taken place, there would have been many more.

Barton Bernstein, fleshing out estimates for the duration of the war under different assumptions, believes that Japan probably would have surrendered before 1 November without atomic bombs if the Soviet Union had entered the war.[13] This is a possible, but hardly ironclad, assumption. Bernstein appeals to the somewhat equivocal testimony of Adm. Toyoda Soemu and Gen. Kawabe Torashiro that Soviet entry was a tremendous shock to Japan. But this is a minority opinion among the Japanese leadership, and Drea's citation of Japanese Army orders to their commanders in Manchuria on 30 May 1945 to withdraw slowly to the Korean border and conduct "protracted defense" is conclusive that Soviet entry was expected by the top Japanese echelons.

Let us suppose that Soviet entry did jar the Japanese into surrender by 1 October. This would be six weeks, and a minimum of 600,000 more Asian deaths later than the atom-caused capitulation. How would one justify the privileging of the Hiroshima-Nagasaki residents over triple the number of totally innocent Chinese, Filipinos, Indonesians, Koreans, and others? What critic in the 1990s can say "Hiroshima was so terrible we should disregard the killing that would have gone on, in the countries Japan invaded, in another two, three, or four months of war?" Simple starvation would have taken much longer to bring surrender; it would have been as horrible as the atom in any case.

All of this reasoning assumes acceptance of a consequentialist moral code. Those who objected to *Enola Gay* before Nitze's finding that the bombs were not needed to get an early surrender will be unpersuaded. In the considerable discussion of this moral question the most noteworthy event was the attempt by G. E. M. Anscombe, at that time a research fellow in philosophy at Somerville College, one of the constituent colleges of Oxford University, to prevent the university from giving an honorary degree to Harry Truman.[14] In the spring of 1956, the governing body of the university considered a proposal to honor Mr. Truman. When Anscombe heard of it, she immediately started agitation. As she wrote in her 1957 pamphlet, *Mr. Truman's Degree,* her inquiry as to the proper procedure in opposing the degree agitated the dons considerably. More than 100 turned out for a meeting that would normally draw less than half that number. The chairman, Lord Bullock, noted that Truman had a claim on England's gratitude for many things, and though "the dropping of the bomb was probably a mistake, as we could now see," at the time it appeared reasonable.[15] Bullock carried the day by voice vote.

Anscombe got back at the misguided dons in her pamphlet. It is still cited by philosophers, and the University of Minnesota Press includes it in the *Collected Philosophical Papers of G. E. M. Anscombe.* It is difficult to call her attack on Truman "reasoning," since it is largely emotive. She had no doubt gotten her distaste for Truman from Blackett, and she goes through the standard claims of the Nitze-Blackett narrative. But ultimately her position is absolutist. The last paragraph of her account gives away the emotional basis of her objection: "It is possible still to withdraw from this shameful business in some slight degree; it is possible not to go to [the awards ceremony]; if it should be embarrassing to someone who would normally go to plead other business, he could take to his bed. I, indeed, should fear to go, in case God's patience suddenly ends."[16] It is difficult to understand how God could wait until 1956 to show his displeasure with Harry Truman.

Most warfighting moralists are not quite so rigid. The ambiguities and complexities of moral decisions in wartime are best expressed in this conclusion of Sir Michael Howard, one of Britain's foremost students of war and morality:

The fundamental moral dilemma remains for me unsolved. The infliction of suffering is in itself an evil, corrupting the agent as well as harming the patient. The conduct of war consists of deploying armed force so as to inflict, or threaten the infliction of suffering on an adversary—which may mean, under contemporary political and economic conditions, on all members of his society. War, thus, is in itself inescapably an evil. But those who renounce the use of force find themselves at the mercy of those who do not, and the value-system which enables us to see the infliction of suffering as an evil is itself the product of a certain kind of society which is as liable as any other social system in history to destruction from without, as it is to corruption and disruption from within. On one horn of the dilemma lies suicide, on the other a moral degradation that may be a more subtle form of self-destruction. There are no easy answers. We have no right to expect them.[17]

All anti-Truman writers point to the noncombatant victims of the Bomb as a major argument against its use; it is perhaps their major contention. It has superficial plausibility; "noncombatant" carries innocuous connotations, but they are more appropriate to bygone days when wars were fought by mercenaries or by volunteers who *chose* to put their lives at risk. In a time of total war, when conscription takes the boy (and girl) next door, and almost all industries have some military connection, it is difficult to agree on a definition of noncombatant. The elderly who no longer participate in economic life and children who have not yet entered the economic system should probably be exempt from classification as belligerents. But if this means a warring power cannot attack munitions factories that happen to be surrounded by workers homes, to use a description invoked by American target committees in 1945, then one cannot destroy the enemy's war-making potential. Furthermore, elderly persons may be as responsible for aggressive acts of the polity as anyone else; only minors could claim undoubted exemption from blame for hostile acts of the state.

Further, those who make the most of noncombatant immunity have a selective approach to invoking it. The NASM curators, and the Nitzeans on whom they depend, seem to be absolutists when the noncombatants in Hiroshima and Nagasaki are invoked, but ignore the larger population of noncombatants who were killed in the major conventional and fire-bombing of Tokyo, Osaka, Kobe, and various German cities destroyed by the Allies. One can say to them with a flawless warrant; "Where were you when London was bombed? Dresden? Shanghai?" It is clear that the outcry over Hiroshima was not caused by sudden awareness that noncombatants were being killed, rather it was because the atomic bombings were so spectacular. How can one defend the position that "Minor instances of noncombatant destruction can be tolerated, but a really outrageous instance has to be opposed?" The hypocrisy of selective application is the most powerful objection to the absolutists who talk as if significant bombing of noncombatants first occurred in Hiroshima.

As to the intrinsic inhumanity of nuclear weapons, no analyst is going to claim that the blast, heat, or radiation generated by those first two atomic bombs offer a pleasant way to die. Some anti-Hiroshima writers, including Paul Nitze, when pushed to cite evidence that Japan was ready to quit, fall back on a claim that starvation would bring it about.[18] Of course it would have, eventually, but the implicit assumption that starvation would have been morally preferable to atomic bombing needs to be argued, not assumed.

John Hersey's *Hiroshima,* the most widely read and influential narrative of death from the atom, left no reader in doubt as to its baleful effects. What Truman's critics omit is any substantive consideration of the horrors of death by starvation. From all positions on the moral compass, death by starvation gets marks as low as bombing.

The NASM curators regarded waiting for the blockade to take effect on Japan as preferable to ending the war quickly with the atom. Admiral William D. Leahy, cited as prescient by NASM, wanted to "defeat Japan by isolation, blockade, and bombardment by sea and air forces."[19] None of Truman's critics engages the considerable evidence that starvation, the ultimate result of blockade, is as morally repulsive a weapon as atom bombs or poison gas.

One of the most vehement of the pacifists engaged in public controversy about the morals of World War II, Vera Brittain, won fame as an incisive opponent of area bombing, and of atomic bombs. Her book *Seed of Chaos* was bitterly assailed in England, and found only Catholic voices defending it when published in the United States. Yet this staunch objector to bombing described the horrors of blockade and starvation, as seen in the British blockade of Germany in 1918, in terms to match any chronicler of Hiroshima: "flesh literally dropped from the bones of the children . . . One boy, a child of nine or ten, had the face of a man of seventy; full of unspeakable suffering and patience; his arms and legs were only bones, partly covered with skin, but the larger part not at all covered, with the few muscles loosening from the bones, completely sore and skinless."[20]

Of a heckler at one of her public appearances, who defended blockades as "more merciful" than R.A.F. bombing raids, Brittain wrote, "He fully believed this, because he knew what bombing meant, but had never experienced starvation."

Michael Walzer, probably the most widely read commentator on the morality of war, devotes sixteen pages of his *Just and Unjust Wars* to "War Against Civilians: Sieges and Blockades." His rejection of this option is compelling: "In this kind of war, once combat begins, noncombatants are more likely to be killed. . . . Fed last, and only with the army's surplus, they die first. More civilians died in the siege of Leningrad than in the modernist infernos of Hamburg, Dresden, Tokyo, Hiroshima, and Nagasaki, taken together. They probably died more painfully too, even in old-fashioned ways."[21]

At the other end of the bellicosity spectrum, one has the word of General of the Army Douglas MacArthur: "No weapon, not even the atomic bomb, is as deadly in its final effect as economic warfare. The atomic bomb kills by the thousands, starvation by the millions."[22]

To *think* about prolonging a war so that blockade and starvation can render an opponent submissive is to reject it. Consider the fact that the official position of the Japanese government was that a hundred million would willingly die for the emperor. Hundreds of Japanese soldiers on isolated Pacific islands did die of starvation rather than surrender. How many civilian starvation deaths would it have taken to induce the Japanese military to surrender? The British blockade of Germany in World War I took three years to produce significant results, and German resentment of this blockade was one of the most pernicious outcomes of that war.[23] As for starving Japan into submission, Spencer Weart's observation holds: "It would not necessarily have been the kindest way to end the war; a blockaded nation feeds it soldiers while its old men, women, and children die lingering deaths."[24]

And had the shocks of August not triggered Japanese surrender, American B-29s would have continued their conventional and incendiary bombing. As of July 1945, U.S. Army Air Forces intended to hit all urban areas with more than 30,000 inhabitants—some 180 Japanese towns, with more than 500,000 inhabitants. They could have been "wiped out by November." Despite lip service paid to a recommendation by the Strategic Bombing Survey that transportation should be the prime target, LeMay and his commanders planned to keep on as they had, destroying every above-ground structure in Japan.[25]

No one knows how long the Japanese would have fought in the absence of atomic shock; no one knows how many would have had to die of starvation before the Japanese government called it quits. It is possible that the total horror caused by continual conventional bombing, blockade, and starvation would have been less than that caused by the atom, but this claim must be argued. What we do know is that the Germans who starved in World War I, and the Russians who starved during the siege of Leningrad, had no John Hersey to present their agony to the world. Harrison Salisbury's *900 Days* never got the attention *Hiroshima* did.

Barton Bernstein appears to feel that judgments about the 1945 atom bombs were more complicated than I believe. He positions himself relative to many writers on Hiroshima as being more concerned with noncombatant immunity, and less impressed with the possibility that using bombs saved lives: "There is a *fundamental ethical* difference between killing soldiers and noncombatants. . . . Such a position . . . does not rest on numbers."[26] But since the Asians other than Japanese who were being killed, assuredly at least several hundred thousand each month, were also noncombatants, it is difficult to see what principle Bernstein invokes. The most significant population of noncombatants at risk was neither American nor Japanese, but Asian and Pacific Islanders.

Here it is appropriate to again view the issue of total casualties through the lens of Michael Walzer. He is a consequentialist: bombing noncombatants is presumptively wrong, but judgment depends on the specific case. Thus, in the early months of World War II, Allied forces had been swept from Europe, and the very existence of Britain was at stake. Walzer says "the decision to bomb cities was made . . . when no other decision seemed possible if there was to be any sort of military offensive against Nazi Germany."[27] By February 1945, however, when Dresden was bombed, the emergency was past and Allied triumph seemed assured. The destruction of Dresden was wrong.

This is all reasonable, but where Walzer goes wrong is in his ignorance of the Pacific war. To Walzer, Japanese militarism was nothing like Nazism: "Japan's rulers were engaged in a more ordinary sort of military expansion, and all that was morally required was that they be defeated, not that they be conquered and totally overthrown."[28] Every single Asian who lived under the control of the Japanese empire would gag at such a statement. Walzer, at the time he wrote this book, apparently had no idea what went on in the so-called Greater East Asia CoProsperity Sphere. He never mentions the Rape of Nanjing, or Burma's Death Railway, or the sacking of Manila, or the Bataan Death March, or Unit 731. He cites no book about the Pacific war. He does not think the Allies were justified in demanding unconditional surrender and the elimination of Japan's military caste. Walzer's gross misrepresentation of what was happening in the Pacific is a case of psychic numbing. It is possible for him to believe the Japanese rampage was benign only because America's collective memory has forgotten, repressed, and marginalized the terrible things that happened to Asians under Japanese rule.

When John Rawls weighed in on the morality of Hiroshima, he too had a limited view of Asian realities in 1945. Accepting Walzer's judgment that British strategic bombing of cities was justified by Britain's peril in 1940, he finds the United States had no such warrant; "Yet it is clear that while the extreme crisis exemption held for Britain in the early stages of the war, it never held at any time for the United States in its war with Japan."[29] Of course, there was no comparable crisis for the United States; the crisis was for Asia and the Pacific.

A look at the history of noncombatant immunity theory must include Arthur L. Goodhart's 1960 volume, *What Acts of War are Justifiable?*[30] Goodhart traces war fighting theory from the ancient Greeks through scholars such as Hugo Grotius, up to the modern conventions such as those adopted in the various Hague peace conferences. Alternatively, historians coming to grips with moral problems of the Vietnam War and the nuclear arms race could well approach the subject with Robert W. Tucker's influential *The Just War* (1960).[31]

Tucker's book is an anguished consideration of the just war doctrine as it related to the twentieth century. His parameters are those of Christian (Protestant and Catholic) teachings. Protestant writers tend to be consequentialists, Catholics tend to be absolutists. Tucker considers the purpose for which a war is fought:

> The aggressor is not looked upon as just another player, entitled to insist upon the observance of rules which set limits to the punishment he may receive at the hands of his opponents. Those states waging a defensive war enjoy a superior moral and legal position and are thereby entitled to respond to aggression in places and with means of their own choosing; hence, their problem in responding to aggression is first and foremost a technical problem, not a moral problem. Still, the manner of employing force is not regarded as free from any moral or legal restraint. Although the aggressor must be defeated, and although peace-loving nations have a right and even a duty to deal with an aggressor so as to insure that he will have neither the inclination nor the ability to pursue his evil design in the future, no more destruction and suffering ought to be inflicted than the necessities of war require.[32]

This brings Tucker, and any analyst of the end of the Pacific war, to a consideration of whether or not Japan was an aggressor whose martial spirit had to be destroyed for the sake of humanity, and whether that martial spirit could have been eradicated by means short of atom bombs. There is no room here for Tucker's full argument, but his conclusion rests on a prima facie warrant: "In this way the use of atomic weapons against Hiroshima and Nagasaki could be and indeed was justified, not only as a military necessity but also as a legitimate application in war of the principle of humanity. There is no reason to question the sincerity of that justification."[33]

The consequentialist principle is difficult to reject. Paul Ramsey, in his *1961 War and the Christian Conscience* analyzes a broad range of doctrine about war, and concludes that absolutist claims cannot allow the necessity recognized by all Christians to participate in war "waged to vindicate what they believe to be an essential Christian principle: to defend the victims of wanton aggression, or to secure freedom for the oppressed."[34] Ramsey does not explicitly say the Pacific war was an event where only dropping two nuclear bombs could defeat wanton aggression, but his treatment of that war implies it.

Other moralists are more specific. R. B. Brandt, in an issue of *Philosophy and Public Affairs* that should be read by all students of the morality of war, explicitly justifies use of atom bombs against Japan if "there is good evidence that it [did] significantly enhance the prospect of victory." I would amend this to read, "If there is good evidence that it did speed Japan's surrender and hence the end of the war."[35] This moral judgment Brandt contrasts with the decision that led to the bombing of Hamburg, which violated the presumptive rule against killing noncombatants because "the destruction of Hamburg did not significantly enhance the prospect of victory."

R. M. Hare, in the same issue of *Philosophy and Public Affairs,* considers the moral situation to be one in which it is not just the noncombatants who might be killed by an act of war who should be factored into one's judgment, but those noncombatants who might be saved: "I would include more people in the class of those whose sufferings are relevant to our moral decisions (for example, in the Hiroshima case, those that will die if the war is not ended quickly, as well as those actually killed by the bombing)."[36] And in his book *Applications of Moral Philosophy,* Hare develops extensively the principle that *consequences are always morally relevant to an act.*[37]

Absolutists are fond of posing hypothetical situations to highlight the sanctity of noncombatant immunity and the irrelevance of consequences. For instance, should one deliberately sacrifice one child in return for avoiding destruction of an entire city? To this the consequentialist must respond, "This is a ridiculous counterfactual; such a choice has never been, and never will be, confronted in the real world."

So we come to the bottom line: the intense preoccupation with the evil of killing noncombatants in Hiroshima and Nagasaki has effectively marginalized or suppressed the moral claims of the millions of totally innocent victims of Japan's aggressive empire. The single-minded concern for the Hibakusha (atom-damaged persons) has preempted the humanitarian action that was due the survivors of Nanjing, of the Death Railway, of the Nauru leper colony. Part of the reason it has taken fifty years for the victims of Japan to capture the attention of the international community is the vehemence of the attacks on *Enola Gay* and the administration that ordered her mission. In this category, one ill-informed zealot stands out: Robert Jay Lifton. The considerable influence of his overly righteous *Hiroshima in America* has turned hundreds toward the belief that the Japanese were really the victims, not the perpetrators, of Pacific war horrors.[38]

Do we then justify the mission of *Enola Gay* as revenge for the atrocities of Tojo's soldiers? Revenge, reprisal, retaliation, retribution are difficult concepts.

Many pundits follow the Old Testament ethic. Norman Cousins invoking revenge as a reason for bombing before Hiroshima has already been noted. A. L. Goodhart asserted in 1940 that what he calls reprisals are morally justified: "It has occasionally been said that no acts of reprisal are ever justifiable because two wrongs cannot make a right. The answer is that one wrongful act can make the other act rightful. International law is therefore correct when it speaks of the *right* to reprisal. This right has been exercised by nearly all belligerents in nearly all wars, so that, whether we like it or not, we cannot close our eyes to its existence."[39]

Many Americans talked as if revenge were their prime motive for bombing the Japanese. Opinion polls showed a healthy minority (twenty-three percent) favored dropping even more atomic bombs on Japan, largely in retaliation for Pearl Harbor. Churchill, Roosevelt, and Truman frequently sought to stimulate enthusiasm for the war by what seem to be calls for revenge. One of FDR's purple passages: "Yes, the Nazis and Fascists have asked for it—and they are going to get it."[40] But this is not necessarily a call for revenge; it is simply a promise to give "them" a hard fight.

The coolly practical men in the American war department, and the politicians of Truman's White House, were not significantly vengeful. Truman recoiled from the possibility of a third atomic bomb on Japan, and ordered that it not be scheduled without his express directive. And try as one might, it is impossible to paint the promises of the Potsdam Declaration as vengeful. Disarmed soldiers were to be able to return home and resume productive lives, in contrast to Japan's enslavement of conquered Europeans and Asians; freedom of speech, religion, and thought were offered. Civilian industries would be permitted, and trade would be allowed on an equitable basis when a responsible civilian government was established. These are not the terms of a conqueror bent on vengeance.

Despite the "eye-for-an-eye" precept of the Old Testament, revenge does not seem to be a legitimate motive for dropping the bombs. The evidence that the bombs were necessary to force an early end to the war simply made revenge, whether legitimate or not, moot.

But this is not the end of the matter; a more sympathetic view of the desire for retaliation expressed by so many Americans in the 1940s comes from reading about Japanese atrocities on Allied prisoners of war and to Asian peoples whom the Japanese conquered. One must also consider this analysis from Sheldon Cohen:

I agree with you in being unhappy with [revenge as a motive for dropping the bombs], but that's not the same thing as being against revenge tout court. In some cases I am not sure how justice and revenge differ. Julius Streicher's execution was just; it may also have been an act of revenge—certainly we weren't trying to reform him. If so, taking revenge can sometimes be morally justified, or even obligatory. Not to punish the miscreant might be, as St. Anselm said in *Cur Deus Homo,* to make light of his crime, and therefore, a moral affront.

I also believe that adult German and Japanese civilians in the 30's and 40's bore some responsibility for the acts agents of their government were performing or soon would be performing. It seems inconsistent to hold a right of national self-determination, and to grant that these were the legitimate governments of Germany and Japan, while denying that the population shares *any* responsibility for the deeds of their governments.[41]

How do justice and revenge differ? Is it not true that the people and factories of Hiroshima and Nagasaki, as well as the rest of Japan, armed Tojo's butchers and sent them forth on their campaigns of pillage, rape, and murder?

Despite the official effort to rehabilitate Japan's wartime record, the passage of time has loosened lips of Japanese who regretted participating in that war—who, in fact, had guilty consciences. One poignant instance is in Haruko Taya Cook and Theodore Cook's volume of interviews with Japanese who lived through the war. The Cooks were talking to Hayashi Shigeo, who had been an engineer in Manchuria, and was sent in late 1945 on a team to Hiroshima and Nagasaki to determine what actually happened there. Hayashi was in Nagasaki:

> One day I went to the Mitsubishi arsenal and was photographing the torpedo plant. I was being escorted around by a Mitsubishi man. At some point he said to me, "This is where we made the first torpedoes, the ones dropped on Pearl Harbor at the onset of the Pacific War." The wrenches and tools used by the workers were lying there, all around me, as if they'd been set down a minute ago. I could have reached out myself and picked them up. Finally he said quietly, "Mr. Hayashi, the very first torpedo was launched from here in Nagasaki, and in the end here's where we were stabbed to death. We fought a stupid war, didn't we?" The two of us just stood there in silence.[42]

It is not the relatively rare Japanese *mea culpas* that are important here, but the overwhelming anguish of the millions of victims of the Japanese empire. While numerous accounts describe what the Japanese did to the other peoples of Asia, these stories are not often recounted in John Hersey's gripping prose. But they are heart-rending accounts nonetheless. Had Hersey visited Nanjing or Manila and written about those catastrophes; had there been no competing and overshadowing spectacle in Japan fueled by supernatural science; had Hiroshima not become a shrine to the peaceminded, the anguish of Japan's victims might be more on our consciences.

In the 27 October 1994 issue of the *Washington Post,* reporter William Branigin tells a story that illustrates the problem:

> MANILA—Vicky Quirino was running to her grandmother's house with her family to take cover from American shelling when a Japanese machine gun nest opened fire on them.

The 13-year-old's mother and elder sister were killed in the hail of bullets, but a 2-year-old lay still alive on the street where her fallen mother had dropped her. A Japanese soldier walked over, tossed the girl in the air and speared her with his bayonet.

Quirino escaped death that morning of February 9, 1945, and lived through three more days of terror. . . . Her father, Elpido Quirino, also survived and went on to become president of the Philippines from 1948 to 1953.

The daughter of one of Manila's most prominent families is now 63 and known as Victoria Quirino-Delgado. For nearly 50 years, she refused to discuss those traumatic memories. But with the commemoration last week of the October 20, 1944 American invasion that ultimately liberated the Philippines from Japanese occupation, she and other survivors of the battle of Manila have decided to speak out.

The survivors' stories illustrate a chapter of World War II that has been largely glossed over by historians. The accounts help to explain lingering distrust in Asia of the Japanese military and resentment of Japan's tendency to portray the populations of Hiroshima and Nagasaki—cities devastated by U.S. atomic bombs—as the principal civilian victims of the war. . . .

According to U.S. Army records, an estimated 100,000 civilians, out of a population of 1 million, died in Manila during this period as about 16,000 Japanese troops put the city to the torch and embarked on an orgy of murder, rape, and atrocities. . . .

Why did Japanese troops behave this way? Juan Jose Rocha, 57, who saw his mother killed by American shelling, then lost 11 other relatives at the hands of the Japanese, said: "It was just total hatred and savagery. You cannot explain it. . ."

Rocha, a former ambassador to Spain and currently president of Memorare-Manila 1945, recently urged the Smithsonian Institution to incorporate Manila's plight in its forthcoming exhibition of the atomic bombings that ended World War II.

"Was the extended 28-day agony of Manila any less of an inhuman tragedy than the lightning incineration of Hiroshima or Nagasaki?" he asked in a letter. "Is death by burning, bayoneting, or slow bleeding any less excruciating than that by radiation . . . We ask you to remember Manila."[43]

There are similar stories from every corner of the Japanese empire. China has the most. There is no room here for the substance of Patrick E. Tyler's "China Villagers Recall Horrors of Germ Attack," in the *New York Times,* 4 February 1997. The conclusion will have to suffice:

Over the years, the United States Government has said little about the atrocities committed in China by the Japanese. The Communist victory in 1949 shifted Asian alliances, pushing postwar Japan and the United States together as a bulwark against Soviet and Chinese Communism.

With the opening of wartime archives in recent years, it is now clear that the United States was willing to exempt Japanese officers who directed chemical and biological programs from war crimes prosecution in exchange for a full rendering of their secret program. . .

The United States renounced its biological warfare programs in 1969 and destroyed its weapons. For all these reasons, a half-century later, many outside China still do not know what happened there.

But the survivors will never forget. On the road out of the village, a stark white pagoda stands on a hilltop that in 1979 was renamed "The Mountain of Remembering Our Hatred."[44]

The NASM curators remembered little and researched nothing that did not indict the Truman-Stimson narrative.

〜 〜 〜

We were the victors in World War II, bursting with pride and arrogance at having defeated two bitter enemies, but also beginning to foment the hatreds and fears that ultimately led us to the terrible excesses of nuclear overkill. In insisting that Japan be held to account for her wrongs, Asian and other critics do not exonerate the United States for terrible excesses of our warfare against the Vietnamese people, or the long series of "interventions" against what we claimed were attempted communist takeovers in Iran, Greece, Chile, Cuba, Guatemala, Indonesia, Nicaragua and several others. Even Louis Allen's account of World War II, *The Campaigns in Asia and the Pacific* does not hold the United States blameless:

> There remains an intractable problem in terms of Japan's relations with other people, and that is the behaviour of her armed forces towards the armies they defeated and the countries they occupied. Inevitably, a certain amount of hypocrisy enters into this. Ruthless, clumsy and brutal though they were, the Japanese had no genocidal master plan to obliterate whole peoples, as the Germans did. Moreover, countries which participated in the International Military Tribunal for the Far East (Tokyo, 1945–1948) and passed sentence on Japan's leaders for preparing aggressive war and committing crimes against humanity fouled themselves by genocidal behaviour in later conflicts, the French in Algeria, the U.S. in Vietnam.[45]

In the hierarchy of blame, the United States does not occupy an enviable position. But the focus here is on the hierarchy of suffering, and where Japan should place compared with Japan's victims. Seiitsu Tachibana's discussion, "The Quest for a Peace Culture: The A-bomb Survivors' Long Struggle and the New Movement for Redressing Foreign Victims of Japan's War" intelligently balances these two arenas. He recognizes that Japan's ills were self-inflicted wounds, and that the atomic casualties must seek redress from their own government. He also knows that the Japanese "have been slow to realize their role as victimizer. Thousands of Asians suffered as a result of Japanese aggression during the war, and during the early 1990s these foreign victims began to voice their long-overdue demands for compensation."[46]

Tachibana sees the invidious aspects of the Tokyo war crimes trials: they ignored the crimes committed against the peoples of Asia, thus "giving the impression that the war's Asian victims were unimportant. Moreover the subsequent execution of seven class-A war criminals produced a general impression that Japan had adequately absolved itself of all war crimes and need not worry about additional compensation in the future."[47] The compensation that Japan did make turns out to be minuscule, and Tachibana sympathizes with the lawsuits filed by the comfort women, those who had been forced laborers for Japanese firms and government, and those who had suffered economic losses due to Japanese currency manipulation and other impositions. He gives the United States credit for granting restitution to its citizens of Japanese extraction who were interned during the war. He concludes with a balanced discussion of the peace movement in Japan, and its struggles against a government that is attempting to rise to the status of a "global power."

As for the peace movement, his conclusion can serve as advice for its American counterpart: "The movement is still to learn how to make common cause with its diverse elements."[48]

Tachibana's picture of the redress movement among Japan's victims was confirmed by events in 2000. Elizabeth Rosenthal's story in the *New York Times* of 2 October 2000 is headed, "Wartime Slaves Use U.S. Law to Sue Japanese."[49] She interviewed residents of Shenyang, claimed to be the first Chinese city occupied by the Japanese. Residents have not forgotten the "brutal 14-year occupation" that started on 18 September 1931. Postwar turmoil, the Communist revolution, and the tumultuous cold war years that followed provided no opportunity for the Chinese citizens to seek redress. The 1978 China-Japan Friendship Treaty seemed to provide an opening, but although Chinese war victims have filed forty-six suits in Japanese courts, none was accepted until 2000. Rosenthal notes that the Japanese say "wartime claims are a matter of international politics, and that the compensation issue was settled in the San Francisco Treaty of 1951."

The development responsible for the current redress activities was the "1999 California law that allowed victims of forced labor during World War II to sue until 2010, [which] provided a new tailor-made opportunity, at a time when Tokyo courts . . . were dismissing Chinese claims." Yang Li, a Shenyang born lawyer now practicing in New York, has filed a class-action suit against Mistubishi and Mitsui, companies that seized some 8,000 Chinese workers and took them to Japan. Retired Shenyang professor Zhang Yibo, who organized the mostly illiterate former laborers, told Rosenthal, "We are taking advantage of the U.S. courts and the chance to be heard in a third country. . . . If this route worked for the Jews, why not for the Chinese? People forget us, but we suffered as much as them."

On 21 December 2000, Howard French reported in the *New York Times* ("Japanese Veteran Testifies in War Atrocity Lawsuit") that Japanese courts are taking evidence from claimants alleging damage from General Ishii's Unit 731. For the first time, a Japanese member of that biological warfare unit appeared in court to describe their gruesome procedures. French explains why this is happening in 2000:

> Japanese legal experts and historians say the floodgate has opened as a result of a complex set of circumstances. For one, the compensation settlements for victims of the Nazis reached in recent years with German and Swiss companies have increased pressure on the Japanese government and Japanese companies to do the same.

But foremost, these experts say, has been the democratization of South Korea and increased freedoms in China that have accompanied the end of the Cold War. This more open atmosphere has for the first time allowed large numbers of individuals to pursue claims for damages against Japan. "During the Cold War situation, Japan just didn't have to face the issues of the past," said Hiroshi Tanaka, a professor of history at Ryukoku University. "We could always get by just ignoring it. Japan was under the umbrella of the United States, and America settled Japan's Asian issues."[50]

The Japanese witness braving condemnation by Japan's still powerful chauvinists to describe what Ishii's unit did was Yoshio Shinozuka. French captured his agonized explanation:

Asked why he had wanted to cooperate with the continuing trial involving Unit 731, Mr. Shinozuka delivered a long and highly personal meditation on guilt and forgiveness. "The government made no apology at the time," he said, "and has kept the same attitude ever since. They remain silent. But all these years I've thought about who received the germs I created, and how much they must have suffered. I thought about the bereaved, and about the survivors, people whose lives were forever damaged. I thought about the victims of vivisection, and I felt these acts must not be buried away, or else we are condemned to go from darkness to darkness."

The victims of Unit 731 had no John Hersey either.

Let us finally look at the American peace movement, or the movement for abolition of nuclear, chemical and biological weapons. I have belonged to this movement since the 1960s, and have followed its permutations from the Vietnam War teach-ins through SANE/Freeze to the present Peace Action. The bottom line objective has always seemed to be reduction and elimination of nuclear weapons. Observing the single-minded devotion of the NASM curators to convincing their visitors that Hiroshima and Nagasaki were mistakes, one wonders, "Why the emphasis on a past that is now irreversible, since this tactic necessarily alienates a whole generation of Americans? Why not deal with the real problems, NSC-68 and the H-bomb decision?"

The pathos of the peaceniks reveals itself in the meeting of peace activists with NASM officials 20 September 1994, organized by Fr. John Dear of Pax Christi. The intent of Dear and representatives of American Friends Service Committee, Physicians for Social Responsibility, and Fellowship of Reconciliation who were present was to persuade Harwit and his curators to restore the tough anti-Truman tone of the original script, which had been modified under pressure from veterans and politicians. Dear wrote of this meeting, "We talked about conscience and morality, and appealed to their integrity. Crouch and the curators did not speak at the meeting, and Harwit seemed exasperated. He said to us, 'Where have you been? You are too late. Why haven't you been in before? Why haven't you talked to the media?' Without making any promises to restore or strengthen the script, he thanked us for coming."[51]

The sign-up sheet Dear passed around at this meeting, recording the name, organization, and phone number of participants is in Accession 96–140, Box 1, Smithsonian Institution Archives. Eleven NASM officials signed, four representatives of peace groups, and seven writers, all of whom presumably agreed with the convener (Dear). It was a gathering of true believers, but half of them spoke with the imprimatur of the federal government, and this half was under attack by the other half, whose loyalty was entirely to the Nitze-Blackett narrative. Obviously this sign-up sheet was not intended to be a mere record. Did Dear think getting the NASM people to sign would stiffen their spines?

This was the first of three such meetings. By Harwit's account, the hottest topic discussed was what figure the script should give as the expected casualties in the scheduled invasion of Japan. The potent question that these people should have been discussing, "How can we convince the world that the existing hydrogen bomb arsenal is so unconscionable that it must be eliminated?" dropped out of sight.[52] Descending to the triviality of Olympic estimates highlights the sterility of the whole process.

Kai Bird, biographer of the cold warrior John McCloy, was present at these meetings. His retrospective judgment on the NASM situation was in the *New York Times* 9 October 1994: "It was a humiliating spectacle, scholars being forced to recant the truth. Curators at the Smithsonian's Air and Space Museum in Washington have been compelled by veterans' groups to rewrite the text for an exhibit on the bombing of Hiroshima. . . . During two closed-door sessions with representatives of the American Legion, they agreed to censor their own historical knowledge."[53]

"Scholars" who confuse the fraudulent Nitze-Blackett narrative with truth deserve humiliation.

The attack on *Enola Gay* was an error. The real task of the peaceminded at the end of the twentieth century was not to obsess on the frightful explosions of 1945, but to concentrate on righting the wrongs done to millions of Asians in that war, and to reduce the power and waste of the nuclear establishment. The most persuasive clientele to get across this message was precisely the crew who had flown the 1945 atomic missions. The fliers of the 509th were not warmongers, just the opposite.

Ted Van Kirk, who navigated *Enola Gay* to her target, said at a 509th reunion, "We're as anti-war and anti-nuclear as anyone you'll ever see in your life." Norris Jernegan, also at a reunion, said "We're here for the camaraderie. . . . None of us celebrates war."[54] General Charles Sweeney, who flew on the Hiroshima mission and piloted *Bock's Car* over Nagasaki, said "It is my fervent hope that there will never be another atomic mission. The bombs we dropped in 1945 were primitive in comparison to nuclear weapons today. As the man who commanded the last atomic mission, I pray that I maintain that singular distinction."[55]

General Paul Tibbets thinks there are too many nuclear weapons in the world: "But we've always had too many, I mean, there's such a thing as overkill."[56] Frank B. Stewart, a navigator in the 509th, wanted *Enola Gay* restored "to serve as a symbol so that this . . . will never happen again. We're not hawks—nobody wants nuclear war."[57] Thomas L. Karnes, adjutant of the 509th, later a Ph.D. in history from Stanford and a history professor the rest of his life, wrote a long letter to the *Journal of American History* protesting the attempt by historians to destroy the memories of those who had fought the Japanese. Karnes remembered Paul Tibbets "as one of the most decent men I have ever met . . . and I remember Chuck Sweeney . . . leaving Tinian immediately after his Nagasaki mission to fly halfway around the world to bring a formal mass to thousands of Catholics on the island. Then he raised money for an orphanage in Hiroshima. Paul Tibbets's co-pilot, the late Bob Lewis, also raised funds for badly burned women. . . . We were not barbarians. Is it not about time to cool the rhetoric?"[58]

By alienating these good men, the peace movement shot itself in the foot. It is unfortunate that commitment to a fraudulent narrative has so alienated a large segment of the World War II generation, those who can talk, on the basis of experience at war, of the need for reducing and perhaps eliminating altogether a class of weapons that no one has dared use since 1945 because we saw then how horrible they were.

Harry Truman, who weakened his case for using the two bombs by claiming to have saved lives that *might* not have been sacrificed, and Henry Stimson, who painted Truman's decision as "the least abhorrent choice" when the bomb decision did not exclude other choices, were not the most effective spokesmen for their cause. But their sins do not begin to rise to the level of those of Paul Nitze, who told us untruths about Japan, and P. M. S. Blackett, who built on Nitze to misrepresent Truman's motives. The World War II cohort, and the Asian victims of Japan, deserve better.

Bruce E. Gronbeck

AFTERWORD
THE RHETORICS OF FOREIGN POLICY
MAKING, IMPLEMENTING,
AND REMEMBERING

As a series editor of Frontiers in Political Communication, I endorsed the publication of this book because of its narrative virtues. It bulges with stories about new and terrible responsibilities for wartime decision-makers, myopic and self-interested construals of world events, the powerful winds of future events that blow back to resculpt the past, the gnarled politics of those looking both back and strategically ahead at times of public remembrance. These tales can rivet a reader to a book whose facts are stranger and more engrossing than fiction. Especially when Newman gives resonant voice to his own outrage and crusade to right some of the wrongs of political actors then and now, the stories open mythopoetic vistas.

I write this Afterword, however, not as an editor but in my academic voice, as a student of political rhetoric. As a rhetorician, I became engrossed in the rhetorical power of stories about bombs, post-hoc assessment, policy making, and, finally, the multiple rememberings of past policy decisions that effectively paralyzed the National Air and Space Museum (NASM). If with Murray Edelman we think of politics as processes of symbolically constructing both collective threats and institutional reassurances that those threats can be thwarted through governmental action, then this book is a mother lode of rhetorical action and reaction in political arenas. In Edelman's words,

> Adequate explanation [of political behavior] must focus on the complex element that intervenes between the environment and the behavior of human beings: creation and change in common meanings through symbolic apprehension in groups of people of

interests, pressures, threats, and possibilities. The understanding of the symbolic process is a long-range challenge. . . . Analysis of the links among political symbols and political behaviors is a facet of the challenge that can contribute both to an understanding of the function of symbols and to a correlative understanding of change in political cognitions and actions.[1]

And that is what rhetorical conceptions of politics in general, and more particularly of policy making, implementing, and remembering are all about: the power of meaning-making in constructing understandings—descriptively, valuatively, performatively—of the world, ourselves, our actions, others, and our relationships to them. Rhetoric is in Edelman's phrase that "complex element that intervenes between the environment and the behavior of human beings." It does so discursively, through coded verbal, visual, acoustic, and even behavioral symbol systems.

Furthermore, Newman's study strongly reinforces the injunction to examine policy decision making, implementation, and assessment from the vantage of multiple contexts. Each context, in greater or lesser detail, provides historian-critics with a different portal through which to see what was done, why, and to what effects in the past. To look at the dropping of the atomic bombs on Japan, at the post-war investigation of that act's impact on war and peace, and then at the force of both the bombing and the assessment of it on future military, political, and memorial events must be an exercise in perspective-taking, and hence in coming to grips with multiple rhetorics.

Newman's work suggests that questions of foreign policy and behaviors flowing from that policy can (and should) be examined from at least five rhetorical perspectives:

1. *Geopolitical postures of the United States.* When the United States acts (or not) internationally, those actions, while having material consequences, nonetheless are conceived of, justified, and interpreted symbolically. We understand ourselves—and so do others—as acting from particular motives in the face of perceived threats and strategically presumed results. Here, the languages of threat and reassurance, action and prediction, ideological accounts and justifications work rhetorically to create (a) a discourse of self-image, (b) an articulation of "needs and wants of the state,"[2] and (c) sets of symbolic linkages or relationships between ourselves and others. *Geopolitical postures* here are understood as public self-identities crafted because of some threat or need in relationship to the symbolic identities of others. The "geo-" prefix suggests that globalized thinking often involves reifying others regionally, as in concepts of "First- and Second World," "the Near- and Far East," "the Americas." Regionalisms stand in discourses as typifications and generalizations of collective cultures. Particular descriptors of geographical units—"the Orient" (vs. the Occident), "the Pacific Rim" (vs. the U.S. presence on the opposite rim), "the Far East" (vs. the neighborly Near West), "East Asia" (vs. Southwest or West Asia, i.e., India)— become reifications that suggest particular understandings of self and imply

reciprocal linkages to others. Even what we call ourselves and others in relationship to ourselves provide bases for constructing the worldviews that background policy decisions. Furthermore, geopolitical postures become parts of larger rhetorical constructions that organize policies and relationships into policy types—e.g., cold war policy, visions of the New World Order. (See below.)

2. *Conventional histories of governmental administrations.* A very different perspective comes through the abstractions resulting from the identification of governmental systems and actions with the system's chief officer, as in the Roosevelt administration or the Truman administration. Policy statements are associated with presidents even though few would ever have drafted them. To discuss foreign policy administratively rather than geopolitically is to focus upon it as driven by a political agency or vision possessed by an individual, personalized in that individual, and hence ultimately tied to citizens of that era who legitimated the individual's office-holding.[3] And, as Newman has shown, the assessment of such individuals' actions and reactions in terms of personalized successes and failures contributes not only to history per se, but also can provide a rhetorical bulldozer for pushing future decisions in particular directions. More, a president's legacy can be changed symbolically with the passage of time and situation, and so can be employed strategically to pressure a successor into a particular policy move for either affirmative or negative reasons.

3. *Future governmental decisions and actions.* And hence, one administration's decisions and rationales for them march into future administrations' situation rooms and the contexts within which they operate. Arguments about parallel cases inevitably rumble through later administrations when similar crises arise. Questions about strategic bombing of North Vietnam and even of the advisability of employing tactical nuclear weapons in that guerrilla war were raised via parallels between the 1940s and the 1960s. The 1980s debate over a nuclear freeze called for a reassessment of the effects of super weapons on civilians, in turn demanding a condemnation of the pro-bomb decision-makers of World War II.

4. *Various special-interest historians.* Political or governmental history is written not only from the viewpoints of administrations but, of course, from many other vantages as well, each serving as a reflecting or refracting lens for examining the past. Histories are discursive constructions of the past, narratives and interpretive arguments about the past written by amateurs and professionals with particular interests and even motives; history-writing itself is a rhetorical exercise.[4] So, we can read historians of World War II itself, the succeeding arms race and the Cold War, relationships among East Asian countries, post-war developments in Europe and East Asia, and Vietnam and post-Vietnam military actions of the U.S., as well as biographers of the principals, moralists pursuing the dynamics of war, peace, and especially nuclear proliferation, and then bands of revisionists who rise to public notice through re-tellings and counter-arguments about the past, the stories of atomic bombings, and their impacts of the future. Special-interest historians multiply historical tales like rabbits. Especially in the

world of politics, I think, historical narratives frame a past broadly or narrowly, setting out a story with a trajectory aimed squarely at the present. We are told time and again that if we forget our past we are doomed to re-live it; and, of course, the re-living of nuclear holocaust is a vision of hell, which assuredly put the defenders of Truman's decision in a hard place. Newman squirms now and then as he sits on that rock. Other historians with other perspectives circle him constantly as he parries their narrative thrusts.

5. *The memorializing of the past.* On top of all the special-interest historians who tell their stories are the public memorialists. To bring events into public memory (remembrance) is an exercise not unlike history-writing, though it differs from especially academic history in some significant ways. Because historians assume evidentiary burdens, their discourses have a forensic quality to them; their stories ride the back of originary documents that provide the base to their narrative superstructures. Acts of collective memory, in contrast, are less forensic and more epideictic, less legalist and more commemorative, even celebratory. We remember the *Enola Gay* and its context not to test its consequences but to celebrate (or condemn) those party to the decisions made. As well, collective remembering always, always is imbued with a presentist purpose; memorial discourses of praise and blame are not articulated simply to reconstitute the past but to guide today. "Lest we forgot" or "Never forget" signals that collective remembrance makes the past into a political servant of today and tomorrow.[5]

Newman's study is a masterful effort to index and comment upon these five contexts—the geopolitical postures of the U.S., administrative histories, the impact of one administration upon later ones, special-interest histories, and public rememberings, especially the controversy over the NASM exhibit. The book is built around a rambling narrative that runs from the original policy decision making and its initial evaluation by Nitze, Stimson, and Blackett, through a series of events (actually, what Newman identifies as "*nonevents*"[6]) that re-symbolized and re-contextualized the policy decision, and on to the rememberings that allowed—even forced—the United States to draw different lessons from that decision. The rhetorics of foreign policy, it becomes clear, operate both historically and transhistorically.

That is, first of all, the discourses coming from the time of the policy debate, construction, implementation, and initial positive and negative evaluations are conditioned by the web of forces operating at the time of their articulation. For example, that the strategic bombing survey would provide the primary criterion for evaluating the use of atomic weapons was a measure appropriate to the time of the decision, even though it might surprise readers of today. "USSBS" likely is an acronym absolutely unknown to any but historians of the war's aftermath. Similarly, one of Newman's favorite subject matters, NSC-68, is another document that was clearly a product of a specific time and place, rhetorically translating statistical representations into hysterical exhortations, products of what becomes labeled "a doomsayer's delusion."[7] Newman's recitation of other environmental factors makes decisions during Truman's presidency prudent but later misunderstood: the President's convictions and actions that were based on predictions from his best prognosticators, the relationship developing between Paul Nitze and Edward Teller, Nitze's association with America First before the war and the Committee on the Present Danger after it, the suppression from the USSBS of dissident voices. Such forces playing upon Truman's decision effectively moved it out of the military and into a political and then a cultural context.

At this point in his book, i.e., after the first four chapters, Newman has sanctified Truman, vilified Nitze, and spun a story that challenges the anti-bomb and anti-Truman historians and moralists, taking on Wander's claim that "the rhetoric of American foreign policy protects us against reality, that is, against the claim on our attention that any event or fact makes by virtue of its existence."[8] He has sought to construct a wall of facts to hold back the naysayers.

But he does not stop there, for if he had, he would have remained in a nest of revisionist hornets buzzing about dead heroes and their enemies, however the various parties construed heroism and villainy. Instead, second of all, the stories wend into new social, economic, military, and political contexts that coerce the reframings and rememberings comprising the bulk of the book. The rhetorics of foreign policy emerging during the periods of the Korean and Vietnam Wars as well as, I would add, the nuclear freeze debates of the early 1980s,[9] combined the ideological force of Cold War antagonisms with a mythically enlarged vision of nuclear holocaust so as to almost completely remake the contexts within which those policies were constructed.[10] And further, as the Cold War framework and orientational metaphors[11] slipped out of the public mind, there was the symbolic manufacture of what we now term the New World Order, and which Hollihan has identified as one of three foreign policy dramas available to those talking about foreign understandings publicly in the late twentieth century.[12] The United States' geopolitical postures—its self-images as well as those symbolized for others important to foreign relations—changed significantly.

The stories that Newman tells of Korea and Vietnam, together with those he could have told us about the nuclear freeze movement and even the globalized Persian Gulf War, fired up new rhetorics of foreign policy. Consonant with Hollihan's (and Stuckey's) construction of the New World Order, the U.S. tried to work in the Bush Sr. and Clinton administrations from collections of multicultural nation-state actors with their own pragmatic and moral bases, giving up some aspects of self-interest so as to share in the management of conflict and the control of rogue nations and terrorists. In such a vision, the Power Politics (see Hollihan) of self-interested foreign activity—evident, for example, in George W. Bush's statements about U.S. interests in Iraq following 9/11—was submerged by internationalist, even globalized, environments for foreign policy activities. With the New World Order as orientational metaphor, any hint that nuclear weaponry was a viable international tool of influence, even as deterrent, was anathema. Nuclear stockpiles were to shrink in a time of arms limitation, with the whole world watching. The very idea of their use—even the history of their use—brought cries of outrage from everywhere.

In such situations, Newman makes clear, new rhetorics dominated foreign policy talk. If with Lemke by "discourse formations" we reference "persistent habits of speaking and acting, characteristic of some group, through which it constructs its worldview,"[13] then the late- and post-Cold War eras brought new discourse formations. They had the power to remake international threats and to require new sorts of assurances. In a period when "rogue nations" and "terrorists" were more to be feared than monolithic Communism and when the Cold War doctrine of mutually assured destruction (M.A.D.) morphed into fear of nuclear triggers touched off in the Middle East, on the India-Pakistan border, or (now) in North Korea, foreign policy discourses had to change, even radically.

What becomes fascinating in and around the *Enola Gay* controversy is the range of conflicts and subsequent negotiations that surfaced—signs of New World Order rhetorics at their shrillest. Because the exhibit script discussed "Historical Controversies," old inter-nation and inter-constituency disputes could be woven into that script. Japanese massacres in pre-war China, along with the Korean comfort women issue, were symbolically attached to the exhibit's narrative by East Asian historians, even as Nippon Television warned exhibitors not to re-open issues likely to chill U.S.-Japanese relations. The Air Force Association wanted fliers valorized even as Japanese children called them Baby Killers and their parents had allies among historians who blamed everything on European imperialism. Newman's accounts of Japanese and American historians of Japan, of military historians and novelists' accounts of nuclear war, and of peaceniks whose imprint was left on unit 5, "THE LEGACY OF HIROSHIMA AND NAGASAKI," were reflected in the *Enola Gay* script:

> The introduction of nuclear weapons into the world, and their first use at Hiroshima, left powerful legacies beyond the long-term radiation effects on the survivors. For Japan, the United States, and its allies a horrific war was brought to an abrupt end, although at a cost debated to this day; for the world, a nuclear arms race that still threatens unimaginable devastation.[14]

Another heading was "A WORLD GONE M.A.D.," evoking the pre-World War II antagonisms heated to dangerous boiling points by nuclear capabilities. Together with the unit 5 script, such discourse emphasized atomic weaponry as evil because of its civilian effects (on survivors and non-survivors), its economic effects (on an arms race creating obscene defense budgets), and, by implication thanks to other discourses circulating in the public sphere, its ecological and cultural effects (on nuclear winter, ethnic barbarity, and anything else that could be encompassed by "unimaginable devastation"). In such a discourse formation, a straightforward, storied exhibit of an airplane, photos, and artifacts from the events of the summer-fall 1945 could not be created. The exhibit's narrative space could not organize all of the issues coherently.

Inevitably, conflict—strong conflict—arose, made the news, troubled the citizenry (at least those portions with a stake in 1945 or in nuclear policy), and deadlocked a memorializing agency not willing or able to take sides. NASM's funding certainly is too fragile to risk exploding its reputation over one exhibit. As well, the epideictic challenge of organizing praise and blame was staggering.

So, readers of this book are rewarded with strange yet wonder-evoking stories about a past that refuses to give up its hold upon the present and future. In Newman, they can witness a man who himself was a participant in World War II (though in the European theatre) mine again the archives for evidence that he hopes will correct the record and call off the revisionist dogs. The book makes for an engaging read.

For rhetoricians, however, for scholars particularly interested in both the grand discursive visions and the strategic manipulations of particular facts that determine foreign policy making, implementing, and later remembering, this book suggests some important ways that rhetorics of foreign policy should be conceptualized. Two stand out:

1. *Rhetorical negotiations in some areas of human life, including governmental policy making, never are over.* They have characteristics of what Thomas Goodnight defines as a controversy.[15] Foreign policy making is an ongoing process that stops but does not end. It is episodic, that is, it comes and goes as needed, as events require a reexamination of relationships between nation-states. There certainly are policy precedents, akin to legal precedents in courts; they may provide guidance but not answers, because changing circumstances make arguments from parallel cases often difficult to sustain. Precedents act much like Aristotle's *Rhetoric*[16] suggested that examples work: reasoning from particular event to particular event is suggestive but not determinative because parallels are not equivalencies. Further, something like a hermeneutic circle develops, as the past is brought in to help with today's decision, but then, as we look back to that past from today, we remake or reinterpret it. Then, when it has been reconstructed symbolically, it now becomes a different sort of precedent that in turn will have an altered relationship to the present and future.

   Foreign policy decisions, episode after episode, are new phases of continuing geopolitical controversies. The revisioning of American orientations to international relations after the Cold War, as Newman has demonstrated, altered both present difficulties and past acts. As Goodnight argued, "the end of the Cold War means the demise of the coherence, power and issue foci of one argument formation and perhaps the rise of another."[17] That is, the rise of the New World Order vision valued different arguments—new geopolitical postures, new administrative moves—than had the bivalenced worldviews of Democracy-Communism confrontations. A bivalenced world became multivalenced, and controversial relationships had to be argued with a new vocabulary. That profoundly affected even Americans' understanding of 1945.

2. *"Rhetoric," in such cases as Newman's, is not simply relativistic—it is not true that anything goes—but it is context-specific, comprised of discourses grounded in the here-and-now of living peacefully (or not) with others.* The ways that human beings engage and understand the world are a product of the means they have available

for assessing it and the material aspects of that world that they seek to account for with those available means. Human events are parts of an evolving present, and rhetoric is a force, what Edelman called an "intervention," manufacturing and remanufacturing discursive, sociopolitically nuanced accounts of that present. Yesterday's discourses assuredly can be made relevant to today; the USSBS and NSC-68 still are worked into today's accountings—but, in the face of today's information, values, concerns, perceived problems, and hoped-for futures.

When Daniel Bell back in 1960[18] argued that the era of ideology was dead, he did not mean that all ideological accounts were closed off from discourses of power. Rather, he meant that overarching discursive structures of tradition and utopia, such as one finds (he said) in Christian and Communist dogma, were not the starting points of human endeavor. Rather, the starting points were people's lived conditions, lived conditions that made information, values, concerns, threats, and reassurances relevant to decision making. Even the rhetorics of foreign policy making, implementing, adjusting, and remembering are subject to the lived conditions of today, grounded in those conditions but then, as Edelman noted, shaped symbolically into political cognitions and reasoned actions. That is not philosophical relativism. It is, simply, a rhetorical fact of life.

And, Robert Newman has made that point patently clear in this book.

Notes

1. Murray Edelman, *Politics as Symbolic Action: Mass Arousal and Quiescence* (New York: Academic Press), 2.
2. Philip Wander, "The Rhetoric of American Foreign Policy," *Quarterly Journal of Speech* 70 (1984), 339.
3. For a discussion of relationships between specific foreign policies and public opinion, see J. Michael Hogan, "Public Opinion and American Foreign Policy: The Case of Illusory Support for the Panama Canal Treaties," *Quarterly Journal of Speech* 71 (1985), 302–317; cf. J. Michael Hogan and Leroy Dorsey, "Public Opinion and the Nuclear Freeze: The Rhetoric of Popular Sovereignty in Foreign Policy Debate," *Western Journal of Communication* 35 (1991), 319–338; and G. Thomas Goodnight, "Public Argument and the Study of Foreign Policy," *American Diplomacy* [online] 3 (Summer 1998), *http://www.unc.edu/depts/diplomat/AD_Issues/8amdipl.html*.
4. See Bruce E. Gronbeck, "The Rhetorics of the Past: History, Argument, and Collective Memory," *Doing Rhetorical History: Concepts and Cases,* ed. Kathleen J. Turner (Tuscaloosa, AL: University of Alabama Press, 1998), 47–60.
5. Ibid.
6. Newman, Chapter 5.
7. Ibid., 73.
8. Wander, 339.
9. See Hogan and Dorsey.

10. On ideological and mythic dimensions of foreign policy, see Jeff D. Bass and Richard Cherwitz, "Imperial Mission and Manifest Destiny: A Case Study of Political Myth in Rhetorical Discourse," *Southern Communication Journal* 43 (1978), 213–232.

11. Mary E. Stuckey, "Competing Foreign Policy Visions: Rhetorical Hybrids After the Cold War," *Western Journal of Communication* 59 (1995), 214–227.

12. Thomas Hollihan, "The Public Controversy over the Panama Canal Treaties: An Analysis of American Foreign Policy Rhetoric," *Western Journal of Communication* 50 (1986), 368–387.

13. Jay L. Lemke, *Textual Politics: Discourse and Social Dynamics* (London: Taylor & Francis, 1995), 24.

14. Newman, quoted in Chapter 6.

15. G. Thomas Goodnight, "Controvery," *Argument in Controversy*, ed. Donn Parson (Washington, DC: National Communication Association, 1991), 1–12.

16. Aristotle, *On Rhetoric: A Theory of Civic Discourse,* intro., trans. George A. Kennedy (New York: Oxford University Press, 1991).

17. Goodnight, "Public Opinion."

18. Daniel Bell, *The End of Ideology: On the Exhaustion of Political Ideas in the Fifties* (1960; rpt. Cambridge, MA: Harvard University Press, 1988).

Sources Cited

Aristotle. *On Rhetoric: A Theory of Civic Discourse*. Intro., Trans. George A. Kennedy. New York: Oxford University Press, 1991.

Bass, Jeff D., and Richard Cherwitz. "Imperial Mission and Manifest Destiny: A Case Study of Political Myth in Rhetorical Discourse." *Southern Communication Journal* 43 (1978): 213–232.

Bell, Daniel. *The End of Ideology: On the Exhaustion of Political Ideas in the Fifties*. 1960; rpt. Cambridge, MA: Harvard University Press, 1988.

Edelman, Murray. *Politics as Symbolic Action: Mass Arousal and Quiescence*. New York: Academic Press, 1971.

Goodnight, G. Thomas. "Controversy," in Donn Parson, ed., *Argument in Controversy*. Washington, DC: National Communication Association, 1991. 1–12.

——. "Public Argument and the Study of Foreign Policy." *American Diplomacy* [online] 3 (Summer 1998). http://www.unc.edu/depts/diplomat/AD_Issues/8amdipl.html.

Gronbeck, Bruce E. "The Rhetorics of the Past: History, Argument, and Collective Memory," in Kathleen J. Turner, ed., *Doing Rhetorical History: Concepts and Cases*. Tuscaloosa, AL: University of Alabama Press, 1998.

Hogan, J. Michael. "Public Opinion and American Foreign Policy: The Case of Illusory Support for the Panama Canal Treaties." *Quarterly Journal of Speech* 71 (1985): 302–317.

Hogan, J. Michael, and Leroy Dorsey. "Public Opinion and the Nuclear Freeze: The Rhetoric of Popular Sovereignty in Foreign Policy Debate." *Western Journal of Communication* 55 (1991): 319–338.

Hollihan, Thomas. "The Public Controversy over the Panama Canal Treaties: An Analysis of American Foreign Policy Rhetoric." *Western Journal of Communication* 50 (1986): 368–387.

Lemke, Jay L. *Textual Politics: Discourse and Social Dynamics*. London: Taylor & Francis, 1995.

Stuckey, Mary E. "Competing Foreign Policy Visions: Rhetorical Hybrids After the Cold War." *Western Journal of Communication* 59 (1995): 214–227.

Wander, Philip. "The Rhetoric of American Foreign Policy." *Quarterly Journal of Speech* 70 (1984): 339–361.

NOTES

Chapter 1. Official Narrative #1—Truman Version

1. United States Atomic Energy Commission, *In The Matter of J. Robert Oppenheimer* (Cambridge, MA: MIT Press, 1970), 171.
2. On Stimson, Conrad C. Crane, *Bombs, Cities, and Civilians* (Lawrence, KS: University Press of Kansas, 1993), 136; on Marshall, Maurice Matloff, *Strategic Planning for Coalition Warfare* (Washington, D.C., 1959), 5.
3. Perry R. Duis, "No Time for Privacy," in Louis A. Erenberg and Susan B. Hirsch, eds., *The War in American Culture* (Chicago: University of Chicago Press, 1996), 33.
4. Omar Bradley and Clay Blair, *A General's Life* (New York: Simon and Schuster, 1983), 172.
5. Papers of John Callan O'Laughlin, Box 171, Post-Presidential Papers, Herbert Hoover Presidential Library, West Branch, Iowa.
6. Charles F. Brower IV, *The Joint Chiefs of Staff and National Policy: American Strategy and the War with Japan, 1943–1945,* Ph.D. dissertation, University of Pennsylvania, 1987, 266. This is the best account of the struggle between army (Marshall, Embick) and navy/air force (Leahy, King, Arnold) over invasion vs. blockade.
7. Letter of 6 January 1945, O'Laughlin Papers, HHPL.
8. P. J. Philip, "6,300 Canadian Soldiers AWOL of 15,600 Called to Go Overseas," *New York Times* (21 January 1945).
9. Geoffrey Perrett, *Days of Sadness, Years of Triumph* (Baltimore: Penguin, 1974), 410.
10. Cited in John Toland, *The Rising Sun* (New York: Bantam, 1970), 745.
11. Toland, *Rising Sun,* 746.

12. Samuel Stouffer et al., *Combat and Its Aftermath,* Vol. 2 (Princeton: Princeton University Press, 1949), 90.

13. Ibid.

14. JIC as quoted in Brower, *The Joint Chiefs,* 271–72.

15. Hanson Baldwin, "The Let-Down Problem." *New York Times* (2 April 1945). The best single discussion of these matters is Michael D. Pearlman, *Unconditional Surrender, Demobilization, and the Atomic Bomb* (Fort Leavenworth, KS: U.S. Army Command and General Staff College, 1996).

16. Brower, *The Joint Chiefs,* 273.

17. Brower, *The Joint Chiefs,* 274.

18. Malvina Lindsay, "War Weariness," *Washington Post* (9 May 1945).

19. Richard A. Briggs, *Black Hawks Over the Danube* (West Point, KY: Richard A. Briggs, 1953), 102.

20. Stouffer et al., *Combat and Its Aftermath,* 469.

21. Maxwell Taylor, *Swords and Plowshares* (New York: Norton, 1972), 110.

22. Manuscript of unpublished autobiography, Ballantine Papers, Box 3, Hoover Institution Archives, Stanford, CA.

23. The military, like other professions, has its own (sometimes competing) functions and bureaucracies, standard operating procedures, jargon, and unarticulated premises. Innocent civilians wandering among the 17,129 tons of U.S. Army records from World War II are easily led astray by the bewildering functions for which casualty estimates are designed. D. M. Giangreco's "Casualty Projections for the U.S. Invasions of Japan, 1945–1946: Planning and Policy Implications," *Journal of Military History* 61 (July 1997), 521–82, is the most authoritative source for understanding that arcane subject. The Society for Military History awarded Giangreco its Moncado Prize in 1998 for this article.

24. John E. Mueller, *War, Presidents, and Public Opinion* (New York: Wiley, 1973), 60.

25. On Okinawa, I depend on Ronald Spector, *Eagle Against the Sun* (New York: Free Press, 1985), 494–502; Roy E. Appleman et al., *Okinawa: The Last Battle* (Washington, D.C.: Department of the Army, 1948); and Ian Gow, *Okinawa 1945: Gateway to Japan* (Garden City, NY: Doubleday, 1985).

26. Spector, *Eagle,* 540, 543.

27. Hanson Baldwin, "Japan's Industrial Power: While Bombing Will Greatly Cut Output, New Denser Defenses Will Need Less," *New York Times* (22 June 1945).

28. W. H. Lawrence, "Japan, Like Okinawa, Will Cost High Price," *New York Times* (24 June 1945).

29. "Japan's Civil Army Gets Suicide Order," *New York Times* (26 June 1945).

30. "Tokyo Chiefs Hail Okinawa Victory," *New York Times* (27 June 1945).

31. Gladwin Hill, "Mass Suicide Corps Trained by Japan," *New York Times* (29 July 1945).

32. Kyle Palmer, "Palmer Warns Nips Set for Murderous Combat," *Los Angeles Times* (8 May 1945).

33. U. S. Department of Defense, *The Entry of the Soviet Union into the War Against Japan* (Washington, D.C.: Government Printing Office, 1955), 76.

34. Robert H. Ferrell, ed., *Off the Record: The Private Papers of Harry S. Truman* (New York: Harper & Row, 1980), 47.

35. Edward J. Drea, *MacArthur's ULTRA: Codebreaking and the War Against Japan* (Lawrence, KS: University Press of Kansas, 1992), 209–210.

36. Ibid., 223. Giangreco has a different opinion of the exchange between Marshall and MacArthur. In "Casualty Projections for the Invasions of Japan," 545–49, he states that

the lengthy and increasingly pointed exchange had nothing to do with any perception on Marshall's part that the casualty estimates emanating from MacArthur's headquarters were too large. Giangreco notes that the original transmission had all the earmarks of a routine staff request from the Pentagon, and that, consequently, the initial reply to Marshall's query did not come from either MacArthur or any of his senior planners; that the numbers represented a simple medical planning analysis which did not answer Marshall's—or the president's—query; and that this was immediately recognized in Washington. This prompted a request for clarification signed by Marshall and directed specifically to MacArthur. Giangreco maintains it was too early in the Pacific headquarters' planning cycle for formulation of the type of estimates requested by Marshall, and MacArthur was forced to answer with generalities.

37. Ibid., 210.
38. Minutes of Meeting Held at the White House on Monday, 18 June 1945 at 1530, *Foreign Relations of the United States* (Hereafter FRUS) *The Conference of Berlin (Potsdam) 1945*, vol. 1 (Washington D.C.: Government Printing Office, 1960), 905.
39. See Giangreco, "Casualty Projections," 576–577.
40. See Drea, *MacArthur's ULTRA*, ch. 8.
41. Denis Warner, Peggy Warner, and Commander Sadao Seno, *The Sacred Warriors: Japan's Suicide Legions* (New York: Van Nostrand Reinhold, 1982), 298.
42. Robert H. Ferrell, "Intelligence Assessments and Assumptions: The View from Washington," paper presented at the 1999 Annual Meeting of the Society for Military History, University Park, PA, 16 April 1999.
43. Herbert Hoover, "Memorandum on Ending the Japanese War," White House Confidential File, Box 43, Harry S. Truman Library, Independence, MO. See also Giangreco,"'A Score of Bloody Okinawas and Iwo Jimas': President Truman and Casualty Estimates for the Invasion of Japan," *Pacific Historical Review* 72 (February 2003), 93–132, esp. 105–114.
44. Memorandum (by General Thomas T. Handy), 4 June 1945, attached to Memorandum for General Hull, War Department, Office of the Chief of Staff, 1 June 1945; my copy obtained from Marshall Center Archives, Lexington, VA. See also Giangreco, "A Score of . . . Okinawas," 114–116.
45. W. B. Shockley to Edward L. Bowles, 21 July 1945, Proposal for Increasing the Scope of Casualty Studies, Edward L. Bowles Papers, Box 34, Library of Congress. The Shockley effort was a major initiative of Secretary Stimson, and included not only the noted historian Quincy Wright, but Dr. Michael DeBakey (then an expert on casualty classification) and Dr. Gilbert Beebe. For a fuller description of Shockley's operation, see Robert P. Newman, *Truman and the Hiroshima Cult* (East Lansing: Michigan State University Press, 1995), 18–19, and Giangreco "Casualty Projections," 564–569.
46. John W. Finney, *Hiroshima Plus 20* (New York, Delacorte Press, 1965); statement of John J. McCloy pp. 121–125.
47. Brower, *Joint Chiefs*, 263.
48. Ellis M. Zacharias, *Secret Missions* (New York: G. P. Putnam's Sons, 1946), 353.
49. Willoughby quoted in Philip Gustavson, "What if We Had Invaded Japan?" *Saturday Evening Post*, 5 January 1946, 18.
50. Drea, *MacArthur's ULTRA*, 216.
51. Those whose memories were (are) quite clear about the half-million figure as the word-of-mouth assumption for casualties expected in a full Japanese invasion, range from a junior OSS officer brought to Washington from the China-Burma-India Theater for

invasion planning (Samuel Halpern) to Arthur Holly Compton of the Manhattan Project and the University of Chicago. It is nonsense to say that all these several dozen people misremembered.

52. This point is made convincingly in Russell Weigley, *The American Way of War* (Bloomington: Indiana University Press, 1977), 310.

53. Edward J. Drea, *In The Service of The Emperor* (Lincoln: University of Nebraska Press, 1998), ch. 11.

54. Drea, *In The Service,* 164.

55. Joint Intelligence Committee, "Japanese Reaction to an Assault Against Northern Honshu," 6 August 1945, JCS/CCS 381, Box 615, RG 218, NA; Joint War Plans Committee 398/1, "Plan for the Invasion of Northern Honshu," 9 August 1945, Box 615, RG 218, NA.

56. Drea, *In The Service,* 165.

57. On Marshall's plan to use A-bombs on the beaches, see Marc Gallicchio, "After Nagasaki: General Marshall's Plan for Tactical Nuclear Weapons in Japan," *Prologue* 23 (Winter 1991), 396–404. Drea summary: *In The Service,* 167–68.

58. Edmund J. Winslett, "Defense of Southern Kyushu," 3 June 1946, Winslett Papers, U.S. Army Military History Institute, Carlisle Barracks, PA., 7.

59. Earl Pomeroy, "Sentiment for a Strong Peace, 1917–1919," *South Atlantic Quarterly* 43 (October 1944), 325–30.

60. John J. Pershing, *My Experiences in the World War* (New York: Frederick A. Stokes, 1931) 368, 369.

61. Laurence Stallings, *The Doughboys* (New York: Harper & Row, 1963), 345.

62. Stallings, *Doughboys,* 374. Hans Bethe, one of the more sophisticated Manhattan Project scientists, who approved the mission of *Enola Gay* but has since fought against nuclear weapons, is quite clear about the dynamics of 1945: "The German slogan 'Im Felde unbesiegt'—Never defeated in the field—was the seed for the Nazi movement. I believe that Roosevelt and likewise the British had this very much in mind when they asked for unconditional surrender." See Mary Palevsky, *Atomic Fragments* (Berkeley: University of California Press, 2000), 25.

63. See Raymond G. O'Connor, *Diplomacy for Victory: FDR and Unconditional Surrender* (New York: Norton, 1971), 2.

64. Pomeroy, 325.

65. Iokibe Makoto, "American Policy Towards Japan's 'Unconditional Surrender,' " *Japanese Journal of American Studies* 1 (1981), 29.

66. Iokibe, 29–30; and Harley A. Notter, *Postwar Foreign Policy Preparation, 1939–1940* (Washington, D.C.: Government Printing Office, 1949), 126–27.

67. *FRUS,* 1942, 1:25–26.

68. *FRUS, The Conferences at Washington, 1941–1942, and Casablanca, 1943,* 506.

69. Ibid., 635.

70. Ibid., 834–35.

71. Ibid., 727.

72. William M. Franklin, "Unconditional Surrender," in Alexander DeConde, ed., *Encyclopedia of American Foreign Policy* (New York: Charles Scribner's Sons, 1978), 991.

73. Churchill, in Robert E. Sherwood, *Roosevelt and Hopkins* (New York: Harper & Brothers, 1948), 696.

74. Roosevelt, in ibid.

75. Ibid., 697. Some students of international affairs reject the belief that any war could stay won; however, Sir Michael Howard believes that at least the abject defeat of Ger-

many in 1945 "was the end of half a century of German wars, and of the Germany which had provoked them." *Lessons of History* (New Haven: Yale University Press, 1991), 128.

76. *FRUS, Casablanca,* 506.

77. U.S. Department of State, *The Axis in Defeat* (Washington, D.C.: Government Printing Office, 1945), 4.

78. Roosevelt in John L. Chase, "Unconditional Surrender Reconsidered," *Political Science Quarterly* 70 (June 1955), 264.

79. Churchill in ibid., 265. See also Warren F. Kimball, *The Juggler: Franklin Roosevelt as Wartime Statesman* (Princeton: Princeton University Press, 1991), 76.

80. Barton Bernstein, "The Perils and Politics of Surrender: Ending the War with Japan and Avoiding the Third Atomic Bomb," *Pacific Historical Review* 46 (November 1977): 5.

81. See Howard Schonberger, "The Japan Lobby in American Diplomacy," *Pacific Historical Review* 46 (August 1977), 327–29.

82. Brian L. Villa, "The U.S. Army, Unconditional Surrender, and the Potsdam Proclamation," *Journal of American History* 63 (June 1976), 75–76.

83. *FRUS, The Conferences at Malta and Yalta, 1945,* 825–26.

84. Villa, 78. Villa notes that the Allies misused unconditional surrender after the war.

85. Villa, 81.

86. Harry S. Truman, *Memoirs,* Vol. One, *Year of Decisions* (Garden City: Doubleday, 1955), 42.

87. Ibid., 207.

88. *FRUS 1945,* 4:547.

89. *Public Papers of the Presidents of the United States: Harry S. Truman, 1945.* (Washington, D.C.: Government Printing Office, 1961), 98. Marc Gallicchio gives the best explanation of Truman's unwillingness to overtly modify unconditional surrender in *The Cold War Begins in Asia* (New York: Columbia University Press, 1988), 16, and chapter 3.

90. Minutes of Meeting of the Committee of Three, 12 June 1945, ASW (McCloy), 334.8, Box 19, RG 17, NA.

91. Minutes of Meeting Held at the White House on Monday, 18 June 1945 at 1530, *FRUS Berlin,* 1:905.

92. Minutes of Meeting of the Committee of Three, 19 June 1945, ASW (McCloy), 334.8, Box 19, RG 107, NA.

93. Gallicchio, *Cold War Begins,* 16–17.

94. Draft Memorandum for Mr. McCloy, 28 June 1945, ASW (McCloy), 385–87, Box 38, RG 107, NA.

95. Appendix "C," Mark Howe's Draft, attached to document cited in note 94.

96. *FRUS Berlin,* 2:1474.

97. Memorandum, Rights and Powers over Japan, 4 September 1945, ASW (McCloy), 387, Box 38, RG 107, NA.

98. Martin J. Sherwin, *A World Destroyed* (New York: Vintage, 1977), 235. Sherwin contends in "Hiroshima and Modern Memory," *The Nation* 233 (October 1981), 352, that unconditional surrender was a mere "political shibboleth." This is a highly deviant opinion.

99. Leon Sigal, *Fighting to a Finish* (Ithaca: Cornell University Press, 1988), 144–45.

100. Togo Shigenori, *The Cause of Japan* (New York: Simon and Schuster, 1956), 311.

101. USSBS papers, M1654, Roll 1, frame 1021, NA.

102. Kase Toshikazu, *Journey to the Missouri* (New Haven: Yale University Press, 1950), 209–210.

103. Kato Masuo, *The Lost War* (New York: Knopf, 1946), 233.

104. Shigemitsu, in Samuel Eliot Morison, *Victory in the Pacific* (Boston: Little, Brown, 1960), 343.

105. Memorandum for the President, 2 August 1945, William J. Donovan Papers, U.S. Army Military History Institute, Carlisle, PA.

106. See Robert J.C. Butow, *Japan's Decision to Surrender* (Stanford: Stanford University Press, 1954), 244. Butow is still a sound account of the end of the war. The landmark analysis, however, using the vast amount of material that became available after Hirohito's death, is Sadao Asada, "The Shock of the Atomic Bomb and Japan's Decision to Surrender—A Reconsideration," *Pacific Historical Review* 67 (November 1998), 477–512, upon which I depend here.

107. Cited in Lisle A. Rose, *Dubious Victory* (Kent, OH: Kent State University Press, 1973), 319. See also Butow, 189–90.

108. A. E. Campbell, "Franklin Roosevelt and Unconditional Surrender," in Richard Langhorne, ed., *Diplomacy and Intelligence during the Second World War* (Cambridge: Cambridge University Press, 1985), 221.

109. The phrase "slight reassurance" is Butow's; 191.

110. John W. Dower, *Embracing Defeat* (New York: W. W. Norton, 1999), 84.

111. Ibid., 83.

112. Dwight MacDonald, "The Decline to Barbarism," *Politics* 2 (August–September 1945), 225.

113. David Lawrence, "What Hath Man Wrought?" *United States News* 19 (17 August 1945), 38–39.

114. "The Horror and the Shame," *Commonweal,* XLII (24 August 1945), 237–38.

115. "America's Atomic Atrocity," *Christian Century* LXII (29 August 1945), 974.

116. Norman Thomas, "When Cruelty Becomes Pleasurable," *Human Events* II (26 September 1945), 3.

117. Stuart Chase, "Atomic Age Balance Sheet," *Common Sense* XIV (October 1945), 28–29; Milton Mayer, "Thomists and Atomists," *Common Sense* XIV (November 1945), 27–28; Lewis Mumford, "Gentlemen: You Are Mad," *Saturday Review of Literature* XXIX (2 March 1946), 5–6.

118. "Report of Protestant Church Leaders on Atomic Warfare," *New York Times* (6 March 1946).

119. Norman Cousins, "The Non-Obliterators," *Saturday Review* 27 (8 April 1944), 14.

120. Norman Cousins and Thomas K. Finletter, "A Beginning for Sanity," *Saturday Review* 29 (15 June 1946), 5–9, 38–40.

121. Hermann Hagedorn, *The Bomb That Fell on America* (Santa Barbara: Pacific Coast Publishing Co., 1946); later editions, Association Press, New York.

122. Hagedorn, 62.

123. Nicholas Roosevelt to Hermann Hagedorn, 24 April 1946, Hagedorn Papers, Box 1, Syracuse University Library, Syracuse, NY.

124. Tibbetts interview in Robert Del Tredici, *At Work in the Fields of the Bomb* (New York: Harper & Row, 1987), 161.

125. Barton J. Bernstein, "Reconsidering 'Invasion Most Costly': Popular-History Scholarship, and the Claim of High U.S. Casualty Estimates to Help Legitimize the Atomic Bombings," *Peace & Change* 24 (April 1999), 237.

Chapter 2. Official Narrative #2—Nitze Version

1. United States Strategic Bombing Survey, *Summary Report (Pacific War)* (Washington, D.C.: Government Printing Office, 1946—Henceforth GPO), 26. An identical paragraph appears in USSBS, *Japan's Struggle to End the War* (GPO, 1946), 13.

2. I take as definitive the study of USSBS by Gian Gentile, *How Effective is Strategic Bombing?* (New York: New York University Press, 2000). David MacIsaac, *Strategic Bombing in World War II* (New York: Garland, 1976) is also useful for the history of USSBS, though it is not critical.

3. John Kenneth Galbraith, *A Life in Our Times* (Boston: Houghton Mifflin, 1981), chap. 14.

4. Results of the British Bombing Survey Unit (BBSU) were so controversial that they were not published in full until 1998: BBSU, *The Strategic Air War Against Germany* (London: Frank Cass, 1998).

5. Paul H. Nitze, *From Hiroshima to Glasnost: At the Center of Decision* (New York: Grove Weidenfeld, 1989), 36–37.

6. James Beveridge, *History of the United States Bombing Survey (Pacific)* (Washington, D.C.: Center of Military History, 1946), unpaginated appendix.

7. Strobe Talbott, *The Master of the Game: Paul Nitze and the Nuclear Peace* (New York: Knopf, 1988), 37.

8. As Gentile makes clear, when one factors in the whole set of USSBS reports, the Nitzean early surrender counterfactual appears to have come from another planet. The raw data contradict it.

9. Beveridge, 22.

10. John J. Driscoll, Major, Air Corps, to Chairman, USSBS, 3 March 1947, Box 29, RG 243, NA.

11. G. L. McMurrin, Lt. Col. Air Corps, for Chairman, USSBS, to Major John J. Driscoll, 6 March 1947, attached to document identified in preceding note.

12. USSBS, *Japan's Struggle*, 1.

13. Arnold Brackman, *The Other Nuremberg* (New York: William Morrow, 1987), 332; and R. John Pritchard and Sonia M. Zaide, eds., *The Tokyo War Crimes Trial*, vol. 13 (New York: Garland, 1981), 31,180.

14. *Japan's Struggle*, 26.

15. Records of the U.S. Strategic Bombing Survey, M1654, Roll 5, frame 0503.

16. USSBS Records, M1654, Roll 5, frame 0315.

17. Pritchard and Zaide, *Tokyo War Crimes Trial*, 31,180.

18. USSBS, Naval Analysis Division, *Interrogations of Japanese Officials*, vol. 2 (Washington, D.C.: GPO, 1946), 320, 322.

19. USSBS Records, M1654, Roll 1, frames 1021–22.

20. Sakomizu's interrogation in the NA microfilm is largely illegible; this is from "The Decision for Peace," *ONI Review* 1 (June 1946), 15.

21. USSBS Records, M1655, Roll 208A, frames 0357–58.

22. USSBS Records, M1655, Roll 208A, frame 0222.

23. USSBS Records, M1654, Roll 1, frame 0317.

24. USSBS Records, M1654, Roll 3, frames 0010, 0011.

25. USSBS, *The Effects of Air Attack on Japanese Urban Economy—Summary Report* (Washington, D.C.: GPO, 1947), iv.

26. Ibid., 47.

27. Ibid., 49.

28. Robert J. C. Butow, *Japan's Decision to Surrender* (Stanford: Stanford University Press, 1954), chapter 10.

29. Pacific War Research Society, *Japan's Longest Day* (Tokyo and Palo Alto: Kodansha International, 1972).

30. *Japan's Longest Day* is the best account of this.

31. Butow, 33.

32. Ibid., 46.

33. Ibid., 124.

34. Ibid., 66. All these judgments of Butow are affirmed in Sadao Asada, "The Shock of the Atomic Bomb and Japan's Decision to Surrender—a Reconsideration," *Pacific Historical Review* 67 (November 1988), 477–512.

35. Franklin D'Olier to President Harry S. Truman, 10 May 1946, Papers of USSBS, OF 651, Harry S. Truman Library, Independence, MO.

36. SRH-084, Russo-Japanese Relations (1–10) July 1945, Records of the National Security Agency, Central Security Service, Box 17, RG 457, NA.

37. SRH-090, Japan's Surrender Maneuvers, 29 August 1945, Records of the National Security Agency, Central Security Service, Box 17, RG 457, NA.

38. Edward Drea, *MacArthur's ULTRA: Codebreaking and the War Against Japan* (Lawrence: University Press of Kansas, 1992).

39. Ibid., 204.

40. MacIsaac, ch. 6.

41. Gian Gentile, "Shaping the Past Battlefield, 'For the Future,': The United States Bombing Survey's Evaluation of the American Air War Against Japan," *Journal of Military History* 64 (October 2000), 1107.

42. Ibid., 1106.

43. Nitze cited in note 5; Talbott cited in note 7; David Callahan, *Dangerous Capabilities: Paul Nitze and the Cold War* (New York: Harper Collins, 1990).

44. Nitze, xiii.

45. Ibid., xviii.

46. Talbott, 31.

47. Ibid., 30.

48. William R. Castle Diary, 12 June 1951, Houghton Library, Harvard University, Cambridge, MA.

49. Nitze interview by author, 25 January 1994.

50. Callahan, 52.

51. Nitze cited in Gian Gentile, *Advocacy or Assessment? The United States Strategic Bombing Survey of Germany and Japan,* Ph.D. dissertation, Stanford University, 1998, 130.

52. Nitze, 37.

53. MacIsaac discusses this temporary anti-atomic position of some airmen, p. 165.

54. Gentile, *Advocacy or Assessment,* 145.

55. Callahan, 76–77.

56. The most comprehensive account of the construction of NSC-68 is Robert P. Newman, "NSC (National Insecurity) 68: Nitze's Second Hallucination," in Martin Medhurst and H. W. Brands, eds., *Critical Reflections on the Cold War* (College Station: Texas A & M University Press, 2000), 55–94.

57. The text of NSC-68 is available in Ernest R. May, ed., *American Cold War Strategy: Interpreting NSC-68* (Boston: Bedford Books of St. Martin's Press, 1993). Quote is from 26.

58. Ibid.
59. Nitze to Secretary of State, 6 April 1950, Policy Planning Staff Papers, Box 54, RG 59, NA.
60. Callahan, 99.
61. Galbraith, 233. See also Fred Kaplan, *The Wizards of Armageddon*.
62. Eisenhower quoted in Gregg Herken, *Counsels of War* (New York: Oxford University Press, 1987), 116.
63. Paul H. Nitze, "Atoms, Strategy and Policy," *Foreign Affairs* 34 (January 1956), 190.
64. Talbott, 101.
65. Gar Alperovitz, *The Decision to Use the Atomic Bomb and the Architecture of an American Myth* (New York: Knopf, 1995) cites the USSBS early surrender hypothesis 17 times.
66. Butow as mentioned in notes 31–34; Barton Bernstein, ed., *The Atomic Bomb: The Critical Issues* (Boston: Little, Brown, 1976), 52–53; William L. O'Neill, *A Democracy at War* (New York: Free Press, 1993), 415.
67. On Stimson's doubts, see McGeorge Bundy, *Danger and Survival: Choices about the Bomb in the First Fifty Years* (New York: Vintage/Random, 1988), 92–93.
68. For an even-handed evaluation of Grew, see Nakamura Masanori, *The Japanese Monarchy: Ambassador Joseph Grew and the Making of the "Symbol Emperor System"* (Armonk, NY: M.E. Sharpe, 1992).
69. Paul Kecskemeti, *Strategic Surrender: The Politics of Victory and Defeat* (Stanford: Stanford University Press, 1958), 193.
70. Zinn incorporates this essay in a later volume; Howard Zinn, "The Politics of History in the Era of the Cold War," in Andre Schiffrin, ed., *The Cold War & The University* (New York: New Press, 1997), 35–72.
71. See note 65.
72. Herbert Feis, *Japan Subdued: The Atomic Bomb and the End of the War in the Pacific* (Princeton: Princeton University Press, 1961); and Feis, *The Atomic Bomb and the End of World War II* (Princeton: Princeton University Press, 1966).
73. Newman, "Ending the War with Japan: Paul Nitze's 'Early Surrender' Counterfactual," *Pacific Historical Review* LXIV (May 1995), 167–194.
74. Barton J. Bernstein, "Compelling Japan's Surrender Without the A-Bomb, Soviet Entry, or Invasion: Reconsidering the US Bombing Survey's Early-Surrender Conclusions," *Journal of Strategic Studies* 18 (June 1995), 101–48.
75. Gian Gentile, "Advocacy or Assessment? The United States Strategic Bombing Survey of Germany and Japan," *Pacific Historical Review* LXVI (February 1997), 53–79.
76. See note 41.
77. See note 51.

Chapter 3. Stimson's Defense

1. Henry Lewis Stimson Diaries, microfilm edition (New Haven: Yale University Library). My account of Stimson's career is taken from Elting E. Morison, *Turmoil and Tradition* (Boston: Houghton Mifflin, 1960), and Godfrey Hodgson, *The Colonel: The Life and Wars of Henry Stimson* (New York: Knopf, 1990). On Stimson's belief system, see John Bonnett, "Jekyll and Hyde: Henry L. Stimson, Mentalité, and the Decision to Use the Atomic Bomb on Japan," *War in History* 4 (1997), 174–212.

2. Stimson Diary, 2 April 1945. For Stimson's remarkable opinion that we should trust the Soviets until clear evidence of aggressiveness appeared see reel 9 of the diaries, frames 1115, 1125, 1144, 1148, 1149, 1155, 1171, 1176, 1200.

3. Diary, 15 January 1945.

4. Diary, 27 February 1945.

5. Diary, 16 May 1945.

6. For a hopelessly uninformed account of Japan's surrender, see Murray Sayle, "Did the Bomb End the War?" *The New Yorker* (31 July 1995), 54.

7. Diary, 19 June 1945.

8. John W. Dower, *Embracing Defeat* (New York: Norton, 1999), 83.

9. Diary, 2 July 1945.

10. This document is in Stimson, "The Decision to Use the Atomic Bomb," *Harper's Magazine* 97 (February 1945), 102–104.

11. The Diary for July 1945 covers this period.

12. Diary, 18 August 1945.

13. See Robert Newman, "Hiroshima and the Trashing of Henry Stimson," *New England Quarterly* 71 (March 1998), 5–32.

14. James G. Hershberg, *James B. Conant* (New York: Knopf, 1993); chapter 16 is a good account of Conant's activism.

15. Ibid., 279.

16. Spencer Weart, *Nuclear Fear* (Cambridge: Harvard University Press, 1988), 107.

17. John Hersey, *Into the Valley* (New York: Knopf, 1943), 20.

18. For an analysis of why Japanese atrocities disappeared from public discourse but those of the Nazis did not, see Robert Newman, *Truman and the Hiroshima Cult* (E. Lansing: Michigan State University Press, 1995), ch. 7.

19. Bernstein, "Seizing the Contested Terrain of Early Nuclear History: Stimson, Conant, and Their Allies Explain the Decision to Use the Atomic Bomb," *Diplomatic History* 17 (Winter 1993), 35–72.

20. "War and the Bomb," *New York Times* (28 January 1947).

21. "Why We used the Atom Bomb," *Washington Post* (28 January 1947).

22. Alperovitz, *The Decision*, 487; all six chapters of Book Two, Part I, derogate Stimson.

23. Gar Alperovitz, *Atomic Diplomacy: Hiroshima and Potsdam* (New York: Vintage/Random, 1965), dedication page.

24. Stimson, "The Decision," 100.

25. Ibid., 106.

26. This belief is accepted by J. Samuel Walker, *Prompt and Utter Destruction: Truman and the Use of Atomic Bombs Against Japan* (Chapel Hill: University of North Carolina Press, 1997), ch. 4.

27. See Herbert Bix, *Hirohito and the Making of Modern Japan* (New York: HarperCollins, 2000), 503 and elsewhere.

28. On Ennis, see Richard B. Frank, *Downfall: The End of the Imperial Japanese Empire* (New York: Random, 1999), 341; and D. M. Giangreco, "Operation Downfall: The Devil Was in the Details," *Joint Force Quarterly* (Autumn 1995), 89.

29. Sadao Asada, "The Shock of the Atomic Bomb. . . " *Pacific Historical Review* 67 (November 1998), 503–04.

30. Thomas R. H. Havens, *Valley of Darkness: The Japanese People and World War Two* (New York: Norton, 1978), 130–32.

31. Yoshida Shigeru, *The Yoshida Memoirs* (Boston: Houghton Mifflin, 1962), 280.

32. Herbert Passin, "The Occupation: Some Reflections," in Carol Gluck and Stephen Graubard, eds., *Showa: The Japan of Hirohito* (New York: Norton 1992), 111.

33. Dower, *Embracing Defeat*, 117.

34. Alperovitz, *The Decision*, 466–67.

35. Bernstein, "Seizing the Contested Terrain," 52.

36. See the discussion of the horrors of starvation in Newman, *Truman and the Hiroshima Cult*, 37–39, 186.

37. See Barton J. Bernstein, "Ike and Hiroshima: Did He Oppose It?" *Journal of Strategic Studies* 10 (September 1987), 375–89.

38. Robert H. Ferrell, ed., *Off The Record: The Private Papers of Harry S. Truman* (New York: Harper & Row, 1980), 56.

39. The Century Association, *Henry L. Stimson: Addresses Made in His Honor* (New York: Printed for the Club, 1950), 25, 28.

40. W. A. Higinbotham to Henry L. Stimson, 24 February 1947, Stimson Papers, Yale University Library, New Haven CT.

41. See McGeorge Bundy, *Danger and Survival* (New York: Vintage/Random, 1988), 92–93.

42. Bernstein, "Seizing the Contested Terrain," 69.

Chapter 4. Blackett's Attack

1. P. M. S. Blackett, *Fear, War, and the Bomb* (New York: Whittlesey House/McGraw-Hill, 1949), 77.

2. Ibid., 138.

3. Sir Bernard Lovell, "Patrick Maynard Stuart Blackett, Baron Blackett of Chelsea," *Biographical Memoirs of Fellows of the Royal Society*, v. 21 (London: The Royal Society, 1975), 1–115.

4. Nitze interview with author, 25 January 1994.

5. P. M. S. Blackett, "C. P. Snow's account of the role of two scientists in government," *Scientific American* 204 (April 1961), 194.

6. Blackett, *Fear, War*, 43.

7. Ibid., 5.

8. Ibid., 133.

9. Kai Bird and Lawrence Lifschultz, eds., *Hiroshima's Shadow* (Stony Creek, CT: Pamphleteer's Press, 1998), 78–89. Twenty-nine pages of this massive collection are by writers generally favorable to Truman's decision; 542 pages are by Truman's opponents.

10. Blackett, *Fear, War*, 127.

11. Ibid., 130.

12. Ibid., 132.

13. Edward J. Drea, "Missing Intentions: Japanese Intelligence and the Soviet Invasion of Manchuria," *Military Affairs* 48 (April 1984), 67.

14. Blackett, *Fear, War*, 136.

15. See the references to Chennault in Nancy Bernkopf Tucker, *Patterns in the Dust* (New York: Columbia University Press, 1983).

16. See Alice Kimball Smith, *A Peril and a Hope* (Chicago: University of Chicago Press, 1965), appendix B.

17. Smith, *Peril*, 561, 565.

18. Ibid., 566.

19. Ibid., 567.

20. Ibid.

21. Ibid., 567–68.

22. Douglas McClean, "The Atom Bomb," *New Statesman and Nation* 36 (16 October 1948), 327.

23. The Morrison review in *New Statesman and Nation* was substantially repeated in the *Bulletin of Atomic Scientists* 5 (January 1949), 37–40, under the title "Blackett's Analysis of the Issues." Quotations from 37, 40.

24. Lord Cherwell, "Atomic Bombing the Decisive Weapon—and Deterrent," *Daily Telegraph* (9 December 1948).

25. "Contemplation of the Atom," *Times Literary Supplement* (19 February 1949), 117.

26. L. Slater to P. M. S. Blackett, 26 October 1948, Folder H29, P. M. S. Blackett Papers, Royal Society, London.

27. Blackett to M. Hodson, 28 October 1948, Folder H29, Blackett Papers, Royal Society, London.

28. Paul S. Erikson to Harold Heslop, 5 November 1948, Folder H29, Blackett Papers, Royal Society, London.

29. R. G. E. Willison to P. M. S. Blackett, 24 November 1948, Folder H29, Blackett Papers, Royal Society, London.

30. Michael Hodson to Blackett, 24 November 1948, Folder H29, Blackett Papers, Royal Society, London.

31. R. G. E. Willison to Blackett, 25 January 1949, Folder H29, Blackett Papers, Royal Society, London.

32. Edward C. Aswell to Blackett, 4 February 1949, Folder H32, Blackett Papers, Royal Society, London.

33. Waldemar Kaempffert, "Fear, War and the Bomb," *New York Times* (3 July 1949).

34. Paul Jarrico to Blackett, 4 May 1949, Folder H29, Blackett Papers, Royal Society, London.

35. Blackett to Hodson, 16 June 1949, Folder H29, Blackett Papers, Royal Society, London.

36. Ibid. The sharp contrast between the generally friendly reception of Blackett's pro-Soviet opinions in Britain and their rejection in the United States (until the turbulent 1960s) is highlighted by the last letter in this series, from Ellison of Turnstile Press to Blackett, 24 November 1949 (Folder H29, Blackett Papers). Ellison suggests that since Blackett's aim is "to get the biggest world audience for any new pronouncement you wish to make," a new, short volume to sell for six shillings might achieve this. And to cushion the disappointment of low American sales, there was this pep-talk: "Your book has probably done more to influence world opinion than any book I can think of, since Keynes' "Economic Consequences," and on strategic thinking you occupy the same unrivalled position which Keynes occupied. . ." It is unlikely that Ellison could imagine that the only place where Blackett would have this influence would be Japan.

37. Thomas Parrish, *The Cold War Encyclopedia* (New York: Henry Holt, 1996), 375–78.

38. Bernard Lovell to author, 9 February 2000.

39. Ibid.

40. Edward Shils, "Blackett's Apologia for the Soviet Position," *Bulletin of the Atomic Scientists* 5 (January 1949), 34–37.

41. Louis N. Ridenour, Jr., "The Bomb and Blackett." *World Politics* 1 (April 1949), 395–403.
42. Mary Jo Nye, "A Physicist in the Corridors of Power: P. M. S. Blackett's Opposition to Atomic Weapons Following the War," *Physics in Perspective* 1 (1999), 136–56.
43. Mary Jo Nye, "What Price Politics? Scientists and Political Controversy," *Endeavor* 23 (4) (1999), 148–154.

Chapter 5. Cold War, Korea, Vietnam

1. Roger Dingman, "Alliance in Crisis: The Lucky Dragon Incident and Japanese-American Relations," in Warren I. Cohen and Akira Iriye, eds., *The Great Powers in East Asia, 1953–1960* (New York: Columbia University Press, 1990), 206. In 1994, Rep. George Miller (D-California) called hearings of the House Natural Resources Committee to probe new material about Bravo; the fallout was far greater than the AEC claimed in 1954. See Gary Lee, "Postwar Pacific Fallout Wider Than Thought," *Washington Post* (24 February 1994).
2. Kristin E. Hussey, "Hiroshima, Nagasaki a Mystery to Americans," *Washington Times* (3 March 1995).
3. Michael Schaller, *The American Occupation of Japan* (New York: Oxford University Press, 1985), 45.
4. Ibid.
5. John W. Dower, *Embracing Defeat* (New York: Norton/New Press, 1999), 445.
6. Ibid., 452.
7. Herbert P. Bix, *Hirohito and the Making of Modern Japan* (New York: HarperCollins, 2000), 583.
8. Ibid., 584.
9. Shiroyama Saburo, *War Criminal: The Life and Death of Hirota Koki* (Tokyo: Kodansha International, 1978).
10. Dower, *Embracing*, 464–65.
11. Sheldon H. Harris, *Factories of Death* (New York: Routledge, 1994).
12. Dower, *Embracing*, 474.
13. Ibid., 508.
14. Howard Schonberger, "The Japan Lobby in American Diplomacy," *Pacific Historical Review* 46 (August 1977), 336.
15. George F. Kennan, *Memoirs, 1925–1950* (Boston: Little, Brown, 1967), 393.
16. Gary May, *China Scapegoat: The Diplomatic Ordeal of John Carter Vincent* (Washington, D.C.: New Republic Books, 1979); Robert P. Newman, *Owen Lattimore and the "Loss" of China* (Berkeley: University of California Press, 1992). Dower, *Embracing*, 471.
17. Dower, *Embracing*, 473.
18. Ibid.
19. Ibid.
20. Martin J. Sherwin, *A World Destroyed: Hiroshima and the Origins of the Arms Race* (New York: Knopf, 1975).
21. Peter Filene, ed., *American Views of Soviet Russia, 1917–1965* (Homewood, IL: Dorsey

Press, 1968.); George C. Herring, Jr., *Aid to Russia, 1941–1946: Strategy, Diplomacy and the Origins of the Cold War* (New York: Columbia University Press, 1973); Ralph B. Levering, *American Opinion and the Russian Alliance, 1939–1945* (Chapel Hill: University of North Carolina Press, 1976); George Sirgiovanni, *An Undercurrent of Suspicion: Anti-Communist and Anti-Soviet Opinion in World War II America* (New Brunswick: Rutgers University, 1988), Ph.D. dissertation.

22. See Robert P. Newman, "Lethal Rhetoric: The Selling of the China Myths," *Quarterly Journal of Speech* 61 (April 1975), 116–21.

23. Ibid.; Shirley Stone Garrett, "Why They Stayed," in John K. Fairbank, ed., *The Missionary Enterprise in China and America* (Cambridge: Harvard University Press, 1974), 309; and Paul Varg, *Missionaries, Chinese, and Diplomats* (New York, Octagon, 1977), passim.

24. The things most forgotten by Americans: The Very Rev. Edmund Walsh, vice-president of Georgetown University "said today that President Truman would be morally justified in striking first with the atomic bomb if this country were on the verge of being attacked"; *New York Times* (25 December 1950); "Dewey Demands Total Mobilizing . . . as a beginning, the nation should set an immediate goal of 35 percent of its productive capacity for defense," *New York Times* (15 December 1950); "Skiers in Northwest Unite as Defense Guerrillas . . . in case of an invasion by an enemy. The movement is headed by Buster Campbell, University of Washington ski coach . . . plans call for training the skiers to guard mountain passes. . . " *New York Times* (19 December 1950).

25. David E. Lilienthal, *The Journals of David E. Lilienthal, Vol II: The Atomic Energy Years* (New York: Harper & Row, 1964), 632–33.

26. Paul H. Nitze, *From Hiroshima to Glasnost* (New York: Grove Weidenfeld, 1989), 90; Barton J. Bernstein, "The H-Bomb Decisions: Were They Inevitable?" in Bernard Brodie et al, eds., *National Security and International Stability* (Cambridge MA: Oelschlager Gunn & Hain, 1983), 338–42.

27. Kennan, *Memoirs 1925–1950*, 473–74.

28. Peter Galison and Barton Bernstein, "In Any Light: Scientists and the Decision to Build the Superbomb, 1942–1954," *Historical Studies in the Physical and Biological Sciences* 19 (1989), 306.

29. David Alan Rosenberg, "American Atomic Strategy and the Hydrogen Bomb Decision" *Journal of American History* 66 (June 1979), 87.

30. Robert P. Newman, "NSC (National Insecurity) 68: Nitze's Second Hallucination," in Martin J. Medhurst and H. W. Brands, eds., *Critical Reflections on the Cold War* (College Station: Texas A & M University Press, 2000). The conventional wisdom is that in the Spring of 1950 NSC-68 was approved in a breeze; the archives tell a different story.

31. John Lewis Gaddis, *Strategies of Containment* (New York: Oxford University Press, 1982).

32. Ibid., ch. 2.

33. (Kennan, George F.) "X," "The Sources of Soviet Conduct," *Foreign Affairs* XXV (July 1947), 566–82.

34. Gaddis, *Strategies*, 49–51.

35. The President to the Secretary of State, 31 January 1950, FRUS, 1950, I, 39.

36. Newman, "NSC (National Insecurity) 68," 64–65.

37. Nitze to the Secretary of State, 6 April 1950, PPS Papers 1947–1953, Box 54, RG 59, NA.

38. Memorandum by Mr. Charles E. Bohlen to the Director of the Policy Planning Staff (Nitze), 5 April 1950, FRUS 1950, I, 221–25.

39. The President to the Executive Secretary of the NSC (Lay), 12 April 1950, FRUS 1950, I, 235.
40. Roger Dingman, "Alliance in Crisis."
41. Robert A. Divine, *Blowing on the Wind* (New York: Oxford University Press, 1978), 11.
42. Ibid.
43. Dingman, "Alliance in Crisis," 198–207.
44. Ralph E. Lapp, *The Voyage of the Lucky Dragon* (New York: Harper and Brothers, 1958), 119.
45. A. M. Halpern, *Changing Japanese Attitudes Toward Atomic Weapons,* Rand Corporation Report RM-1331 (Santa Monica: Rand Corporation, 1954), 21.
46. Lapp, *Voyage,* 119.
47. Sadao Asada, "Japanese Perceptions of the A-Bomb Decision," in Joe C. Dixon, ed., *The American Military and the Far East* (Colorado Springs: U.S. Air Force Academy, 1980), 203.
48. Tanaka Yasumasu, "Japanese Attitudes Toward Nuclear Arms," *Public Opinion Quarterly* 34 (Spring 1970), 29.
49. Dingman, "Alliance in Crisis," 206.
50. Sheila K. Johnson, *The Japanese Through American Eyes* (Stanford: Stanford University Press, 1991), 48–49.
51. Ibid., 46.
52. Michael R. Beschloss, *Mayday: Eisenhower, Khrushchev and the U-2 Affair* (New York: Harper & Row, 1986).
53. See Peter Wyden, *Bay of Pigs* (New York: Simon & Schuster, 1979); Trumbull Higgins, *The Perfect Failure: Kennedy, Eisenhower, and the CIA at the Bay of Pigs* (New York: Norton, 1987).
54. Theodore Draper, *The Dominican Revolt* (New York: Commentary, 1968).
55. Charles Roberts, "LBJ's Credibility Gap," *Newsweek* (19 December 1966), 24–25.
56. "Editors Assert Administration Practices Deceit for its Own Sake," *New York Times* (16 April 1968).
57. Stewart L. Udall, *The Myths of August* (New York: Pantheon, 1994).
58. Ibid., 17.
59. "Izzy vs. a Mendacious Agency," *Washington Journalism Review* 10 (May 1988), 50.
60. This account of the Mancuso affair is taken from the author's conversation with Mancuso 1 November 1994; Robert Alvarez, "Mancuso Affair," *Bulletin of the Atomic Scientists* 36 (February 1980), 61–62; and Robert del Tredici, *At Work in the Fields of the Bomb* (New York: Harper & Row, 1987), 138–41.
61. Author conversation with Mancuso.
62. J. Carson Mark, "Research, Development and Production," *Bulletin of the Atomic Scientists* 39 (March 1983), 50.
63. See H. Jack Geiger, "Generations of Poison and Lies," *New York Times* (5 August 1990); George Wald, "The Nuclear-Power-Truth Maze," *New York Times* (29 February 1976); Daniel Ford, *The Cult of the Atom* (New York: Simon and Schuster, 1982).
64. Schaller, *American Occupation,* chapters 5, 9.
65. Dower, *Embracing,* 553.
66. Nishi Toshio, *Unconditional Democracy: Education and Politics in Occupied Japan* (Stanford: Stanford University Press, 1982), xxxi.
67. Michael Schaller, *Altered States: The United States and Japan Since the Occupation* (New York: Oxford University Press, 1997), ch. 11.

68. Thomas R. H. Havens, *Fire Across the Sea: The Vietnam War and Japan* (Princeton: Princeton University Press, 1987) 3–4.

69. Ibid., 133.

70. See ch. 2.

71. Udall, *Myths*, 15–17.

72. Barton J. Bernstein, "The Atomic Bomb and American Foreign Policy. . . " *Peace and Change* 2 (Spring 1974), 6.

73. Ibid., 9–10.

74. Barton J. Bernstein, lecture at Truman State University, 1 May 2000.

75. For a book brimming with moral indignation, the absence of any attempt to engage the significant literature on the morality of war fighting—including nuclear war—is disconcerting. Boyer cites fourteen poets and literary figures, a few theologians, and a dozen or so popular periodicals. Apparently the entire corpus of professional philosophers is unworthy of his attention.

76. Barton J. Bernstein, ed., *The Atomic Bomb: The Critical Issues* (Boston: Little, Brown, 1976), 52.

77. Barton J. Bernstein, "Roosevelt, Truman, and the Atomic Bomb, 1941–1945: A Reinterpretation," *Political Science Quarterly* 90 (Spring 1975).

78. Barton J. Bernstein, "Ike and Hiroshima: Did He Oppose It?" *Journal of Strategic Studies* 10 (September 1987), 377–89.

79. Barton J. Bernstein, "The author replies," *International Security* 116 (Winter 1991–1992), 214-21.

Chapter 6. *Enola Gay* at Air and Space: Anonymity, Hypocrisy, Ignorance

1. Gregg Herken to Tom Crouch and Michael Neufeld, 8 December 1993, Smithsonian Institution Archives (Henceforth SIA), *Enola Gay* Exhibition Records (Henceforth EGER), Accession 96–140, Box 4.

2. Michael Neufeld to Wayne Dzwonchyk, 12 May 1994, SIA-EGER, Accession 96–140, Box 9.

3. The most useful account of the NASM *Enola Gay* event is Martin Harwit, *An Exhibit Denied* (New York: Springer-Verlag, 1996).

4. *Presenting History: Museums in a Democratic Society* (Washington, D.C.: Smithsonian Institution, 1995), 30.

5. Daniel Seltz, *The* Enola Gay *Exhibition and the Challenge to American Memory* (Providence: East Asian Studies, Brown University, 1996), 67.

6. Pamela Walker Laird, "The Public's Historians," *Technology and Culture* 39 (July 1998), 476.

7. Harwit, *Denied*, 51.

8. Ibid.

9. Ibid., 206.

10. Gregg Herken, *The Winning Weapon* (Princeton: Princeton University Press, 1981), 329.

11. See note 1.

12. Michael Neufeld to Edward Drea et al., 21 April 1994, *Enola Gay* Records, U.S. Naval Historical Center, Washington Navy Yard, D.C.

13. Neufeld to author, 25 September 1999.
14. Wayne Dzwonchyk to Michael Neufeld, 28 April 1944, SIA-EGER, Accession 96–140, Box 9.
15. See note 2.
16. M. K. Stone to Smithsonian Institution, 22 May 1994; Tom Crouch to Stone, 17 June 1994; Stone to Crouch, 23 June 1994; Crouch to Stone, 28 June 1994; all in SIA-EGER, Accession 96–140, Box 4.
17. Mark Jacobson to Alfred Goldberg, 18 July 1994, *Enola Gay* Records, Naval Historical Center, Washington Navy Yard, D.C.
18. Martin Harwit to Ruth Adams, 1 November 1988, SIA, Record Unit 355, Office of Cooperative Programs. Box 2.
19. Attachment to document listed in note 18.
20. Ibid.
21. Ibid.
22. Harwit, *Denied*, 59.
23. Ibid., 56.
24. Martin Harwit to Bob Adams, 16 April 1993, SIA-EGER, Accession 96–140, Box 2.
25. Harwit to Akihiro Takahashi, 18 May 1993, SIA-EGER, Accession 96–140, Box 2.
26. Harwit to Bill Constantine et al, 26 April 1994, SIA-EGER, Accession 96–140, Box 1.
27. Report of the National Air and Space Review Team, 25 May 1994, *Enola Gay* Records, Box 3, Naval Historical Center, Washington Navy Yard, D.C.
28. Ibid.
29. Michael Neufeld to Tiger Team, 25 April 1994, cited in *Denied*, 281.
30. Tom Crouch to David Blasco, 17 August 1994, SIA-EGER, Accession 96–140, Box 4.
31. Harwit to Tom Crouch, 2 July 1993, SIA-EGER, Accession 96–140, Box 1.
32. *Denied*, viii.
33. Richard Hallion to Tom Crouch, 9 August 1994, SIA-EGER, Accession 96–140, Box 4.
34. Preble Stolz to I. Michael Heyman, 2 September 1994, SIA-EGER, Accession 96–140, Box 1.
35. Lance Morrow, "Hiroshima and the Time Machine," *Time* 144 (19 September 1994), 94.
36. Tom Crouch to Harwit, 21 July 1993, SIA-EGER, Accession 96–140, Box 4.
37. Charles S. Maier, *The Unmasterable Past: History, Holocaust, and German National Identity* (Cambridge: Harvard University Press, 1988), 83.
38. Barton J. Bernstein, "Reconsidering 'Invasion Most Costly': Popular-History Scholarship, Publishing Standards, and the Claim of High U.S. Casualty Estimates to Help Legitimate the Atomic Bombings," *Peace & Change* 24 (April 1999), 238.
39. Tami Davis Biddle to Paul Nitze, 29 June 1990, SIA, Record Unit 355, Office of Cooperative Programs, Box 2.
40. Helen Claire McMahon to Paul Nitze, 26 June 1990, SIA, Record Unit 355, Office of Cooperative Programs, Box 4.
41. Tami Davis Biddle to Lord Zuckerman, 23 August 1990, SIA, Record Unit 355, Office of Cooperative Programs, Box 2.
42. Helen Claire McMahon to Gregg (Herken), 31 July 1990, SIA, Record Unit 355, Office of Cooperative Programs, Box 2.
43. Ibid.
44. For Nitze's intense support of more and bigger bombs, see Strobe Talbott, *The Master of the Game* (New York: Knopf, 1988); David Callahan, *Dangerous Capabilities* (New

York: HarperCollins, 1990); and Robert P. Newman, "NSC (National Insecurity) 68: Nitze's Second Hallucination," in H.W. Brands and Martin Medhurst, eds., *Public Discourse in Cold War America* (College Station: Texas A & M University Press, 2000), 55–94.

45. Paul F. Boller, Jr., "Hiroshima and the American Left: August 1945," *International Social Science Review* 57 (Winter 1982) 13–27.
46. Harwit, *Denied,* 339.
47. Robert P. Newman, Letter to editor, *Journal of American History* 83 (June 1996), 305–06.
48. Martin Harwit, Letter to editor, *Journal of American History* 83 (June 1996), 307.
49. Von Hardesty to Martin Harwit, 28 December 1987, SIA-EGER, Accession 96–140, Box 2.
50. Harwit, *Denied,* 212.
51. Otto Mayr, "The *Enola Gay* Fiasco: History, Politics, and the Museum," *Technology and Culture* 39 (1998), 464.
52. *Enola Gay* Exhibit text as printed in Philip Nobile, ed., *Judgment at the Smithsonian* (New York: Marlowe, 1995), 37–38.
53. Nakamura Masanori, *The Japanese Monarchy* (Armonk, NY: M. E. Sharpe, 1992).
54. See notes 100 through 105, ch. 1.
55. Sadao Asada, "The Shock of the Atomic Bomb and Japan's Decision to Surrender—A Reconsideration," *Pacific Historical Review* 67 (November 1998), 477–512.
56. Harwit, *Denied,* 158.
57. Akira Iriye to Martin Harwit, 25 February 1993, SIA-EGER, Accession 96–140, Box 2.
58. Sadao Asada et al., eds., *Japan and the World, 1853–1952* (New York: Columbia University Press, 1989).
59. Donald S. Detwiler, ed., *War in Asia and the Pacific* Vol. 1 (New York: Garland, 1980), vii.
60. *Enola Gay* text in Nobile, 3.
61. Geoffrey M. White, "Memory Wars: The Politics of Remembering the Asia-Pacific War," *Asia-Pacific Issues* 21 (July 1995), 5.
62. Toshio Iritani, *Group Psychology of the Japanese in Wartime* (London: Kegan Paul, 1991), 237–40.
63. Kitahara Michio, *Children of the Sun: The Japanese and the Outside World* (New York: St. Martin's, 1989).
64. Saburo Ienaga, *The Pacific War* (New York: Pantheon, 1978). Ienaga is very clear that the bombs ended the war, however much he deplores them. See 231.
65. Tsurumi Shunsuke, *An Intellectual History of Wartime Japan* (London: Kegan Paul International, 1986), 81.
66. Nobuya Bamba and John F. Howes, *Pacifism in Japan* (Vancouver: University of British Columbia Press, 1978), 263.
67. Maruyama Masao, *Thought and Behaviour in Modern Japanese Politics* (London: Oxford University Press, 1963), xii, 88.
68. Edward Drea to Commander L. Smith, 13 April 1994, SIA-EGER, Accession 96–140, Box 9.
69. Toshiaki Kawahara, *Hirohito and His Times* (Tokyo: Kodansha, 1990), 201.
70. Michael A. Barnhart, review of books by Hosoya, Hiwatari, Hara, Asada, *Journal of American History* 83 (March 1997), 1478.
71. John W. Dower, *Embracing Defeat* (New York: Norton, 1999), especially chapters 1 and 4.

72. See Richard H. Kohn, ed., "The Scholarship on World War II: Its Present Condition and Future Possibilities," *Journal of Military History* 55 (July 1991), 365–93.

73. One can understand, though not agree with, Harwit's disdain for military historians employed by the armed forces; that he allowed this to justify ignoring the topflight military historians in this AMI panel cannot be understood.

74. See Günter Bischof and Robert L. DuPont, eds., *The Pacific War Revisited* (Baton Rouge: Louisiana State University Press, 1997).

75. Harwit, *Denied*, 53.

76. Richard Kohn to Tom Crouch, 8 August 1994, SIA-EGER, Accession 96–140, Box 4.

77. Richard Kohn to Martin Harwit, 18 June 1994, SIA-EGER, Accession 96–140, Box 4.

78. Ibid.

79. The last version of the script pleased hardly anyone. The Nitzeans thought it much too favorable to *Enola Gay;* the veterans and politicians thought it still too hostile to *Enola Gay;* and the scholars who knew something about the Pacific war thought it simply incompetent.

80. Gregg Herken to Martin Harwit, 31 August 1994, SIA-EGER, Accession 96–140, Box 8. The "fever pitch" in the media was largely Harwit's fault. He blamed others, such as Editor John Correll of *Air Force* magazine, who was charged with distributing a copy of the script furnished him in confidence; but Correll merely shared a script previously furnished him by an NASM employee. Harwit's shop leaked like a sieve. Harwit charged the *Washington Post* with biased reporting, which it did not deserve; the significant biased (and incompetent) reporting was the postmortem in the *American Journalism Review:* Tony Capaccio and Uday Mohan, "Missing the Target" in the issue of July–August 1995. The closest these writers got to significant research was an interview with Ronald Spector, but even that was underreported.

81. *Enola Gay* text in Nobile, 117.

82. Barton J. Bernstein, "The H-Bomb Decisions: Were They Inevitable?" in Bernard Brodie et al., eds., *National Security and International Stability* (Cambridge MA: Oelgeschlager, Gunn & Hain, 1983), 338–42.

83. David Alan Rosenberg, "American Atomic Strategy and the Hydrogen Bomb Decision," *Journal of American History* 66 (June 1979), 62–87.

84. See especially David Holloway, *Stalin and the Bomb* (New Haven: Yale University Press, 1994).

85. Martin J. Sherwin, *A World Destroyed* (New York: Vantage/Random, 1987), 227.

86. Vladislav M. Zubok, "Stalin and the Nuclear Age," in John Lewis Gaddis et al., eds., *Cold War Statesmen Confront the Bomb* (Oxford: Oxford University Press, 1999), 39–61.

87. See especially John Lewis Gaddis, *The Long Peace* (New York: Oxford University Press, 1987).

88. Richard Rhodes to Michael Neufeld, 25 February 1994, SIA-EGER, Accession 96–140, Box 9.

89. Spencer Weart and Gertrude Weiss Szilard, *Leo Szilard: His Version of the Truth* (Cambridge: MIT Press, 1978), 186.

90. Michael S. Sherry to Martin Harwit, 2 June 1994, SIA-EGER, RU 355, Box 2.

91. Martin Harwit to Michael Sherry, 9 June 1944, SIA-EGER, RU 355, Box 2.

92. Victor Bond to Michael Neufeld, 3 March 1994, SIA-EGER, Accession 96–140, Box 9.

93. "Statement of Mr. Charles Bohlen before the Voorhees Group on 3 April 1950." Because of the complexities of FOIA processing, this document cannot now be traced to a specific box in the PPS Papers, RG 59, NA.

94. Y. C. L. Susan Wu to Martin Harwit, 13 September 1994, SIA-EGER, Accession 96–140, Box 9. Wu was not the only person to attempt to convince Harwit that others than American and Japanese were suffering during the Pacific War. NASM ethnocentrism will be covered more fully in chapter 7.

95. Michael Walzer, *Just and Unjust Wars* (New York: Basic Books, 1977).

96. Michael Walzer, "50 Years After Hiroshima," *Dissent* 42 (Summer 1995), 331.

97. Sheldon M. Cohen, *Arms and Judgment* (Boulder, CO: Westview, 1988).

98. Harwit, *Denied*, 347.

99. Martin Sherwin to Michael Neufeld, 11 April 1994, SIA-EGER, Accession 96–140, Box 9.

100. Michael Neufeld to Martin Sherwin, 19 May 1994, SIA-EGER, Accession 96–140, Box 9.

101. See especially Barton Bernstein, "The author replies," *International Security* 16 (1991/1992), 214–221.

102. Hallion comments printed in Harwit, *Denied*, 222–24.

103. John W. Dower, "Rethinking World War II in Asia," *Reviews in American History* 12 (June 1994), 161, 165.

104. Akira Iriye to Martin Harwit, 24 September 1994, SIA-EGER, Accession 96–140, Box 9.

105. Linenthal's essay, "Anatomy of a Controversy," in Tom Englehardt and Edward T. Linenthal, eds., *History Wars* (New York: Henry Holt, 1996), 9–62, is a perceptive analysis of the dynamics of the controversy.

106. Sherwin to panel on *Enola Gay*, Organization of American Historians Convention, Washington, D. C. 30 March 1995. Tape recording arranged by OAH.

107. "Hiroshima Exhibit Opens Quietly at University," *New York Times* (10 July 1995).

108. Harwit, *Denied*, 219.

109. Richard Rhodes to Michael Neufeld, 25 February 1994, SIA-EGER, Accession 96–140, Box 4.

110. Harwit, *Denied*, 219.

111. "Suggestions for Further Reading," Draft #2, July 1994, SIA-EGER, Accession 96–140, Box 8.

112. Barton J. Bernstein, "Seizing the Contested Terrain," 69.

113. Barton J. Bernstein, "Ike and Hiroshima: Did He Oppose It?" *Journal of Strategic Studies* 10 (September 1987), 375–89.

114. Laird, "The Public's Historians," 476.

Chapter 7. A Transnational Narrative: Recognizing the Claims of Japan's Victims

1. Astrid Pei to Martin Harwit, 18 September 1994, Smithsonian Institution Archives, *Enola Gay* Exhibit Records, Accession 96–140, Box 3.

2. Yukiko Koshiro, *Trans-Pacific Racisms* (New York: Columbia University Press, 1999), 107, 121, 219.

3. Sheldon H. Harris, *Factories of Death* (New York: Routledge, 1994).

4. George Hicks, *The Comfort Women* (New York: Norton, 1994).

5. Seiitsu Tachibana, "The Quest for a Peace Culture . . ." in Michael J. Hogan, ed., *Hiroshima in History and Memory* (Cambridge: Cambridge University Press, 1996), 184; Toshio Iritani, *Group Psychology of the Japanese in Wartime* (London: Kegan Paul, 1991), 237.

6. Gavan Daws, *Prisoners of the Japanese* (New York: Morrow, 1994), 363.

7. See the publications of the Alliance for Preserving the Truth of Sino-Japanese War, available from P.O. Box 2066, Cupertino, CA 95015.

8. John W. Dower, *Embracing Defeat* (New York: Norton, 1999), 72.

9. R. J. Rummel, *China's Bloody Century* (New Brunswick: Transaction Publishers, 1991), 150.

10. Shi Young and James Yin, *The Rape of Nanking: Japanese Carnage in China During World War Two* (Chicago: Innovative Publishing Group, 1977), 242, 248, 250, 267.

11. Laurens van der Post, *The Prisoner and the Bomb* (New York: Morrow, 1971), 22.

12. Anthony Reid, "Indonesia: From Briefcase to Samurai Sword," in Alfred W. McCoy, ed., *Southeast Asia Under Japanese Occupation* (New Haven: Yale University Southeast Asia Studies, 1980), 21.

13. Barton J. Bernstein, "Compelling Japan's Surrender . . . ," *Journal of Strategic Studies* 18 (June 1995), 131–137.

14. For a fuller account of this fascinating affair, see Robert P. Newman, *Truman and the Hiroshima Cult* (E. Lansing: Michigan State University Press, 1995), 123–27.

15. "Congregation," *Oxford Magazine* 76 (3 May 1956), 382.

16. G. E. M. Anscombe, *Collected Philosophical Papers,* Vol. II (Minneapolis: University of Minnesota Press, 1981), 62. As this was in press, Anscombe's obituary appeared in the *New York Times;* it features her crusade against Harry Truman (13 January 2001).

17. Michael Howard, *Studies in War and Peace* (New York: Viking, 1971), 16–17.

18. Author interview with Nitze, 25 January 1994.

19. Leahy's opinion is in Ernest J. King and Walter M. Whitehill, *Fleet Admiral King* (New York: Norton, 1952), 621.

20. Vera Brittain, *Humiliation With Honor* (New York: Fellowship Publications, 1943), 64–66.

21. Michael Walzer, *Just and Unjust Wars* (New York: Basic/HarperCollins, 1992), 160.

22. MacArthur quoted in Nishi Toshio, *Unconditional Democracy* (Stanford: Stanford University Press, 1982), 69.

23. Walzer, *Just and Unjust,* 172–74.

24. Spencer Weart, *Nuclear Fear* (Cambridge MA: Harvard University Press, 1988), 93.

25. Michael Sherry, *The Rise of American Airpower* (New Haven: Yale University Press, 1987), 312.

26. Barton J. Bernstein, "The Struggle Over History," in Nobile, *Judgment,* 197.

27. Walzer, *Just and Unjust,* 258.

28. Ibid., 267–68.

29. John Rawls, "50 Years After Hiroshima," *Dissent* 42 (Summer 1995), 325.

30. A. L. Goodhart, *What Acts of War are Justifiable?* (Oxford: Clarendon Press, 1940), 25.

31. Robert W. Tucker, *The Just War* (Baltimore: Johns Hopkins University Press, 1960).

32. Ibid., 85.

33. Ibid., 90.

34. Paul Ramsey, *War and the Christian Conscience* (Durham, Duke University Press, 1961), 88.

35. R. B. Brandt, "Utilitarianism and the Rules of War," *Philosophy and Public Affairs* 1 (Winter 1972), 156.

36. R. M. Hare, "Rules of War and Moral Reasoning," *Philosophy and Public Affairs* 1 (Winter 1972), 181.

37. R. M. Hare, *Applications of Moral Philosophy* (Berkeley: University of California Press, 1972), 14–19.

38. Robert J. Lifton and Greg Mitchell, *Hiroshima in America: Fifty Years of Denial* (New York: G. P. Putnam's Sons, 1995).

39. Goodhart, *What Acts of War*, 25.

40. Franklin D. Roosevelt, *The War Messages of Franklin D. Roosevelt* (Washington, D.C.: GPO, 1943), 32.

41. Cohen to author, 21 April 1994.

42. Hayashi, in Haruko and Theodore Cook, *Japan at War* (New York: Free Press, 1992), 40–43.

43. William Branigan, "50 Years Later, Survivors of Battle of Manila Speak Out," *Washington Post* (27 October 1994).

44. Patrick E. Tyler, "China Villagers Recall Horrors of Germ Attack," *New York Times* (4 February 1997).

45. Louis Allen, "The Campaigns in Asia and the Pacific," *Journal of Strategic Studies* 13 (March 1990), 183.

46. Tachibana, "Quest," 168.

47. Ibid., 169.

48. Ibid., 186.

49. Elisabeth Rosenthal, "Wartime Slaves Use U.S. Law to Sue Japanese," *New York Times* (2 October 2000).

50. Howard French, "Japanese Veteran Testifies in War Atrocity Lawsuit," *New York Times* (21 December 2000).

51. Dear as quoted in Harwit, *Denied*, 343.

52. Harwit, *Denied*, 342.

53. Kai Bird, "The Curators Cave In," *New York Times* (9 October 1994).

54. Van Kirk and Jernegan quoted in Eugene L. Meyer, "The Bombers Who Flew Into History," *Washington Post* (3 September 1994).

55. Charles Sweeney, *War's End* (New York: Avon, 1997), xiii.

56. Tibbets quoted in Eugene L. Meyer, "Target: Smithsonian," *Washington Post* (30 January 1995).

57. Stewart as quoted in Harwit, *Denied*, 17.

58. Thomas L. Karnes, letter to editor, *Journal of American History* 83 (June 1996), 313–14. There is much more testimony to the anti-nuclear attitudes of members of the 509th. See the warning against the dangers of nuclear destruction in "Thomas Ferebee Dies at 81: Dropped First Atomic Bomb," *New York Times* (18 March 2000); and the extensive reports of the attitudes of 509th members in Bob Greene, *Duty* (New York: William Morrow, 2000).

BIBLIOGRAPHY

Allen, Louis. "The Campaigns in Asia and the Pacific." *Journal of Strategic Studies* 13 (March 1990).

Alperovitz, Gar. *Atomic Diplomacy: Hiroshima and Potsdam*. New York: Vintage/Random, 1965.

——*The Decision to Use the Atomic Bomb and the Architecture of an American Myth*. New York: Knopf 1995.

Alvarez, Robert. "Mancuso Affair." *Bulletin of the Atomic Scientists* 36 (February 1980).

"America's Atomic Atrocity." *Christian Century* LXII (29 August 1945).

Anscombe, G. E. M. *Collected Philosophical Papers*, vol II. Minneapolis: University of Minnesota Press, 1981.

Appleman, Roy E., et al. *Okinawa: The Last Battle*. Washington, D.C.: Department of the Army, 1948.

Asada, Sadao, et al., eds. *Japan and the World, 1853–1952*. New York: Columbia University Press, 1989.

——"Japanese Perceptions of the A-Bomb Decision," in Joe C. Dixon, ed. *The American Military and the Far East*. Colorado Springs: U.S. Air Force Academy, 1980.

——"The Shock of the Atomic Bomb and Japan's Decision to Surrender—A Reconsideration." *Pacific Historical Review* 67 (November 1998).

Baldwin, Hanson. "Japan's Industrial Power . . ." *New York Times*, 22 June 1945.

——"The Let-Down Problem." *New York Times*, 2 April 1945.

Bamba, Nobuya, and John F. Howes. *Pacifism in Japan*. Vancouver: University of British Columbia Press, 1978.

Barnhart, Michael A. Review of books by Hosoya, Hiwatari, Hara, Asada. *Journal of American History* 83 (March 1997).

Bernstein, Barton. "The Atomic Bomb and American Foreign Policy . . ." *Peace and Change* 2 (Spring 1974).

——*The Atomic Bomb: The Critical Issues*. Boston: Little, Brown, 1976.

——"The author replies," *International Security* 116 (Winter 1991–1992).

——"Compelling Japan's Surrender Without the A-Bomb, Soviet Entry or Invasion . . ." *Journal of Strategic Studies* 18 (June 1995).

——"The H-Bomb Decisions: Were They Inevitable?" in Bernard Brodie, et al, eds., *National Security and International Stability*. Cambridge MA: Oelschlager, Gunn & Hain, 1983.

——"Ike and Hiroshima: Did He Oppose It?" *Journal of Strategic Studies*. 10 (September 1987).

——"The Perils and Politics of Surrender: Ending the War with Japan and Avoiding the Third Atomic Bomb." *Pacific Historical Review* 48 (November 1977).

——"Reconsidering 'Invasion Most Costly': Popular History Scholarship . . ." *Peace & Change* 24 (April 1999).

——"Roosevelt, Truman, and the Atomic Bomb, 1941–1945: A Reinterpretation." *Political Science Quarterly* 90 (Spring 1975).

——"Seizing the Contested Terrain of Early Nuclear History . . . " *Diplomatic History* 17 (Winter 1993).

——"The Struggle Over History," in Philip Nobile, ed. *Judgment at the Smithsonian*. New York: Marlowe, 1995.

Beschloss, Michael R. *Mayday: Eisenhower, Khrushchev and the U-2 Affair*. New York: Harper & Row, 1986.

Beveridge, James. *History of the United States Bombing Survey (Pacific)*. Washington, D.C.: Center of Military History, 1946.

Bird, Kai, and Lawrence Lifschultz, eds. *Hiroshima's Shadow*. Stony Creek, CT: Pamphleteer's Press, 1998.

——"The Curators Cave In." *New York Times*, 9 October 1994.

Bischof, Günter, and Robert L. DuPont, eds., *The Pacific War Revisited*. Baton Rouge: Louisiana State University Press, 1997.

Bix, Herbert. *Hirohito and the Making of Modern Japan*. New York: HarperCollins, 2000.

Blackett, P. M. S. "C. P. Snow's Account of the Role of Two Scientists in Government." *Scientific American* 204 (April 1961).

——*Fear, War and the Bomb*. New York: Whittlesey House/McGraw-Hill, 1949.

Boller, Paul F. "Hiroshima and the American Left: August 1945," *International Social Science Review* 57 (Winter 1982).

Bonnett, John. "Jekyll and Hyde: Henry L. Stimson, Mentalité, and the Decision to Use the Atomic Bomb on Japan." *War in History* 4 (1997).

Brackman, Arnold. *The Other Nuremberg*. New York: William Morrow, 1987.

Bradley, Omar and Clay Blair. *A General's Life*. New York: Simon and Schuster, 1983.

Brandt, R. B. "Utilitarianism and the Rules of War." *Philosphy and Public Affairs* 1 (Winter 1972).

Branigan, William. "50 Years Later, Survivors of Battle of Manila Speak Out." *Washington Post*, 27 October 1994.

Briggs, Richard A. *Black Hawks Over the Danube*. West Point, KY: Richard A. Briggs, 1953.

British Bombing Survey Unit. *The Strategic Air War Against Germany*. London: Frank Cass, 1998.

Brittain, Vera. *Humiliation With Honor*. New York: Fellowship Publications, 1943.

Brower, Charles F. IV. *The Joint Chiefs of Staff and National Policy.* Philadelphia: University of Pennsylvania, 1987, Ph.D. dissertation.

Bundy, McGeorge. *Danger and Survival: Choices About the Bomb in the First Fifty Years.* New York: Vintage/Random, 1998.

Butow, Robert J.C. *Japan's Decision to Surrender.* Stanford: Stanford University Press, 1954.

Callahan, David. *Dangerous Capabilities: Paul Nitze and the Cold War.* New York: Harper-Collins, 1990.

Campbell, A. E. "Franklin Roosevelt and Unconditional Surrender," in Richard Langhorne, ed., *Diplomacy and Intelligence During the Second World War.* Cambridge: Cambridge University Press, 1985.

Capaccio, Tony and Uday Mohan. "Missing the Target." *American Journalism Review* 17 (July–August 1995).

Century Association. *Henry L. Stimson: Addresses Made in His Honor.* New York: Printed for the Club, 1950.

Chase, John L. "Unconditional Surrender Reconsidered." *Political Science Quarterly* 70 (June 1955).

Chase, Stuart. "Atomic Age Balance Sheet." *Common Sense* XIV (October 1945).

Cherwell, Lord. "Atomic Bombing the Decisive Weapon—and Deterrent." London: *Daily Telegraph* 9 December 1948.

Cohen, Sheldon. *Arms and Judgment.* Boulder, CO: Westview, 1988.

"Congregation." *Oxford Magazine,* 76 (3 May 1956).

"Contemplation of the Atom." *Times Literary Supplement* 19 February 1949.

Cousins, Norman. "The Non-Obliterators." *Saturday Review of Literature* 27 (8 April 1944).

Cousins, Norman, and Thomas K. Finletter. "A Beginning for Sanity." *Saturday Review of Literature* 29 (15 June 1946).

Crane, Conrad C. *Bombs, Cities, and Civilians .* Lawrence: University Press of Kansas, 1993.

Daws, Gavan. *Prisoners of the Japanese.* New York: Morrow, 1994.

"The Decision for Peace." *ONI Review* 1 (June 1946).

Del Tredici, Robert. *At Work in the Fields of the Bomb.* New York: Harper & Row, 1987.

Detwiler, Donald S., ed. *War in Asia and the Pacific,* vol 1. New York: Garland, 1980.

Dingman, Roger. "Alliance in Crisis: The Lucky Dragon Incident and Japanese-American Relations," in Warren I. Cohen and Akira Iriye, eds., *The Great Powers in East Asia, 1953–1960.* New York: Columbia University Press, 1990.

Divine, Robert. *Blowing on the Wind.* New York: Oxford University Press, 1978.

Dower, John W. *Embracing Defeat.* New York: W. W. Norton, 1999.

——— "Rethinking World War II in Asia." *Reviews in American History* 12 (June 1994).

Draper, Theodore. *The Dominican Revolt.* New York: Commentary, 1968.

Drea, Edward J. *In the Service of the Emperor.* Lincoln: University of Nebraska Press, 1998.

———*MacArthur's ULTRA: Codebreaking and the War Against Japan.* Lawrence: University Press of Kansas, 1992.

——— "Missing Intentions: Japanese Intelligence and the Soviet Invasion of Manchuria." *Military Affairs* 48 (April 1984).

Duis, Perry R. "No Time for Privacy," in Louis A. Erenberg and Susan B. Hirsch, eds., *The War in American Culture.* Chicago: University of Chicago Press, 1996.

"Editors Assert Administration Practices Deceit for its Own Sake." *New York Times,* 16 April 1968.

Feis, Herbert. *The Atomic Bomb and the End of World War II.* Princeton: Princeton University Press, 1966.

——*Japan Subdued*. Princeton: Princeton University Press, 1961.

Ferrell, Robert H. "Intelligence Assessments and Assumptions: The View from Washington." Paper presented at the 1999 Annual Meeting of the Society for Military History, University Park, PA, 16 April 1999.

——*Off the Record: The Private Papers of Harry S. Truman*. New York: Harper & Row, 1980.

Filene, Peter ed. *American Views of Soviet Russia, 1917–1965*. Homewood, IL: Dorsey Press, 1968.

Finney, John W. *Hiroshima Plus 20*. New York: Delacorte Press, 1965.

Ford, Daniel. *The Cult of the Atom*. New York: Simon and Schuster, 1982.

Frank, Richard B. *Downfall: The End of the Imperial Japanese Empire*. New York: Random, 1999.

Franklin, William M. "Unconditional Surrender," in Alexander DeConde, ed., *Encyclopedia of American Foreign Policy*. New York: Charles Scribner's Sons, 1978.

French, Howard. "Japanese Veteran Testifies in War Atrocity Lawsuit." *New York Times*, 21 December 2000.

Gaddis, John Lewis. *The Long Peace*. New York: Oxford University Press, 1987.

——*Strategies of Containment*. New York: Oxford University Press, 1982.

Galbraith, John K. *A Life in Our Times*. Boston: Houghton Mifflin, 1981.

Galison, Peter, and Barton Bernstein. "In Any Light: Scientists and the Decision to Build the Superbomb." *Historical Studies in the Physical and Biological Sciences* 19 (1989).

Gallicchio, Marc. "After Nagasaki: General Marshall's Plan for Tactical Nuclear Weapons in Japan." *Prologue* 23 (Winter 1991).

——*The Cold War Begins in Asia*. New York: Columbia University Press, 1988.

Garrett, Shirley Stone. "Why They Stayed," in John K. Fairbank ed., *The Missionary Enterprise in China and America*. Cambridge: Harvard University Press, 1974.

Geiger, H. Jack. "Generations of Poison and Lies." *New York Times*, 5 August 1990.

Gentile, Gian. "Advocacy or Assessment? The United States Strategic Bombing Survey of Germany and Japan." *Pacific Historical Review* LXVI (February 1997).

——*How Effective is Strategic Bombing?* New York: New York University Press, 2000.

——"Shaping the Past Battlefield, 'For the Future,'. . ." *Journal of Military History* 64 (October 2000).

Giangreco, D. M. "Casualty Projections for the U.S. Invasions of Japan, 1945–1946: Planning and Policy Implications," *Journal of Military History* 61 (July 1997).

——"Operation Downfall: The Devil Was in the Details." *Joint Force Quarterly* (Autumn 1995).

——"Victory Rides the Divine Wind: The Kamikaze and the Invasion of Japan," in Peter G. Tsouras, ed., *Rising Sun Victorious*. London: Greenhill Books, 2001.

—— "'A Score of Bloody Okinawas and Iwo Jimas': President Truman and Casualty Estimates for the Invasion of Japan." *Pacific Historical Review* 72 (February 2003).

——"To Bomb or Not to Bomb." *Naval War College Review* 51 (Spring 1998).

——"The Truth About Kamikazes." *Naval History* 11 (May 1997).

——"Letters to the Editor." *Journal of American History* 84 (June 1997).

Giangreco, D.M. and Kathryn Moore. *Dear Harry . . . Truman's Mailroom, 1945–1953: The Truman Administration Through Correspondence with "Everyday Americans."* Mechanicsburg PA: Stackpole Books 1999.

——"Half a Million Purple Hearts." *American Heritage* 51 (December/January 2000).

Goodhart, A. L. *What Acts of War are Justifiable?* Oxford: Clarendon Press, 1940.

Gow, Ian. *1945: Gateway to Japan.* Garden City, NY: Doubleday, 1985.

Greene, Bob. *Duty.* New York: William Morrow, 2000.

Gustavson, Philip. "What if We Had Invaded Japan?" *Saturday Evening Post,* 5 January 1946.

Hagedorn, Hermann. *The Bomb That Fell on America.* Santa Barbara: Pacific Coast Publishing Company, 1946.

Halpern, A. M. *Changing Japanese Attitudes Toward Atomic Weapons.* Rand Corporation Report RM-1331. Santa Monica: Rand Corporation, 1954.

Hare, R. M. *Applications of Moral Philosophy.* Berkeley: University of California Press, 1972.

——"Rules of War and Moral Reasoning." *Philosophy and Public Affairs* 1 (Winter 1972).

Harris, Sheldon. *Factories of Death.* New York: Routledge, 1994.

Harvey, Robert. *The Undefeated.* London: Macmillan, 1994.

Harwit, Martin. *An Exhibit Denied.* New York: Springer-Verlag, 1996.

Havens, Thomas R. H. *Fire Across the Sea: The Vietnam War and Japan.* Princeton: Princeton University Press, 1987.

——*Valley of Darkness: The Japanese People and World War Two.* New York: Norton, 1978.

Herken, Gregg. *The Winning Weapon.* Princeton: Princeton University Press, 1981.

—— *Counsels of War.* New York: Oxford University Press, 1987.

Herring, George C. Jr. *Aid to Russia, 1941–1946.* New York: Columbia University Press, 1973.

Hersey, John. *Into the Valley.* New York: Knopf, 1943.

Hershberg, James G. *James B. Conant.* New York: Knopf, 1993.

Hicks, George. *The Comfort Women.* New York: Norton, 1994.

Higgins, Trumbull. *The Perfect Failure: Kennedy, Eisenhower, and the CIA at the Bay of Pigs.* New York: Norton, 1987.

Hill, Gladwin. "Mass Suicide Corps Trained by Japan." *New York Times,* 29 July 1945.

"Hiroshima Exhibit Opens Quietly at University." *New York Times,* 10 July 1995.

Hodgson, Godfrey. *The Colonel: The Life and Wars of Henry Stimson.* New York: Knopf, 1990.

Holloway, David. *Stalin and the Bomb.* New Haven: Yale University Press, 1994.

"The Horror and the Shame." *Commonweal* XLII (24 August 1945).

Howard, Michael. *Lessons of History.* New Haven: Yale University Press, 1991.

——*Studies in War and Peace.* New York: Viking, 1971.

Hussey, Kristin E. "Hiroshima, Nagasaki, a Mystery to Americans." *Washington Times,* 3 March 1995.

Ienaga, Saburo. *The Pacific War.* New York: Pantheon, 1978.

Iokibe, Makoto. "American Policy Towards Japan's Unconditional Surrender." *Japanese Journal of American Studies* 1 (1981).

Iritani, Toshio. *Group Psychology of the Japanese in Wartime.* London: Kegan Paul, 1991.

"Izzy vs. A Mendacious Agency." *Washington Journalism Review* 10 (May 1988).

"Japan's Civil Army Gets Suicide Order." *New York Times,* 26 June 1945.

Johnson, Sheila K. *The Japanese Through American Eyes.* Stanford: Stanford University Press, 1991.

Kaempffert, Waldemar. "Fear, War and the Bomb." *New York Times,* 3 July 1949.

Kaplan, Fred. *The Wizards of Armageddon.* Stanford: Stanford University Press, 1983.

Kase, Toshikazu. *Journey to the Missouri.* New Haven: Yale University Press, 1950.

Kawahara, Toshiake. *Hirohito and His Times*. Tokyo: Kodansha, 1990.

Keckskemeti, Paul. *Strategic Surrender: The Politics of Victory and Defeat*. Stanford: Stanford University Press, 1958.

Kennan, George F. *Memoirs, 1925–1950*. Boston: Little, Brown, 1967.

——"The Sources of Soviet Conduct." *Foreign Affairs* XXV (July 1947).

Kimball, Warren F. *The Juggler: Franklin Roosevelt as Wartime Statesman*. Princeton: Princeton University Press, 1991.

King, Ernest, and Walter M. Whitehill. *Fleet Admiral King*. New York: Norton, 1952.

Kitahara, Michio. *Children of the Sun: The Japanese and the Outside World*. New York: St. Martin's, 1989.

Kohn, Richard H., ed. "The Scholarship on World War II: Its Present Condition and Future Possibilities." *Journal of Military History* 55 (July 1991).

Koshiro, Yukiko. *Trans-Pacific Racisms*. New York: Columbia University Press, 1999.

Laird, Pamela Walker. "The Public's Historians." *Technology and Culture* 39 (July 1998).

Lapp, Ralph E. *The Voyage of the Lucky Dragon*. New York: Harper and Brothers, 1958.

Lawrence, David. "What Hath Man Wrought?" *United States News* 19 (17 August 1945).

Lawrence, W. H. "Japan, Like Okinawa, Will Cost High Price." *New York Times*, 24 June 1945.

Lee, Gary. "Postwar Pacific Fallout Wider Than Thought." *Washington Post*, 24 February 1994.

Levering, Ralph. *American Opinion and the Russian Alliance, 1939–1945*. Chapel Hill: University of North Carolina Press, 1976.

Lifton, Robert J. and Greg Mitchell. *Hiroshima in America*. New York: G. P. Putnam's Sons, 1995.

Lilienthal, David E. *The Journals of David E. Lilienthal*. Volume 2. New York: Harper & Row, 1964.

Lindsay, Malvina. "War Weariness." *Washington Post*, 9 May 1945.

Linenthal, Edward. "Anatomy of a Controversy," in Tom Englehardt and Edward Linenthal, eds., *History Wars*. New York: Henry Holt, 1996.

Lovell, Bernard. "Patrick Maynard Stuart Blackett, Baron Blackett of Chelsea." *Biographical Memoirs of Fellows of the Royal Society*, 21. London: The Royal Society, 1975.

MacDonald, Dwight. "The Decline to Barbarism." *Politics* 2 (August–September 1945).

MacEachin, Douglas J. *The Final Months of the War with Japan*. Washington, D.C.: Central Intelligence Agency, 1998.

Maddox, Robert J. *Weapons for Victory*. Columbia: University of Missouri Press, 1995.

Maier, Charles S. *The Unmasterable Past: History, Holocaust, and German National Identity*. Cambridge: Harvard University Press, 1988.

Maga, Tim. *America Attacks Japan*. Lexington: The University Press of Kentucky, 2002.

Mark, J. Carson. "Research, Development and Production." *Bulletin of the Atomic Scientists* 39 (March 1983).

Maruyama, Masao. *Thought and Behaviour in Modern Japanese Politics*. London: Oxford University Press, 1963.

Masanori, Nakamura. *The Japanese Monarchy*. Armonk, NY: M.E. Sharpe, 1992.

Matloff, Maurice. *Strategic Planning for Coalition Warfare*. Washington, D.C.: GPO, 1959.

May, Ernest R., ed. *American Cold War Strategy: Interpreting NSC 68*. Boston: Bedford Books, 1993.

May, Gary. *China Scapegoat: The Diplomatic Ordeal of John Carter Vincent*. Washington, D.C.: New Republic Books, 1979.

Mayer, Milton. "Thomists and Atomists." *Common Sense* XIV (November 1945).

Mayr, Otto. "The *Enola Gay* Fiasco: History, Politics, and the Museum." *Technology and Culture* 39 (1998).

McClean, Douglas. "The Atom Bomb." *New Statesman and Nation* 36 (16 October 1948).

Meyer, Eugene L. "The Bombers Who Flew Into History." *Washington Post,* 3 September 1994.

——"Target: Smithsonian." *Washington Post,* 30 January 1995.

Morison, Elting. *Turmoil and Tradition.* Boston: Houghton Mifflin, 1960.

Morison, Samuel Eliot. *Victory in the Pacific.* Boston: Little, Brown, 1960.

Morrison, Philip. "Blackett's Analysis of the Issues." *Bulletin of the Atomic Scientists* 5 (January 1949).

Morrow, Lance. "Hiroshima and the Time Machine." *Time* 144 (19 September 1994).

Mueller, John E. *War, Presidents, and Public Opinion.* New York: Wiley, 1973.

Mumford, Lewis. "Gentlemen: You Are Mad." *Saturday Review of Literature* XXIX (2 March 1946).

Newman, Robert. "Ending the War With Japan: Paul Nitze's 'Early Surrender' Counterfactual." *Pacific Historical Review* LXIV (May 1995).

——"Hiroshima and the Trashing of Henry Stimson." *New England Quarterly* (March 1998).

——"Lethal Rhetoric: The Selling of the China Myths." *Quarterly Journal of Speech* 61 (April 1975).

——"NSC (National Insecurity) 68: Nitze's Second Hallucination," in Martin Medhurst and H. W. Brands, eds., *Critical Reflections on the Cold War.* College Station: Texas A & M University Press, 2000).

——*Owen Lattimore and the "Loss" of China.* Berkeley: University of California Press, 1992.

——*Truman and the Hiroshima Cult.* East Lansing: Michigan State University Press, 1995.

Nitze, Paul H. "Atoms, Strategy and Policy." *Foreign Affairs* 34 (January 1956).

——*From Hiroshima to Glasnost: At the Center of Decision.* New York: Grove Weidenfeld, 1989.

Nishi, Toshio. *Unconditional Democracy.* Stanford: Stanford University Press, 1982.

Nobile, Philip, ed. *Judgment at the Smithsonian.* New York: Marlowe, 1995.

Notter, Harley A. *Postwar Foreign Policy Preparation, 1939–1940.* Washington, D.C.: GPO, 1949.

Nye, Mary Jo. "A Physicist in the Corridors of Power: P. M. S. Blackett's Opposition to Atomic Weapons Following the War." *Physics in Perspective* 1 (1999).

——"What Price Politics? Scientists and Political Controversy." *Endeavor* 23 (1999).

O'Connor, Raymond G. *Diplomacy for Victory: FDR and Unconditional Surrender.* New York: Norton, 1971.

O'Neill, William L. *A Democracy at War.* New York: Free Press, 1993.

Pacific War Research Society. *Japan's Longest Day.* Tokyo and Palo Alto: Kodansha International, 1972.

Palevsky, Mary. *Atomic Fragments.* Berkeley: University of California Press, 2000.

Palmer, Kyle. "Palmer Warns Nips Set for Murderous Combat." *Los Angeles Times,* 8 May 1945.

Parrish, Thomas. *The Cold War Encyclopedia.* New York: Henry Holt, 1996.

Passin, Herbert. "The Occupation: Some Reflections," in Carol Gluck and Stephen Graubard, eds., *Showa: The Japan of Hirohito.* New York: Norton, 1992.

Pearlman, Michael D. *Unconditional Surrender, Demobilization, and the Atomic Bomb.* Ft. Leavenworth: U.S. Army Command and General Staff College, 1996.

——*Warmaking and American Democracy*. Lawrence: University Press of Kansas, 1999.

Perrett, Geoffrey. *Days of Sadness, Years of Triumph*. Baltimore: Penguin, 1974.

Pershing, John J. *My Experiences in the World War*. New York: Frederick A. Stokes, 1931.

Philip, P. J. "6,300 Canadian Soldiers AWOL. . ." *New York Times*, 21 January 1945.

Pomeroy, Earl. "Sentiment for a Strong Peace." *South Atlantic Quarterly* 43 (October 1944).

Presenting History: Museums in a Democratic Society. Washington, D. C.: Smithsonian Institution, 1995.

Pritchard, R. John and Sonia M. Zaide, eds. *The Tokyo War Crimes Trial*, vol. 13. New York: Garland, 1981.

Public Papers of the Presidents of the United States: Harry S. Truman. Washington, D.C.: GPO, 1961.

Ramsey, Paul. *War and the Christian Conscience*. Durham: Duke University Press, 1961.

Rawls, John. "50 Years After Hiroshima." *Dissent* 42 (Summer 1995).

Reid, Anthony. "Indonesia: From Briefcase to Samurai Sword," in Alfred W. McCoy, ed., *Southeast Asia Under Japanese Occupation*. New Haven: Yale Southeast Asia Studies, 1980.

"Report of Protestant Church Leaders on Atomic Warfare." *New York Times*, 6 March 1946.

Ridenour, Louis, Jr. "The Bomb and Blackett." *World Politics* 1 (April 1949).

Roberts, Charles. "LBJ's Credibility Gap." *Newsweek* 19 December 1966.

Roland, Alex. "Keep the Bomb." *Technology Review* 98 (August/September 1995).

Rose, Lisle A. *Dubious Victory*. Kent: Kent State University Press, 1973.

Rosenberg, David Alan. "American Atomic Strategy and the Hydrogen Bomb Decision." *Journal of American History* 66 (June 1979).

Rosenthal, Elisabeth. "Wartime Slaves Use U.S. Law to Sue Japanese." *New York Times*, 2 October 2000.

Rummel, R. J. *China's Bloody Century*. New Brunswick: Transaction Publishers, 1991.

Sayle, Murray. "Did the Bomb End the War?" *The New Yorker*, 31 July 1995.

Schaller, Michael. *Altered States*. New York: Oxford University Press, 1977.

——*The American Occupation of Japan*. New York: Oxford University Press, 1985.

Schonberger, Howard. "The Japan Lobby in American Diplomacy." *Pacific Historical Review* 46 (August 1977).

Seltz, Daniel. *The Enola Gay Exhibition and the Challenge to American Memory*. Providence: East Asian Studies, Brown University, 1996.

Sherry, Michael. *The Rise of American Airpower*. New Haven: Yale University Press, 1987.

Sherwin, Martin J. "Hiroshima and Modern History." *The Nation* 233 (October 1981).

——*A World Destroyed*. New York: Vintage, 1975.

Sherwood, Robert E. *Roosevelt and Hopkins*. New York: Harper & Brothers, 1948.

Shils, Edward. "Blackett's Apologia for the Soviet Position." *Bulletin of the Atomic Scientists* 5 (January 1949).

Shirayama, Saburo. *War Criminal: The Life and Death of Hirota Koki*. Tokyo: Kodansha International, 1978.

Sigal, Leon. *Fighting to a Finish*. Ithaca: Cornell University Press, 1988.

Sirgiovanni, George. *An Undercurrent of Suspicion: Anti-Communist and Anti-Soviet Opinion in World War II America*. New Brunswick: Rutgers University, 1988, Ph.D. dissertation.

Smith, Alice Kimball. *A Peril and a Hope*. Chicago: University of Chicago Press, 1965.

Spector, Ronald. *Eagle Against the Sun*. New York: Free Press, 1985.

Stallings, Laurence. *The Doughboys*. New York: Harper & Row, 1963.

Stimson, Henry L. "The Decision to Use the Atomic Bomb." *Harper's Magazine* 97 (February 1947).

Stoler, Mark. Review of Leon Sigal, "Fighting to a Finish." *Journal of American History* 16 (June 1989).

——*George C. Marshall.* New York: Twayne Publishers, 1989.

Stouffer, Samuel et al. *Combat and Its Aftermath,* Vol. 2. Princeton: Princeton University Press, 1949.

Sweeney, Charles. *War's End.* New York: Avon, 1997.

Tachibana, Seiitsu. "The Quest for a Peace Culture. . ." in Michael J. Hogan, ed., *Hiroshima in History and Memory.* Cambridge: Cambridge University Press, 1996.

Talbott, Strobe. *The Master of the Game: Paul Nitze and the Nuclear Peace.* New York: Knopf, 1988.

Tanaka, Yasumasu. "Japanese Attitudes Toward Nuclear Arms." *Public Opinion Quarterly* 34 (Spring 1970).

Taylor, Maxwell. *Swords and Plowshares.* New York: Norton, 1972.

"Thomas Ferebee Dies at 81: Dropped First Atomic Bomb." *New York Times,* 18 March 2000.

Thomas, Norman. "When Cruelty Becomes Pleasurable." *Human Events* II (26 September 1945).

Togo, Shigenori. *The Cause of Japan.* New York: Simon and Schuster, 1956.

"Tokyo Chiefs Hail Okinawa Victory." *New York Times,* 27 June 1945.

Toland, John. *The Rising Sun.* New York: Bantam, 1970.

Truman, Harry S. *Memoirs, Vol 1: Year of Decisions.* Garden City: Doubleday, 1955.

Tsurumi, Shunsuke. *An Intellectual History of Wartime Japan.* London: Kegan Paul International, 1986.

Tucker, Nancy Bernkopf. *Patterns in the Dust.* New York: Columbia University Press, 1983.

Tucker, Robert W. *The Just War.* Baltimore: Johns Hopkins University Press, 1960.

Tyler, Patrick E. "China Villagers Recall Horrors of Germ Attack." *New York Times,* 4 February 1997.

Udall, Stewart. *The Myths of August.* New York: Pantheon, 1994.

U.S. Department of Defense. *The Entry of the Soviet Union into the War Against Japan.* Washington, D.C.: GPO, 1955.

U.S. Department of State. *The Axis in Defeat.* Washington, D.C.: GPO, 1945.

United States Atomic Energy Commission. *In the Matter of J. Robert Oppenheimer.* Cambridge, MA: MIT Press, 1970.

United States Strategic Bombing Survey. *The Effects of Air Attack on Japanese Urban Economy—Summary Report.* Washington, D.C.: GPO, 1947.

——Naval Analysis Division. *Interrogations of Japanese Officials,* vol. 2. Washington, D.C.: GPO, 1946.

——*Japan's Struggle to End the War.* Washington, D.C.: GPO, 1946.

——*Summary Report (Pacific War).* Washington, D.C.: GPO, 1946.

van der Post, Laurens. *The Prisoner and the Bomb.* New York: Morrow, 1971.

Villa, Brian L. "The U.S. Army, Unconditional Surrender, and the Potsdam Proclamation." *Journal of American History* 63 (June 1976).

Wald, George. "The Nuclear-Power-Truth Maze." *New York Times,* 29 February 1976.

Walker, J. Samuel. *Prompt and Utter Destruction: Truman and the Use of Atomic Bombs Against Japan.* Chapel Hill: University of North Carolina Press, 1997.

Walzer, Michael. "50 Years After Hiroshima." *Dissent* 42 (Summer 1995).

——*Just and Unjust Wars.* New York: Basic Books, 1977.

"War and the Bomb." *New York Times,* 28 January 1947.

Warner, Dennis, Peggy Warner, and Sadao Seno. *The Sacred Warriors: Japan's Suicide Legions*. New York: Van Nostrand Reinhold, 1982.

Weart, Spencer. *Nuclear Fear*. Cambridge: Harvard University Press, 1988.

Weart, Spencer and Gertrude Weiss Szilard. *Leo Szilard: His Version of the Truth*. Cambridge: MIT Press, 1978.

Weigley, Russell. *The American Way of War*. Bloomington: Indiana University Press, 1977.

Weinberg, Gerhard. *A World at Arms*. Cambridge: Cambridge University Press, 1994.

Weintraub, Stanley. *The Last Great Victory*. New York: Dutton, 1995.

White, Geoffrey M. "Memory Wars: The Politics of Remembering the Asia-Pacific War." *Asia-Pacific Issues* 21 (July 1995).

"Why We Used the Bomb." *Washington Post,* 28 January 1947.

Wyden, Peter. *Bay of Pigs*. New York: Simon & Schuster, 1979.

Yoshida, Shigeru. *The Yoshida Memoirs*. Boston: Houghton Mifflin, 1962.

Young, Shi and James Yin. *The Rape of Nanking: Japanese Carnage in China During World War Two*. Chicago: Innovative Publishing Group, 1997.

Zacharias, Ellis M. *Secret Missions*. New York: G. P. Putnam's Sons, 1946.

Zinn, Howard. "The Politics of History in the Era of the Cold War," in Andre Schiffrin, ed., *The Cold War and the University*. New York: New Press, 1997.

Zubok, Vladislav M. "Stalin and the Nuclear Age," in John Lewis Gaddis et al., eds., *Cold War Statesmen Confront the Bomb*. Oxford: Oxford University Press, 1999.

INDEX

Acheson, Dean, 28, 81
Adams, Robert, 105
Air Force Association, 104, 122, 128
Akahiro Tadahashi 105
Alison, Thomas, 106
Allen, Louis, 148
Allied War Graves Registration Unit, 157
Alperovitz, Gar, 48, 56, 59, 94–95, 100, 103
Alvarez, Robert, 177
Ambrose, Stephen, 96, 120
America First, 44
American Council on Japan 18, 78
American Friends Service Committee, 150
American Legion, 111, 151
American Society of Newspaper Editors, 89
American University, 130
Anami Korechika, 32, 57
Anderson, Orvil a., 43
Anscombe, G. E. M., 139
Appleman, Roy E., 121
Arneson, Gordon, 82
Arnold, H.H. (Hap), 29
Asada Sadao, xiii, 58, 87, 114, 115, 131
Asia First, 80

Aswell, Edward, 70
Atlantic Charter, 17
Atomic Energy Commission, 85–88

Baldwin, Hanson, 4, 7
Ball, George, 30, 103, 131
Ballantine, Joseph, 77
Bamba Nobuya, 118
Barnhart, Michael, 119
Bataan Death March, 116, 134
Battle of the Bulge, 2
Bearss, Edwin, 130
Bell, Daniel, 160
Bernstein, Barton, xiii, 27, 48, 56. 59, 81, 74, 94–96, 101, 129, 138. 142
Beschloss, Michael, 177
Bethe, Hans, 166
Beveridge, James, 32
Biddle, Tami Davis, 110
Bikini Atoll, 85–88
Bilibid Prison, 135
Bird, Kai, 151
Bischof, Gunter, 181
Bix, Herbert, 77, 132

Blackett, P. M. S., xiii, 62–74, 93, 139, 152
Blasco, David, 107
Bohlen, Charles "Chip", 46, 84, 127
Boller, Paul F., Jr., 180
Bond, Victor, 126, 130
Bonesteel, Chrles, 20
Bonnett, John, 171
Bowles, Edward L., 11
Boyer, Paul, 94–95
Brackman, Arnold, 169
Bradley, Omar, 2
Brandt, R. B., 144
Branigin, William, 146
BRAVO, 85–86
Bridge on the River Kwai, 134
Brtiggs, Richard A., 164
British Bombing Survey Unit, 30
Brittain, Vera, 141
Brokaw, Tom, 134
Brower, Charles F. IV, 163
Bullock, Alan, 139
Bundy, Harvey, 52, 54
Bundy, McGeorge, 56
Bush, George W., xiv
Butow, Robert J. .C. 39–40, 48, 120, 121, 131
Byrnes, James F., 23, 59

Cairo Conference, 62
Callahan, David, 43, 47
Campbell, A. E., 23
Capaccio, Tony, 181
Casablanca Conference, 15
Castle, William, 44–45
Chennault, Claire, 65–66
Cherwell, Lord, 68–69
China, 81
Chinese Alliance for Memorial and Justice, 137
Chinese Holocaust, 134
Christian Century, 24
Churchill, Winston, 15–16
Clinton, William J., 90
Cochran, Bert, 124
Cochran, Thomas B., 125
Cohen, Sheldon M., 128, 145–6
Cohen, Warren, 175
Cole, W. Sterling, 87
Comfort Women, 149

Commonweal, 24
Committee on the Present Danger, 47
Compton, Karl T., 97
Conant, James B., 54–5
Congress, 107
Constantine, William, 106
Conventional histories, 155
Cook, Haruko and Theodore, 146
Coox, Alvin D., 120
Correll, John T., 124
Costello, John, 121
Cousins, Norman, 25, 55, 88, 145
Craig, William, 121
Crane, Conrad C., 121
Credibility Gap, 88
Crouch, Thomas, xiii, 97, 100, 102, 108, 115, 122, 133

Dagley, Hugh, 112
Davis, Norman, 15
Daws, Gavan, 136–7
Dear, Father John, 150
Del Tredici, Robert, 168
Department of Energy, 90
Detwiler, Donald, 115
Dewey, Thomas, 81
Dietz, Thomas, 100
Dingman, Roger, 121
Divine, Robert, 86
D'Olier, Franklin, 30, 31, 40
Donovan, Robert, 124
Dooman, Eugene, 77
Dower, John W., 23, 59, 76, 78–9, 93, 120–1, 129–30, 132, 135, 137
Draper, Theodore, 89
Drea, Edward, 8, 12, 42, 65, 119–20, 132, 139
Dresden, 27, 51, 122, 142
Driscoll, John, 33
Duis, Perry, 2
Dulles, John Foster, 85, 92
Dzwonchyk, Wayne, 97, 102

Edelman, Murray, 153
Eisenbud, Merrill, 87
Eisenhower, Dwight, xii, 3, 60, 88, 95, 132
Ennis, R. F., 58
Enola Gay exhibit, 97–133
Enola Gay Restoration Association, 98

Federal Council of Churches in America, 25
Feis, Herbert, 48, 96
Feller, Bonner, 77
Fellowship of Reconciliation, 150
Ferrell, Robert H., 124
Field, Norma, 120
Filene, Peter, 80
Finletter, Thomas, 25–6
509th Composite Group, 98
Forrestal, James, 20, 44, 83–4
Franck, James, 66–8
Frank, Richard B., 132
Franklin, William, 16
French, Howard, 149
Fussell, Paul, 124, 131

Gaddis, John L., 123, 132
Gaither Commission, xii, 47
Galbraith, John Kenneth, 30, 47, 103
Galison, Peter, 82
Gallicchio, Marc S., 166–7
Garrett, Shirley Stone, 176
Geiger, H. Jack, 92
Gentile, Gian, xii, 33, 43, 48
Geopolitical postures, 154
Gernstein, Joanne, 100
Giangreco, D. M., 6, 132, 164–5
Gibney, Frank, 132
Gingrich, Newt, 107
Gluck, Carol, 120
Gofman, John, 92
Goldberg, Stanley, 130
Goodhart, A. L., 143
Goodnight, Thomas, 159
Graebner, Norman, 124
Grassley, Charles, ix
Greene, Bob, 184
Grew, Joseph, 10, 19, 48, 57, 77, 110, 113
Gronbeck, Bruce E., 153–62
Groves, Leslie, 1, 13
Gustafson, Philip, 11

Hagedorn, Hermann, 26
Haldane, J. B. S., 73
Hallion, Richard, 108, 129
Halpern, A. M., 87
Halpern, Samuel, 166
Hamby, Alonzo, 124

Handy, Thomas T., 10
Hardesty, Von, 112
Hare, R. M., 144
Harriman, Averell, 84
Harris, Sheldon H., 175
Harrison, George, 52
Harwit, Martin, xiii, 97–133
Hata Ikuhiko, 114
Hata Shunroku 37
Hatana Sumio, 115
Havens, Thomas R. H., 59, 93
Hayashi Shigeo, 146
Heller, Joseph, 104
Herken, Gregg, 97, 100, 106, 123
Herring, George, 80
Hersey, John, 141–2, 146
Heyman, I. Michael, 108
Hickerson, John D.
Hicks, George, 183
Higinbotham, W. A., 61
Higgins, Trumbull, 177
Hill, Gladwin, 7
Hiranuma Kiichiro, 21, 36
Hirohito, 23
Hiroshima Maidens, 88
Hirota, Koki, 41, 77
Hiss. Alger, 81
Ho Chi Minh, 81
Hollihan, Thomas, 157
Holloway, David, xiii, 125, 131
Hoover, Herbert, 2, 10, 19, 52. 77–8
Hosoya, Chihiro, 115
Howard, Michael, 121, 139–40, 166
Howe, Mark, 20
Howes, John, 118
Hull, Cordell, 10
Hussey, Kristin E. 175

Ichigo offensive, 138
Ienaga Saburo, 117
Inoculation argument, 126, 128
International Military Tribunal for the Far
    East, 32, 76–8
Iokibe Makoto, 15, 114
Iritani Toshio, 117, 136
Iriye, Akira, 114, 129
Ishii Shiro, 77, 135, 149
Iwo Jima, 3, 6

Jacobsen, Mark, 102–3
Japanese as victims, 63
Jaranilla, Delfin, 79
Jarrico, Paul, 174
Jernegan, Norris, 151
Johnson, Lyndon, 89, 131
Johnson, Sheila, 88
Joint Intelligence Committee, 4
Just War doctrine, 143

Kaempffert, Walter, 70–1
Kamikazi tactics, 7
Kaplan, Fred, 171
Karnes, Thomas, 152
Kase Shunichi, 22
Kase Toshikazu, 21–2
Kato Masuo, 22
Kawabe, Torashiro, 138
Kawahara Toshiaki, 119
Kecksmeti, Paul, 48
Kennan, George F., 46, 78, 82–4, 127
Kennedy, John F., 89
Kern, Harry, 77
Kido Koichi, 33–6
Kimball, Warren F., 167
King, Ernest, 1, 11
Kirk, Grayson, 15
Kirkendall, Richard, 124
Kitahara Michio, 117
Kitamura Kojiro, 22
Kohn, Richard, 120, 121–3
Konoye Fumimaro, 34–5, 41
Korean War, 6, 85. 93
Koshiro Yukiko, 132, 135
Kurin, Richard, 99
Kyoto, 118, 151

Lacey, Michael, 124
Laird, Pamela Walker, 100, 132
Lapp, Ralph, 87
Lattimore, Owen, 78
Lawrence, David, 24
Lawrence, W. H., 7
Leahy, William, 3, 8, 132, 141
Lee, Gary, 175
LeMay, Curtis, 12, 122, 131
Lemke, Jay, 158
Levering, Ralph, 80

Leviero, Anthony, 29
Lewis, Bob, 152
Liddell Hart, Basil Henry, 118.
Lifton, Robert Jay, 145
Lilienthal, David E., 81, 90
Lincoln, George, 122
Lindsay, Malvina, 5
Linenthal, Edward, 130, 133
Locke, Edwin, 41
Lopez, Donald, 106
Lovell, Bernard, 63, 72
Lovett, Robert, 30
Luce, Henry, 80
Lucky Dragon, 75, 85–88

MacArthur, Douglas, 8, 141
MacArthur Foundation, 103–4
MacDonald, Dwight, 24
MacIsaac, David, 43, 110
Maddox, Robert, 132
MAGIC, 114
Maier, Charles S., 109–10
Mancuso, Thomas F., 91–2
Manhattan Engineer District, 52, 90
Mao Tse-tung, 80
Mark, J. Carson, 92
Marshall, George C., 2, 8–9, 12, 51
Maruyama Masao, 118–9
Matloff, Maurice, 163
Maud Committee, 63
May, Gary, 175
Mayr, Otto, 113
McCarthy, Joseph, 81
McCloy, John J., 11, 20, 52, 76, 151
McCullough, David, 124
McGraw-Hill, 69–70
McIntosh, Denise, 103
McLellan, David, 124
McMahon, Helen Claire, 111
Mearshimer, John, 123
Mee, Charles, 96
Memorializing the past, 156
Messer, Robert, 96
Meyer, Eugene L., 184
Michio Saito, 116
Mohan, Uday, 181
Molotov, Vyacheslav, 41
Morgenthau, Henry, 53

Morison, Samuel Eliot, 22
Morrison, Philip, 68, 73
Morrow, Lance, 108–9
Mueller, John, 6
"Murderer, Hello!", 109
Mylai, 94

Nagano Osami, 37–8
Nagasaki, 36
Nakamura Masanori, 114
Nakatsuji Keiji, 114
Nanking (Nanjing), Rape of, 116, 134
National Air and Space Museum (NASM),
    xiii, 29, 94, 97–133
Nauru, 145
Naval Historical Center, 101
Neufeld, Michael, 97, 100, 102, 106, 128–9
Nevada Test Site, 90–1
Niebuhr, Reinhold, 15
Nishi Toshio, 93
Nitze, Paul H., xi, 28–49, 60, 63, 72, 81, 90,
    111, 125, 152
Norris, Robert Standish, 125
NSC-68, 46, 60, 83
Nye, Mary Jo, 73

O'Connor, Raymond G., 166
Office of Strategic Services, 22
Okamura, 41
Okinawa, 4, 6, 19, 23
O'Laughlin, John Callan, 2
O'Leary, Helen, 90
OLYMPIC, 7, 13
O'Neill, William L., 48
Oppenheimer, J. Robert, 92

Pacific War Research Society, 40
Pal, Rodhabinod, 78
Palevsky, Mary166
Palmer, Kyle, 7
Parrish, Thomas, 72
Passin, Herbert, 59
Peace Action, 150
Pearl Harbor, 134
Pearlman, Michael, 132, 164
Pei, Astrid, 134
Perrett, Geoffrey, 3–4
Pershing, John J. 14–5

Pettee, George, 44
Physicians for Social Responsibility, 150
Potsdam Conference, 5, 20, 76
Potts, Ramsey, 110
Powers, Francis Gary, 89
Pritchard, R. John, 169
Protestant missions, 80

Quirino, Vicky, 146–7

Ramsey, Paul, xiii, 144
Rawls, John, 143
Reid, Anthony, 138
Retired Officers Association, 123
Rhodes, Richard, 96, 126, 130–1
Ridenour, Louis N., 41
Robert, Kenneth, 106
Roberts, Charles, 89
Rocha, Juan Jose, 147
Roosevelt. Elliott, 16
Roosevelt, Franklin D., 3, 14–18, 145
Roosevelt, Nicholas, 26
Roosevelt, Theodore, 14
Rose, Lisle, 168
Rosenberg, David Alan, 83, 125
Rosenthal, Elizabeth, 149
Rummel, R. J., 137
Rusk, Dean, 20

Sakharov, Andrei, 85
Sakomizu Hisatsume,36
Salisbury, Harrison, 142
SANE/Freeze, 150
Sato Eisaku, 93
Sayle, Murray, 172
Schaller, Michael, 76, 92
Schonberger, Howard, 77–8
Searles, Fred, 34
Seltz, Daniel, 99
Seno Sadao, 10
Sherry, Michael, 121–2, 126
Sherwin, Martin, 21, 79, 95, 101, 124, 130
Sherwood, Robert E., 16
Shigemitsu Mamoru, 22
Shils, Edward, 73
Shinozuka, Yoshio, 150
Shockley, William B., 10–1
Sigal, Leon, 21

Sirgiovanni, George, 80
Smith, Alice Kimball, 174
Social Science Research Council, 4
Soter, Steven, 106
Soviet Union, 23, 65
Spector, Ronald, xiii, 7, 120, 131
Stalin, Joseph, 15, 46
Stallings, Laurence, 14–5
Starvation as cause of surrender, 141
Stephan, John J., 121
Stewart, Alice, 91
Stewart, Frank B. 151
Stimson, Henry L., 10, 48, 50–61, 152
Stoler, Mark, 121
Stolz, Preble, 108
Stone, I. F., 91
Stone, M. K., 102
Stouffer, Samuel, 4–5
Strauss, Lewis L., 85–7
Strong, George, 18
Suzuki Kantaro, 37
Sweeney, Charles, 151
Szilard, Leo, 126

Tachibana Seeitsu, 136, 14
Takagi Morihisa, 105
Takashima Tatsuhiko, 51–2, 120
Takata Toshitani, 52
Talbott, Strobe, 31, 43
Tamplin, Arthur, 92
Tanaka, Hiroshi, 150
Tanaka Yasumasu, 87
Taylor, Maxwell, 5
Teller, Edward, 46, 81, 91, 125
Thomas, Norman, 25
Thompson, Llewellyn, 46, 84
Thorne, Christopher, 121
Thorpe, Elliott, 76
Tibbets, Paul, 123, 151
Tiger Team, 100
Togo Shigenori, 21, 41
Tokyo Imperial University, 38–9
Toland, John, 4
Tomioka Sadatoshi, 38
Toyoda Soemu, 36, 138
Truman, David B., 36
Truman, Harry S., 8, 10, 27, 46, 96, 127, 139, 152

Tsurumi Shunsuke, 118
Tucker, Nancy Bernkopf, 173
Turner, Robert W., 143
Turnstile Press, 69–71
Tyler, Patrick, 147–8

Udall, Stewart, 90, 94
ULTRA, 9, 12, 40, 65, 120
Unconditional surrender, 14–24
Unit 731, 77, 135, 149
Umited Nations, 55
U. S. Strategic Bombing Survey (USSBS), xi, 28–49, 103

Van der Post, Laurens, 138
Van Dusen, Henry P., 25
Van Kirk, Ted, 151
Varg, Paul, 176
Veterans of Foreign Wars, 123
Vietnam War, 93, 131
Villa, Brian Loring, 121
Vincent, John Carter, 78
Vinson, Fred, 4
Vonnegut, Kurt, 104, 122

Wainwright, Jonathon, 116
Wald, George, 92
Waldorf Conference on World Peace, 71
Walker, J. Samuel, 101
Walsh, Edmund, 81
Walzer, Michael, 128, 141, 142.
Wander, Philip, 157
War weariness, 2–6
Warfighting theorists, 127
Warner, Dennis and Peggy, 10
Warnke, Paul, 47
Weart, Spencer, 142
Weinberg, Gerhard, 121
Weintraub, Stanley, 132
Weld, S. L., 26
White, Geoffrey M., 116
Williams, William Appleman, 94, 124
Willoughby, Charles, 11
Wilson, Harold, 63
Wilson, Woodrow, 14, 23
Winslett, Edmund, 14
Wolk, Herman, 129
Woodward, E. L., 16

Wright, Quincy, 11
Wu, Y. C. L., Susan, 127–8
Wyden, Peter, 177

Yibo Zhang, 149
Yin, James, 137
Yoshida Shigeru, 59
Young, Shi, 137

Zacharias, Ellis, 11, 57
Zaide, Sonia, 169
Zaloga, Steven, 125
Zhukov, Georgi, 125
Zinn, Howard, 48
Zubok, Vladimir, 125
Zuckerman, Solly, 110–1

POLITICAL COMMUNICATION

FRONTIERS IN

General Editors
Lynda Lee Kaid and Bruce Gronbeck

At the heart of how citizens, governments, and the media interact is the communication process, a process that is undergoing tremendous changes as we embrace a new millennium. Never has there been a time when confronting the complexity of these evolving relationships been so important to the maintenance of civil society. This series seeks books that advance the understanding of this process from multiple perspectives and as it occurs in both institutionalized and non-institutionalized political settings. While works that provide new perspectives on traditional political communication questions are welcome, the series also encourages the submission of manuscripts that take an innovative approach to political communication, which seek to broaden the frontiers of study to incorporate critical and cultural dimensions of study as well as scientific and theoretical frontiers.

For more information or to submit material for consideration, contact:

BRUCE E. GRONBECK
Obermann Center for Advanced Studies
N134 OH
The University of Iowa
Iowa City, IA 52242-5000

LYNDA LEE KAID
Political Communication Center
Department of Communication
University of Oklahoma
Norman, OK 73109

To order other books in this series, please contact our Customer Service Department:

    (800) 770-LANG (within the U.S.)
    (212) 647-7706 (outside the U.S.)
    (212) 647-7707 FAX

Or browse online by series:
    WWW.PETERLANGUSA.COM